797, ᴊᴏᴏks

are available to read at

www.ForgottenBooks.com

Forgotten Books' App
Available for mobile, tablet & eReader

ISBN 978-1-331-51904-1
PIBN 10200928

Similar Books Are Available from
www.forgottenbooks.com

WALT WHITMAN

BY

RICHARD MAURICE BUCKE, M.D.

TO WHICH IS ADDED

ENGLISH CRITICS ON WALT WHITMAN

EDITED BY

EDWARD DOWDEN, LL.D.

PROFESSOR OF ENGLISH LITERATURE IN THE UNIVERSITY OF DUBLIN

GLASGOW

WILSON & McCORMICK, Saint Vincent Street

1884

CONTENTS.

(3)

PART II.

ILLUSTRATIONS.

Frontispiece.—PORTRAIT OF WALT WHITMAN, FROM LIFE, IN 1864. Photo-Intaglio. Drawn by Herbert H. Gilchrist, England.

Facing Page 13.—HOUSE AT WEST HILLS IN WHICH W. W. WAS BORN. Drawn by Joseph Pennell. Eng. by Photo Eng. Co., N. Y.

Facing Page 15.—ANCIENT BURIAL GROUND OF THE VAN VELSORS at Cold Spring Harbor, L. I., on the Homestead Farm. Drawn by Pennell. Eng. by P. E. Co., N. Y.

Facing Page 17.—ANCIENT BURIAL GROUND OF THE WHITMANS at West Hills, L. I., on the Homestead Farm. Drawn by Pennell. Eng. by P. E. Co., N. Y.

Facing Page 26.—PORTRAIT FROM LIFE OF WALTER WHITMAN, the Poet's Father.

Facing Page 46.—PORTRAIT FROM LIFE OF LOUISA (VAN VELSOR) WHITMAN, the Poet's Mother.

Facing Page 48.—PORTRAIT FROM LIFE OF WALT WHITMAN in 1880. Photo by Edy Bro.'s, London, Canada.

Facing Page 54.—W. W.'S HANDWRITING. Fac-simile.

(6)

INTRODUCTION.

Now just entering his sixty-fifth year, Walt Whitman has become the object, in America and Europe, of such pronounced attacks, defences, inquiries, and of comments, assumptions, and denials, so various and inconsistent—with a certainty of steadily increasing interest, perhaps of still more pronounced attack and defence. in the future—that a field may well be presumed to exist for statements about him from observation at first hand. Such contemporaneous statements, executed in their own way, form the purpose of the following pages. To arrest, at the time, some otherwise evanescent facts and features of the man—to sketch him on the spot, in his habit as he lived, and give a few authentic items of his ancestry, youth, middle life, and actual manners and talk, is the primary object of this volume; secondly, to put forth in regard to *Leaves of Grass* my own deliberate constructions of that work. I make no pretence that they are other than from a friendly point of view. "As it seems to me," might doubtless have served as heading for all I have written.

To balance, however, any proclivity, or danger of proclivity, in that direction, I have freely included in my book (Appendix, Part II.) the fullest representation from the enemies and most outspoken fault-findings and denunciations of *Leaves of Grass* and their author. I know that the poet himself welcomes such searching attacks and trials. He has told me that he considers them the means whereby Nature and Fate try the right of any thing or ambition, book or what-not, to exist. "If my light can't stand such gales," he once said to me, "let it go out—as it will then deserve to go out."

In short, and while I have no final authority to speak for Walt Whitman (who has himself more opposed than favored my enterprise), I do not hesitate to send forth the following pages, not only as the *bonâ fide* results of my own knowledge of the poet and study of his writings for many years past, but as direct testimony from the days and actualities among which he lives, and certainly representing the last feeling and verdict of persons (I have had correspondence or face-to-face meetings with many of them), who have been closest and longest in contact with him.

William D. O'Connor's "Good Gray Poet," of 1865–'6, and, after eighteen years, his letter now written (1883), in confirmation and re-statement of that pamphlet, occupy a considerable part of the ensuing volume; but they are both in courteous response to my solicitations, and will prove invaluable contributions to the future. They come from a scholar who has absorbed to its very depths the literature of the Elizabethan age, as illustrated by Shakespeare and Bacon —an ardent familiar of the great geniuses of all times—and a personal knower of Walt Whitman's life for the last twenty-five years. The judgments such a man, after such opportunities, has to announce, deserve, indeed, to be recorded.

Walt Whitman said not long since to a friend that he did not want his life written, that he did not care in any way to be differentiated from the common people, of whom he was one. "Then," said his friend, "why did you differentiate yourself from ordinary men by writing *Leaves of Grass?*" According to the poet himself, he has lived a common life; and this is true, not in the sense that it has been like other lives, but that other lives in future are to be like it, and that his life is to be the common property of humanity. For this man, who has absorbed the whole human race, will, in the future, in turn, be absorbed by each individual member of the race who aspires to attain complete spiritual growth.

The claim made throughout the present work, both in that First Part of it which deals with the man Walt Whitman, and in the Second, which deals with the book *Leaves of Grass*, is, that the leading fact in both, the one as much as the other, is *moral elevation;* that this is their basic meaning and value to us. The true introduction, therefore, to this volume, is the author's previous work, "Man's Moral Nature."* In that book he has discussed the moral nature in the abstract, pointed out its physical basis, and shown its historic development; while the sole object of the present work is to depict an Individual moral nature, perhaps the highest that has yet appeared.

And now, before entering on the various subjects attempted and more fully detailed in my volume, it will essentially serve the reader to run his or her eyes over an authentic and brief

Chronological forecast of WALT WHITMAN'S *life, and the successive publications of* LEAVES OF GRASS.

1819. Born at West Hills—(see *Specimen Days*).
1820, '21, '22, and early half of '23. At West Hills.
1823–'24. In Brooklyn, in Front street.
1825–'30. In Cranberry, Johnson, Tillary, and Henry streets. Went to public schools.
1831–'32. Tended in a lawyer's office; then, a doctor's.
1833–'34. In printing offices, learning the trade.
1836–'37. Teaching country schools on Long Island. "Boarded round."
1840–'45. In New York city, printing, etc. Summers in the country. Some farm-work.

---

* "Man's Moral Nature, an Essay." G. P. Putnam's Sons: N.Y., 1879.

1846–'47. In Brooklyn, editing daily paper, the " Eagle."

1848–'49. In New Orleans, on editorial staff of daily paper, the " Crescent."

"1848–'49. About this time went off on a leisurely journey and working expedition (my brother Jeff with me) through all the Middle States, and down the Ohio and Mississippi Rivers. Lived a while in New Orleans, and worked there. After a time, plodded back northward, up the Mississippi, the Missouri, etc., and around to, and by way of, the great lakes, Michigan, Huron, and Erie, to Niagara Falls and Lower Canada—finally returning through Central New York, and down the Hudson."—*Personal Notes, W. W.*

1850. Publishing " The Freeman " newspaper in Brooklyn.

1851, '52, '53, '54. Carpentering—building houses in Brooklyn, and selling them.

1855. *First issue of Leaves of Grass. Small quarto*, 94 *pages. Eight or nine hundred copies printed. No sale.*

1856. *Second issue of Leaves of Grass. Small* 16mo., 384 *pages—32 poems— published by Fowler & Wells*, 308 *Broadway, New York. Little or no sale.*

1860. *Third issue of Leaves of Grass*, 456 *pages*, 12mo., *published by Thayer & Eldridge*, 116 *Washington Street, Boston.*

1862. W. W. leaves Brooklyn and New York permanently. Goes down to the field of war. Winters partly in Army of the Potomac, camped along the Rappahannock, Virginia. Begins his ministrations to the wounded.

1863–'64. In the field, and among the army hospitals—(see *Specimen Days*).

1865. At Washington City, as government clerk.

1866. Prints " Drum Taps " and "Sequel to Drum Taps," poems written during the war, " President Lincoln's Funeral Hymn," and other pieces. 96 pages, 12mo. Washington. No publisher's name.

1867. *Fourth edition of Leaves of Grass*, 338 *pages*, 12mo. *The poems now begin the order and classification eventually settled upon. New York. No publisher's name.*

1868, '69, '70. Employed in Attorney-General's Department, Washington.

1871. Delivers " After all, not to Create only," (" Song of the Exposition "), at the opening of the American Institute, New York.

1871. *Fifth issue of Leaves of Grass*, 384 *pages, and Passage to India*, 120 *pages, both in one volume*, 12mo. *Washington, D. C. Includes Drum Taps, Marches now the War is over, etc. A handsome edition.*

1872. Delivers " As a Strong Bird on Pinions Free," at the commencement, Dartmouth College, Hanover, N. H. (now, in 1882–'83 edition, entitled " Thou Mother with thy Equal Brood.")

"1872. Took a two months' trip through the New England States, up the Connecticut valley, Vermont, the Adirondacks region—and to Burlington, to see my dear sister Hannah once more. Returning, had a pleasant day-trip down Lake Champlain—and, the next day, down the Hudson."—*Notes.*

1873. Opening of this year, W. W. prostrated by paralysis, at Washington. Loses his mother by death.

1874–'75. Living in Camden, New Jersey, disabled and ill.

1876. *Sixth or Centennial issue of Leaves of Grass (printed from the plates of the fifth, 1871, edition). Also another volume, Two Rivulets, composed of prose and poems alternately.*

1877–'78. Health and strength now moderately improving.

1879. Journeys west to Missouri, Kansas, Colorado, etc. (see *Specimen Days*).

1880. Journeys to Canada, and summers there.

1881. *Seventh issue of Leaves of Grass, 382 pages, 12mo. James R. Osgood & Co., Boston. Six months after issue, J. R. Osgood & Co. are threatened with prosecution by Massachusetts District Attorney Stevens, and abandon the publication.*

1882–'83. *Eighth and final edition of Leaves of Grass, from same plates as 1881, Boston, edition, with last touches and corrections of the author, containing all the poems from first to last—two hundred and ninety-three—printed under W. W.'s direct supervision. Published by David McKay, 23 South Ninth Street, Philadelphia (formerly Rees Welsh & Co.).*

1882–'83. *Prose writings, autobiography, etc., entitled Specimen Days and Collect. The author's parentage, early days on Long Island, and young manhood in New York city. Three years' experience in the Secession War, especially the army hospitals. Convalescent notes afterward. Also, some literary criticisms, and jaunts west and north. The latter part, Collect, includes Democratic Vistas, the successive Prefaces of Leaves of Grass, with many notes, and prose compositions of various years. 374 pages, 12mo. Published by David McKay, 23 South Ninth Street, Philadelphia.*

1882–'83. *English edition of Leaves of Grass. Published by Wilson & McCormick, 73 Saint Vincent Street, Glasgow, Scotland.*

1882–'83. *English edition of Specimen Days and Collect. Published by Wilson & McCormick, 73 Saint Vincent Street, Glasgow, Scotland.*

PART I.

IF Taine, the French critic, had done no other good, it would be enough that he has brought to the fore the first, last, and all-illuminating point, with respect to any grand production of literature, that the only way to finally understand it is to minutely study the personality of the one who shaped it—his origin, times, surroundings, and his actual fortunes, life, and ways. All this supplies not only the glass through which to look, but it is the atmosphere, the very light itself. Who can profoundly get at Byron or Burns without such help? Would I apply the rule to Shakespeare? Yes, unhesitatingly; the plays of the great poet are not only the concentration of all that lambently played in the best fancies of those times—not only the gathering sunset of the stirring days of feudalism, but the particular life that the poet led, the kind of man he was, and what his individual experience absorbed. I don't wonder the theory is broached that other brains and fingers (Bacon's, Raleigh's, and more) had to do with the Shakespearian work—planned main parts of it, and built it. The singular absence of information about the *person* Shakespeare leaves unsolved many a riddle, and prevents the last and dearest descriptive touches and dicta of criticism.

WALT WHITMAN in " The Critic," Dec. 3d, 1881.

(12)

CHAPTER I.

BIOGRAPHICAL SKETCH.

WALT WHITMAN was born at West Hills, Huntington Township, Suffolk County, Long Island, New York State, May 31, 1819— the second of a family of nine children, seven boys and two girls.* The earliest lineal ancestor I am at present able to trace was Abijah W., born in England about 1560. The Rev. Zechariah W., his son, born 1595, came from England in the ship "True-Love" in 1635, and lived at Milford, Connecticut, whence his son Joseph W. some time before 1660 passed over to Huntington and settled there. From him (Savage's "Genealogical Dictionary," vol. 4, p. 524) the Long Island Whitmans descended. Although Joseph W. does not appear to have been very well off in 1660, there is evidence in the town records that he afterwards became so. It is probable that he or one of his sons purchased the farm at West Hills on which the poet's great grandfather, grandfather, and father lived.

The Whitmans were, and are still, a solid, tall, strong-framed, long-lived race of men, moderate of speech, friendly, fond of their land and of horses and cattle, sluggish in their passions, but

---

* Here is a list of the immediate family:

The Parents.	Born.	Died.
Walter Whitman, ...	July 14, 1789.	July 11, 1855.
Louisa Van Velsor, . . .	Sept. 22, 1795.	May 23, 1873.
Sons and Daughters.		
Jesse Whitman, ...	March 2, 1818.	March 21, 1870.
Walt Whitman, ...	May 31, 1819.	
Mary Elizabeth, ...	Feb. 3, 1821.	
Hannah Louisa, ...	Nov. 28, 1823.	
An Infant, ...	March 2, 1825.	Sept. 14, 1825.
Andrew Jackson, ...	April 7, 1827.	December, 1863.
George Washington, . .	Nov. 28, 1829.	
Thomas Jefferson, ...	July 18, 1833.	
Edward, ...	Aug. 9, 1835.	

Remote Ancestry of Walt Whitman.

ABIJAH WHITMAN, born in Eng.and about 1560.

ROBERT WHITMAN, born 1615, came from England in the "Abigail" in 1635, married in 1648, was living in 1679.

JOHN WHITMAN, born in Eng and, 1602, came over in the "True Love," 1640; died, 1692; had five sons, Thomas, John, Abijah, Zechariah, and Samuel (latter lived o be a hundred years o d), and five daughters, Hannah, Sarah, Mary, Elizabeth, and Judi h. All ch ldren were liv ng in 1685, as all mentioned in father's will made that year. Savage remarks that "John Whitman may well seem to be he ancestor o the larger portion of he thousands bearing that name in America."

ZECHARIAH WHITMAN, born 1595, came from England in the "True Love," 1635. Settled at M l-ford, Connecticut; a clergyman.

JOSEPH WHITMAN, son of Rev. Zech. Whitman, came to Huntington, L. I., before 1660; was still living in Huntington, 1690. His signature to a document bearing that date may still be seen in the town records. From him descended all the Long Island Whitmans.

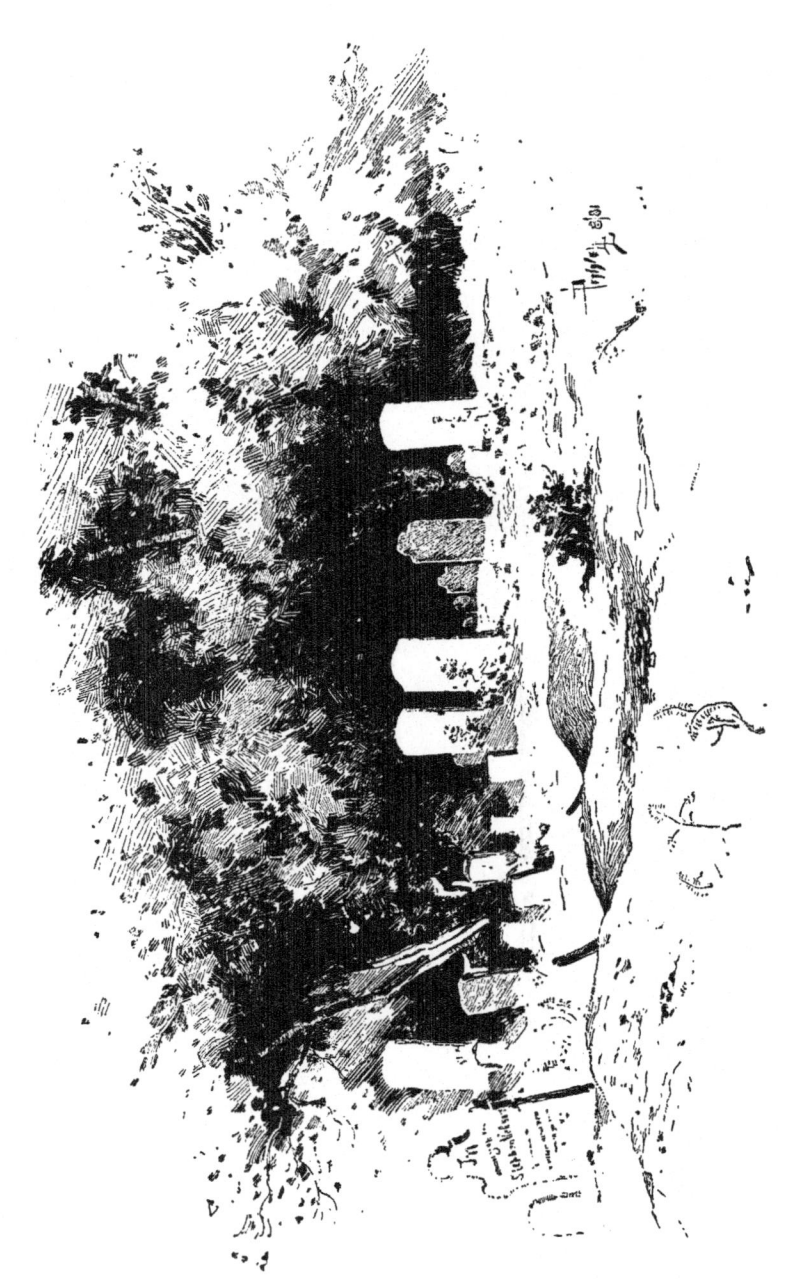

fearful when once started. During the American Revolution of 1776–'83, they were staunch patriots or "rebels," and several of the name were soldiers under Washington, two of them officers of some rank.

The poet's father, Walter W., after a childhood passed at West Hills on his parents' farm, when about 15 was put apprentice to the carpenter's trade in New York City, and lived and worked there as youth and young man. He married in 1816. His business afterwards for many years extended into various parts of Long Island. He was a large, quiet, serious man, very kind to children and animals, and a good citizen, neighbor and parent. In his trade he was noted as a superior framer. Not a few of his barn and house frames, with their seasoned timbers and careful braces and joists, are still standing in Suffolk and Queen's counties and in Brooklyn, strong and plumb as ever.

On his mother's side the poet is descended from the Van Velsors, a family of farmers settled also on their own land near Cold Spring Harbor, three or four miles from West Hills. They seem to have been a warm-hearted and sympathetic race. An aged man who had known them well, said to me one day at Huntington, "Old Major Van Velsor was the best of men; there are no better men than he was—and his wife was just as good a woman as he was a man." Walt Whitman's mother, Louisa Van Velsor, was their daughter. The family was of Holland Dutch descent. The men and boys were fond of horses, the raising of which from blooded stock was a large part of their occupation, and Louisa, when young, was herself a daring and spirited rider. As a woman and mother she was of marked spiritual and intuitive nature, remarkably healthy and strong, had a kind, generous heart, good sense, and a cheerful and even temper. Walt Whitman himself makes much of the feminine side of his ancestry. Both his grandmothers (with each of whom he spent a part of every year until he was quite a big lad), appear to have been specially noble and endearing characters. At the death of his own mother he spoke of her, and his sister-in-law Martha, as "the best and sweetest women I ever saw, or ever expect to see."

Not a little of the significance of the poet's Whitman and

Immediate Ancestry of Walt Whitman.

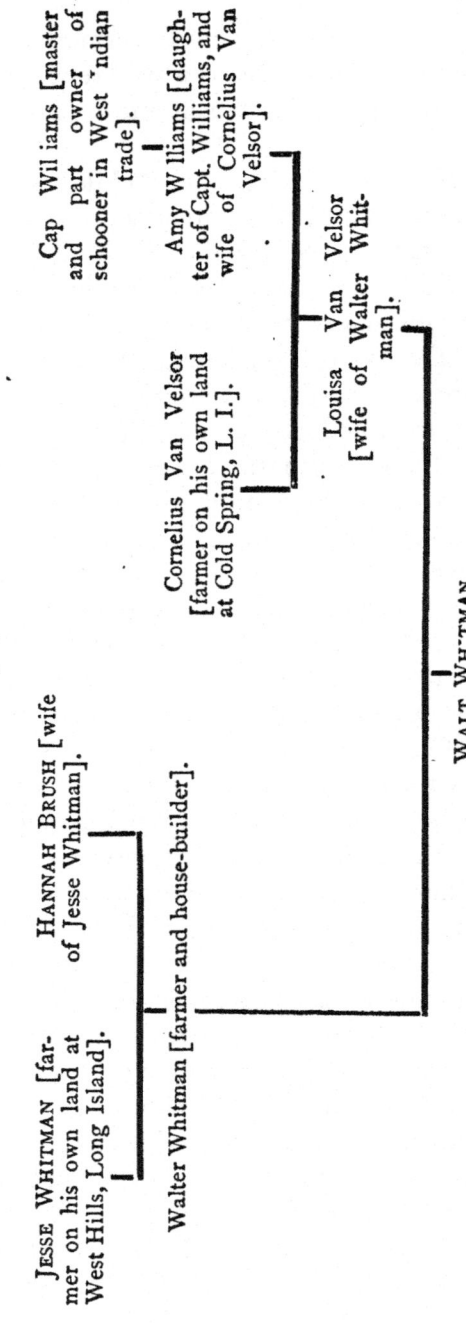

Cap Wil iams [master and part owner of schooner in West ndian trade].

Amy W lliams [daughter of Capt. Williams, and wife of Cornelius Van Velsor].

Cornelius Van Velsor [farmer on his own land at Cold Spring, L. I.].

Louisa Van Velsor [wife of Walter Whitman].

Hannah Brush [wife of Jesse Whitman].

Walter Whitman [farmer and house-builder].

Jesse Whitman [farmer on his own land at West Hills, Long Island].

WALT WHITMAN.

Van Velsor ancestry may be found in the ancient, grim, and crowded cemeteries of the two families and their branches, running back for many generations. To any "Old Mortality" these cemeteries—one at West Hills, the other about a mile from Cold Spring Harbor—would fully repay the trouble to visit. Looking on them as I did a couple of summers since, I thought them the most solemn, natural, impressive burial-places I had ever seen.

There is no doubt that both Walt Whitman's personality and writings are to be credited very largely to their Holland origin through his mother's side. A faithful and subtle investigation (and a very curious one it would be) might trace far back many of the elements of *Leaves of Grass,** long before their author was born. From his mother also he derived his extraordinary affective nature, spirituality and human sympathy. From his father chiefly must have come his passion for freedom, and the firmness of character which has enabled him to persevere for a lifetime in what he has called "carrying out his own ideal." I have heard him say, more than once, that all the members of his father's family were noted for their resolution (which he called obstinacy), and that nothing ever could or did turn any of them

* Washington Irving taught the people of New York to laugh at their Dutch ancestors. John Lothrop Motley has made them proud of them as the connecting link between themselves and the heroic founders of the Dutch Republic. It is full time that the New Netherlands colonists should be rescued from the limbo of absurdity into which Irving's wit cast them. They deserve rehabilitation and a serious history. The merits of their descendants speak for them The old Knickerbocker families are still—and have been ever since the day when stout old Sir Robert Holmes seized the New Netherlands for England—among the first and best people in New York. If all the truth were known, we should be as proud of the ship "Goot Vrow" and the landing at Communipaw, as New Englanders are of the "May Flower" and Plymouth Rock. In Motley's pages what a noble people lives again! No grander fight than theirs for freedom was ever fought. In the cases of Greece against Persia, Switzerland against Austria and Burgundy, the American Colonies against England, the first French Republic against Monarchial Europe, certain special advantages were on the weaker though winning sides, and brilliant victories in the field decided the struggle. But the poor and peaceable little Dutch Provinces in their stand against bitter religious persecution, plus intolerable tyranny, from the wealthiest and most warlike Kingdom in Europe, were beaten repeatedly; yet they fought on, and when at last, wearied with slaughter, Spain gave over, and let them go free, it was not because she was defeated or lacked either men or means to carry on the contest, but because she saw that complete conquest of the Netherlands would mean the last Hollander dead in the last ditch, and the country the Dutch had reclaimed from the ocean once more sunk beneath its waves. Who can read that history and not think of it with pride, if the blood of those heroic people flows in his veins?—*New York Tribune.*

from a course they had once positively decided upon. From father and mother alike, he derived his magnificent physique, and (until he lost it in 1873 through special causes to be spoken of later) his almost unexampled health and fulness of bodily life. Walt Whitman* could say with perhaps a better right than almost any man for such a boast, that he was

> Well-begotten, and rais'd by a perfect mother.

The other main element which has to be taken into account in the formation of the character of the poet, is that he was brought up on Long Island, or as he often calls it, giving the old Indian name, Paumanok, a peculiar region, over a hundred miles long, "shaped like a fish, plenty of sea-shore, the horizon boundless, the air fresh and healthy, the numerous bays and creeks swarming with aquatic birds, the south-side meadows covered with salt hay, the soil generally tough, but affording numberless springs of the sweetest water in the world." In certain parts the scenery, especially about West Hills and Huntington, and along the north side, is very picturesque. Here and there inland or along the coast are magnificent views, among them a grand one from the summit of "Jayne's Hill," about a mile from the old Whitman farm. On the broad top of this eminence the boy Walt Whitman must have lingered many an hour looking far over the slopes, the crests covered with trees, and the valleys between dotted with farm-houses—to the south far off the just visible waters of the Atlantic, to the north glimpses of Long Island Sound. Perhaps, indeed, there are few regions on the face of the earth better fitted for the concrete background of such a book as *Leaves of Grass.* After seeing and exploring it, the mind appreciates what was said by William O'Connor, after spending some weeks on Long Island and its shores, "that no óne can ever really get at Whitman's poems, and their finest lights and shades, until he has visited and familiarized himself with the freshness, scope, wildness and sea-beauty of this rugged Island."

While Walt Whitman was still a child his parents moved to

---

* At home, through infancy and boyhood, he was called "Walt," to distinguish him from his father "Walter," and the short name has always been used for him by his relatives and friends.

Brooklyn.   Here he grew up, but as lad and young man made frequent and long visits to his birth-place, and all through Queen's and Suffolk counties.   He attended the common schools of Brooklyn until he was thirteen years of age, and then he went into a printing office and learned to set type.   While still a youth of sixteen or seventeen he taught school in the country, and even then was writing for the newspapers and magazines. When he was about nineteen or twenty years of age (in 1839 and 1840) I find him publishing and editing the "Long Islander," a weekly newspaper at Huntington.   Then he came to New York city to live.

For the next twelve years he seems to have been employed chiefly in printing offices as compositor, and quite often as newspaper and magazine writer.   It was during those twelve and a few immediately following years—say from the age of 19 to 34 or '5— that he acquired his especial education ; and only those who know *Leaves of Grass* can understand the full meaning of that word in his case.   It was perhaps the most comprehensive equipment ever attained by a human being, though many things that the schools prescribe were left out.   It consisted in absorbing into himself the whole city and country about him, New York and Brooklyn, and their adjacencies ; not only their outside shows, but far more their interior heart and meaning.   In the first place he learned life—men, women, and children ; he went on equal terms with every one, he liked them and they him, and he knew them far better than they knew themselves.   Then he became thoroughly conversant with the shops, houses, sidewalks, ferries, factories, taverns, gatherings, political meetings, carousings, etc.   He was first the absorber of the sunlight, the free air and the open streets, and then of interiors.   He knew the hospitals, poorhouses, prisons, and their inmates.   He passed freely in and about those parts of the city which are inhabited by the worst characters ; he knew all their people, and many of them knew him ; he learned to tolerate their squalor, vice, and ignorance ; he saw the good (often much more than the self-righteous think) and the bad that was in them, and what there was to excuse and justify their lives.   It is said that these people, even the worst of them, while entire strangers to Walt Whitman, quite invariably received him without discourtesy and treated him well. Perhaps only those who have known the man personally, and have felt the peculiar magnetism of his presence, can fully understand this. Many of the worst of those characters became singularly attached to him. He knew and was sociable with the man that sold peanuts at the corner, and the old woman that dispensed coffee in the market. He did not patronize them, they were to him as good as the rest, as good as he, only temporarily dimmed and obscured.

True, he knew, and intimately knew, the better off and educated people as well as the poorest and most ignorant. Merchants, lawyers, doctors, scholars and writers, were among his friends. But the people he knew best and liked most, and who knew him best and liked him most, were neither the rich and conventional, nor the worst and poorest, but the decent-born middle-life farmers, mechanics, carpenters, pilots, drivers, masons, printers, deckhands, teamsters, drovers, and the like. These and their wives and children, their old fathers and mothers, he knew as no one I think ever knew them before, and between him and them (especially the old folks, the mothers and fathers) in numberless instances existed the warmest attachments.

He made himself familiar with all kinds of employments, not by reading trade reports and statistics, but by watching and stopping hours with the workmen (often his intimate friends) at their work. He visited the foundries, shops, rolling mills, slaughterhouses, woollen and cotton factories, shipyards, wharves, and the big carriage and cabinet shops—went to clam-bakes, races, auctions, weddings, sailing and bathing parties, christenings, and all kinds of merry-makings. (In their amplitude, richness, unflagging movement and gay color, *Leaves of Grass*, it may be said, are but the putting in poetic statements of the Manhattan Island and Brooklyn of those years, and of to-day.)

Amid the rest of his training and exercise he was a frequent speaker at debating societies. On Sundays he occasionally went to the churches of the various sects of Christians, and sometimes the synagogues of the Jews, and if there had been Buddhist tem ples, Mohammedan Mosques, and Confucian Joss-houses accessible, he would undoubtedly have visited those with the same interest and sympathy. Then he went occasionally to the libraries and museums of all sorts. For instance, there was at this time in New York a very fine and full collection of Egyptian antiquities, and for over two years off and on he spent many an hour there; he became friends with the proprietor, Dr. Abbott, a learned Egyptologist, and gleaned largely from his personal narrations. Reading did not go for so very much in Walt Whitman's education—he found he could get more from the things themselves than from pictures or descriptions of them drawn by others; still his aim was to absorb humanity and modern life, and he neglected no means, books included, by which this aim could be furthered. A favorite mode of study with him was, after an early breakfast, to reach by stage or sometimes on foot, several miles from the city, some solitary spot by the sea-shore, generally Coney Island (a very different place then from what it is now), taking with him a knapsack containing a bite of plain food, a towel and a book. There he would spend the day in solitude with Nature, walking, thinking, observing the sea and sky, bathing, reading, or perhaps reciting aloud Homer and Shakespeare as he strode along the beach. These years he used to watch the English quarterlies and Blackwood, and when he found an article that suited him he would buy the number, perhaps second-hand, for a few cents, tear it out, and take it with him on his next sea-beach excursion to digest. Walt Whitman's life at this time was perhaps the happiest that has ever been lived; he speaks of himself as

Wandering, amazed at my own lightness and glee.

Whatever he did or saw seemed to give him pleasure. At one period of his life a special enjoyment in New York was riding up and down Broadway on an omnibus, sitting in front, watching the crowds and vehicles, and the limitless life of the swarming streets. Or crossing the East River, half the day or half the night in the pilot-houses of Brooklyn ferry-boats, watching the multitudes coming and going, observing the sights on the waters, feeling the quiver of the boat, the strong beat of the paddles, and the rush through the yielding water.   Other times he would go out to sea with his friends of the pilot-boats, and all day and all night enjoy the salt air, the motion of the waves, the speed of the boat, the isolation, the deep feeling of communion with free Nature and the great brine.   The simplest and most common- place pursuits (and yet perhaps something *rushing*) suited him best; the main thing with him was that he was perfectly sound and well, and all life's delights were matters of course.

At one time, (I think along in his twenty-third year or there- abouts,) he became quite a speaker at the Democratic mass-meet- ings.   He spoke in New York City and down at country gather- ings on Long Island.   He was quite popular at Jamaica, in Queen's County.   (He had been a student at the Academy there when a big lad.)   Though he took (in Brooklyn and New York, 1840 – '55,) no strenuous personal part in "politics"—in the City, State and National elections—he watched their progress carefully, sometimes aided in the nomination of candidates, per- haps voted at the municipal elections, and always at the Con- gressional and Presidential ones.

Though all this practical, tumultuous, varied and generally outdoor life was enjoyment to Walt Whitman, there had come to his young maturity one supreme enjoyment, the Italian opera. And the climax of the opera to him was the singing of the famous contralto Alboni.   It was during the time of which I am now speaking that she came to New York, and he did not miss hear- ing her one single night.   I have heard him say that the influence of Alboni's singing upon him was a most important factor in his poetic growth.   He speaks of her in *Leaves of Grass,* as

> The lustrous orb, Venus contralto, the blooming mother,
> Sister of loftiest gods.

Throughout all his life indeed the opera and the best music has been one of his chief delights.   He heard all the good bands, orchestras, or soloists who came to New York from 1840 to 1860, and I know that many passages of his poetry were suggested or inspired by one or other of them, and often written down at the moment, or immediately afterwards.

To use the simple and hearty old scripture phrase, "the love of women" has, of course, been, and is in a legitimate sense, one of the man's elementary passions. I can only touch upon this subject, which is sufficiently set forth in the latter lines of the following extract from John Burroughs's "Notes":

For a few years he now seems to be a member of that light battalion of writers for the press who, with facile pen, compose tale, report, editorial, or what-not, for pleasure and a living; a peculiar class, always to be found in any large city. Once in a while he appears at the political mass meetings as a speaker. He is on the Democratic side, at the time going for Van Buren for President, and, in due course, for Polk. He speaks in New York, and down on Long Island, where he is made much of. Through this period (1840 – '55), without entering into particulars, it is enough to say that he sounded all experiences of life, with all their passions, pleasures and abandonments. He was young, in perfect bodily condition, and had the city of New York and its ample opportunities around him. I trace this period in some of the poems of "Children of Adam," and occasionally in other parts of his book, including "Calamus."

In 1847 and '48 he was occupied in Brooklyn as editor of the "Daily Eagle" newspaper. (It is said to have been his strenuous and persistent advocacy that secured to the city the old Fort Greene battle-ground, now known as Washington Park.) About 1849, being now thirty years of age, having lived so far entirely on Long Island and Brooklyn and in New York, and besides the invariable though moderate labor necessary to pay his way, occupied himself enjoying and absorbing their shows, life and facilities, he started on a long tour through the Middle, Southern and Western States. He passed slowly through Pennsylvania and Virginia, crossed the Alleghany Mountains, took a steamboat at Wheeling, descended by leisurely stages the Ohio and Mississippi Rivers to New Orleans, and lived there some time, employed editorially on a newspaper, the "Crescent." Outside of work hours he occupied himself observing Southern life, people, the river, with its miles of levee and its multitudinous and peculiar scenes. He seems to have passed much the same sort of a time as in New York—that is, a life of the open streets and public places, hotels, theatres, evening drives and social meetings—(and I know no city where such a life may be more enjoyable than

New Orleans). He liked to go to the great French market for an early morning walk, for the sake of the peculiar stir and shows of the place—often took his breakfast at a coffee-stand there kept by a large, handsome mulatto woman. All who have lived in the Southern States, and love them (and who that has ever lived there can think of them without affection and longing?) will feel in a hundred places, in reading *Leaves of Grass,* that Walt Whitman has caught and transferred to his pages the true atmosphere of that delicious and sunny region.

After staying about a year in New Orleans, he visited various other parts of the South, and then turned North again. Ascending the Mississippi to St. Louis, he stayed there for a time, then journeyed to Chicago, to Milwaukee, and so up to the Straits of Mackinaw. From there, turning east and south, after lingering awhile at Detroit, he slowly descended the great lakes to Niagara, and, with many lags and stoppages, crossed New York State and returned to Brooklyn.

In 1851 and '52 he published and edited a newspaper of his own, the "Freeman," in Brooklyn. He afterward built and sold moderate-sized houses. At this last business he made money, and if he had continued would probably have become rich. (He seems to have thought there was danger of this, and that was one reason, no doubt, why he gave it up.) Early in the fifties *Leaves of Grass* began to take a sort of unconscious shape in his mind. In 1854 he commenced definitely writing out the poems that were printed in the first edition. Though most of this period was occupied with the house-building speculations, he made frequent excursions down Long Island, and at times would remain away in some solitary place, by the sea-shore or in the woods, for weeks at a time. The twelve poems which make up the original 1855 edition finished, they were printed at the establishment of Andrew and James Rome, corner of Fulton and Cranberry Streets, Brooklyn, the poet himself assisting to set the type.

I insert here a short account furnished me (in Brooklyn in July, 1881) by a person who knew Walt Whitman soon after

1849—that is, subsequent to his 30th year. I give it in the nar-   x
rator's own words as I jotted them down at the time :

Walt Whitman had a small printing office and book store on Myrtle Avenue,
Brooklyn, where after his return from the South he started the "Freeman"
newspaper, first as weekly, then as daily, and continued it a year or so. The
superficial opinion about him was that he was somewhat of an idler, "a
loafer," but not in a bad sense. He always earned his own living. I
thought him a very natural person. He wore plain, cheap clothes, which
were always particularly clean. Everybody knew him, everyone almost
liked him. We all of us (referring to the other members of his family,
brothers, sisters, father and mother), long before he published *Leaves of
Grass*, looked upon him as a man who was to make a mark in the world. He
was always a good listener, the best I ever knew—of late years, I think, he
talks somewhat more—in those early years (1849-'54) he talked very little
indeed. When he did talk his conversation was remarkably pointed, attractive, and clear. When *Leaves of Grass* first appeared I thought it a great
work, but that the man was greater than the book. His singular coolness
was an especial feature. I have never seen him excited in the least degree :
never heard him swear but once. He was quite gray at thirty. He had a
look of age in his youth, as he has now a look of youth in his age.

The great International Exhibition or World's Fair of 1853 in
New York, in that vast structure (Sixth Avenue and Fortieth
Street) of glass and iron, never excelled for architectural sentiment and beauty, with its rare and ample picture collection from
Europe, its statues, specimens of the fabrics of all nations, silver
and gold plate, machinery, ores, woods of different countries,
with its immense streams of visitors day and night, had for him
a powerful attraction, kept up for nearly a year. Among his
favorite haunts through the building were the area containing
Thorwaldsen's colossal group of Christ and the twelve apostles,
the department of woods and timber, the thousand works in the
long picture gallery—a collection never surpassed in any land—
and then occasionally to stand a long while under the lofty
heavy glass dome.

-Early in 1855 he was writing *Leaves of Grass* from time to
time, getting it in shape. Wrote at the opera, in the street, on
the ferry-boat, at the sea-side, in the fields, sometimes stopped
work to write. Certainly no book was ever more directly written
from living impulses and impromptu sights, and less in the

abstract. Quit house-building in the spring of 1855 to print
and publish the first edition. Then, "when the book aroused
such a tempest of anger and condemnation everywhere," to
give his own words as he has since told me, " I went off to the
" east end of Long Island, and spent the late summer and all the
" fall—the happiest of my life—around Shelter Island and Peco-
" nic Bay. Then came back to New York with the confirmed
" resolution, from which I never afterwards wavered, to go on
" with my poetic enterprise in my own way, and finish it as well
" as I could."

Early in July this year had occurred the death of his father,
after a suffering of many years, from serious illness and prostra-
tion.

The memoranda which follow were written for this volume in
1881 by a lady—Miss Helen E. Price, of Woodside, Long
Island—whose acquaintance with Walt Whitman, and his frequent temporary residence in her parents' family, make her pecu-
liarly competent to present a picture of the man in those periods
of middle life:

My acquaintance with Walt Whitman began in 1856, or about a year after
he published the first edition of *Leaves of Grass.* I was at that time living
with my parents in Brooklyn, and although hardly more than a child in years,
the impression made upon my girlish imagination by his large, grand presence, his loose, free dress, and his musical voice will never be effaced. From
that date until the death of his mother, in 1873, he was often a visitor at our
house, as I at his, his mother being only less dear to me than my own.

So many remembrances of him in those by-gone years come crowding to
my mind that to choose what will be most characteristic, and most likely to
interest those who know him only from his books, is a task to which I fear I
shall prove unequal. On the other hand, *anything* I might write of him, his
conversation especially, when deprived of the magnetism of his presence and
voice, and of the circumstances and occasions which called forth the words,
will, I am painfully aware, seem poor and tame.

I must preface my first anecdote of him with some description of a gentleman with whom many of my early recollections of his conversations are
connected. At that time Mr. A. was living with his daughter's family, who
occupied with us the same house. A. was a man of wide knowledge and
the most analytical mind of any one I ever knew. He was a Swedenborgian,
not formally belonging to the church of that name, but accepting in the

main the doctrines of the Swedish seer as revealed in his works. Although the two men differed greatly on many points, such was the mutual esteem and forbearance between them, that during the many talks they had together, in which I sat by a delighted listener, it was only on one occasion (at the outbreak of our civil war) that I ever noticed the slightest irritation between them. Each, though holding mainly to his own views, was large enough to see truth in the other's presentation also. The subject of many of their early conversations was Democracy. No one who has even the slightest acquaintance with Walt Whitman's writings needs to be told what were and are his ideas on that subject—with what passionate ardor he espouses the cause of the people, and the fervent and glowing faith he has in their ultimate destiny. Mr. A. rather inclined to the Carlylean and perhaps Emersonian idea, that from among the masses are to be found only here and there individuals capable of rightly governing themselves and others, as in myriads of grains of sand, there are only occasional diamonds—or in innumerable seeds, only a very few destined to develop into perfect plants. Some months after our first meeting with Mr. Whitman, my mother invited Mrs. Eliza A. Farnum (former matron of Sing Sing prison) to meet him at our house. In the beginning of conversation he said to her, " I know more about you, Mrs. Farnum, than you think I do ; I have heard you spoken of often by friends of mine at Sing Sing at the time you were there." Then turning to Mr. A., who sat near by, he added in a lower tone, half seriously, half quizzically, " Some of the prisoners." This was said solely for Mr. A.'s benefit, as a kind of supplement to their talks on Democracy.

No one could possibly have more aversion to being lionized than Mr. Whitman. I could not say how many times, after getting his consent to meet certain admirers at our house, he has vexed and annoyed us by staying away. At one time an evening was appointed to meet General T., of Philadelphia, and a number of others. We waited with some misgivings for his appearance, but he came at last. Soon as the introductions were over, he sidled off to a corner of the room where there was a group of young children, with whom he talked and laughed and played, evidently to their mutual satisfaction. Our company, who had come from a distance to see Mr. Whitman, and did not expect another opportunity, were quite annoyed, and my mother was finally commissioned to get him out of his corner. When she told her errand, he looked up with the utmost merriment, and said, " O, yes—I'll do it—where do you want me to sit ? On the piano ?" He went forward very good-naturedly, however, but I knew that his happy time for that evening was over.

A friend of ours, a very brilliant and intellectual lady, had often expressed a great desire to see him—but as she lived out of town it was difficult to arrange a meeting. One day she came to our house full of animation and triumph. " I have seen Walt Whitman at last," she said. " I was sitting in the cabin of the Brooklyn ferry-boat when he came in. I knew it was he; it couldn't be any one else; and as he walked through the boat with such an elephantine roll and swing, I could hardly keep from getting right up and rolling after him." The next time he called we related this to him; he laughed heartily, and frequently afterward alluded to his "elephantine roll."

Mr. Whitman was not a smooth, glib, or even a very fluent talker. His ideas seemed always to be called forth or suggested by what was said before, and he would frequently hesitate for just the right term to express his meaning. He never gave the impression that his words were cut and dried in his mind, or at his tongue's end, to be used on occasion; but you listened to what seemed to be freshly thought, which gave to all he said an indescribable charm. His language was forcible, rich and vivid to the last degree, and even when most serious and earnest, his talk was always enlivened by frequent gleams of humor. (I believe it has been assumed by the critics that he has no humor. There could not be a greater mistake.) I have said that in conversation he was not fluent, yet when a little excited in talking on any subject very near his heart, his words would come forth rapidly, and in strains of amazing eloquence. At such times I have wished our little circle was enlarged a hundred-fold, that others might have the privilege of hearing him.

As a listener (all who have met him will agree with me) I think that he was and is unsurpassed. He was ever more anxious to hear your thought than to express his own. Often when asked to give his opinion on any subject, his first words would be, " Tell me what you have to say about it." His method of considering, pondering, what Emerson calls " entertaining," your thought was singularly agreeable and flattering, and evidently an outgrowth of his natural manner, and as if unconscious of paying you any special compliment. He seemed to call forth the best there was in those he met. He never appeared to me a conceited or egotistical man, though I have frequently heard him say himself that he was so. On the contrary, he was always unassuming and modest in asserting himself, and seemed to feel, or at least made others feel, that their opinions were more valuable than his own. I have heard him express serious doubt as to what would be the final judgment of posterity on his poems, or " pieces" as he sometimes called them.

I have, however, seen in his character something that, for wan⁴ of a better word, I would call vanity. I think it arose from his superabundant vitality and strength. All through those years he gloried in his health, his magnificent physical proportions, his buoyant and overflowing life (this was in the first ten years of my acquaintance with him), and whatever so-called oddity there was in his dress and looks arose, I think, from this peculiar consciousness or pride. We all thought that his costume suited him, and liked every part of it except his hat. He wore a soft French beaver, with rather a wide brim and a towering crown, which was always pushed up high. My sister would sometimes take it slyly just before he was ready to go, flatten the crown, and fix it more in accordance with the shape worn by others. All in vain; invariably on taking it up his fist would be thrust inside, and it would speedily assume its original dimensions.

One day, in 1858 I think, he came to see us, and after talking awhile on various matters, he announced, a little diffidently I thought, that he had written a new piece. In answer to our inquiries, he said it was about a mocking bird, and was founded on a real incident. My mother suggested that he bring it over and read to us, which he promised to do. In some doubt, in spite of this assurance, we were, therefore, agreeably surprised when a few days after he appeared with the manuscript of " Out of the Cradle Endlessly Rocking" in his pocket. At first he wanted one of us to read it. Mr. A. took it and read it through with great appreciation and feeling. He then asked my mother to read it, which she did. And finally, at our special request, he read it himself. That evening comes before me now as one of the most enjoyable of my life. At each reading fresh beauties revealed themselves to me. I could not say whose reading I preferred ; he liked my mother's, and Mr. A. liked his. After the three readings were over, he asked each one of us what we would suggest in any way, and I can remember how taken aback and nonplussed I was when he turned and asked me also.

He once (I forget what we were talking about—friendship, I think) said there was a wonderful depth of meaning (" at second or third removes," as he called it) in the old tales of mythology. In that of Cupid and Psyche, for instance ; it meant to him that the ardent expression in words of affection often tended to destroy affection. It was like the golden fruit which turned to ashes upon being grasped, or even touched. As an illustration, he mentioned the case of a young man he was in the habit of meeting every morning where he went to work. He said there had grown up between them a delightful silent friendship and sympathy. But one morning when he went as usual to the office, the young man came forward, shook him violently by the hand, and expressed in heated language the affection he felt for him. Mr. Whitman said that all the subtle charm of their unspoken friendship was from that time gone.

He was always an ardent lover of music, and heard all the operas, oratorios, bands, and all the great singers who visited New York during those years. I heard him very frequently speak of Grisi, Mario, Sontag, La Grange, Jenny Lind, Alboni, Bosio, Truffi, Bettini, Marini, Badiali, Mrs. Wood, Mrs. Seguin ; and I was never tired of listening to his accounts of them. Alboni he considered by far the greatest of them all, both as regards voice and emotional and artistic power. If I remember rightly, he told me that during her engagament in the city he went to hear her twenty nights. Brignoli in his prime he thought superior to Mario. Bettini, however, was his favorite tenor, and Badiali, the baritone, was another favorite. In talking to him once about music I found he had read George Sand's "Consuelo," and enjoyed it thoroughly. One passage he liked best was where Consuelo sings in church at the very beginning of her musical career. He said he had read it over many times. I remember hearing him mention other books of George Sand's, "the Journeyman Joiner" and the " Devil's Pool," which he liked much.

But although he talked of music and books with me, and of politics, patriotism, and the news of the day with Mr. A., it was in talking with my mother on the spiritual nature of man, and on the reforms of the age and kindred themes, that he took special delight. These appeared to be his favorite topics, and she, having similar sympathies and tastes, would take an equal pleasure with himself in discussing them. It was the society of my mother that was certainly Walt Whitman's greatest attraction to our house. She had a nature in many respects akin to his own—a broad, comprehensive mind, which enabled her to look beyond and through externals into the essence of things —a large, generous spirit in judging whoever she came in contact with, always recognizing the good and ignoring the evil—a strong deep faith in an infinite overruling goodness and power, and a most tender and loving heart. How many times has she taken in outcasts who have come to our door, and treated them to the best the house afforded, regardless of dirt, disease, everything but their humanity and suffering. How many times (not always however) has she been most wofully deceived and drawn into much trouble thereby. It made no difference, the next one that came would be treated with the same hospitality in spite of all remonstrance and argument. She has gone to that unknown world she was so fond of speculating upon, and never will the memory of her unselfish life, her exceeding love and charity, fade from the hearts of her children and friends. It was in her friendship, and in this *women's circle*—a mother and two daughters—that Mr. Whitman passed not a few of his leisure hours during all those years.

Walt Whitman, the most intuitive man I ever knew, had the least regard for mere verbal smartness. While seeing him listening with bent head to Mr. A.'s arguments upon some point on which they radically differed, I have often been reminded of that passage in his book,

> Logic and sermons never convince ;
> The damp of the night drives deeper into my soul.

While admitting and appreciating the force of reason and logic, yet if they were in conflict with what he *felt* in the depths of his soul to be true, he would hold fast to the latter, even though he could give no satisfactory reason for so doing. Though he would himself pooh-pooh the assumption, I have no doubt also he had spells of singular abstraction and exaltation. I remember hearing my mother describe an interview she once had with him while we were living in Brooklyn during the early years of our acquaintance. Death was the subject of their conversation. For a few minutes, she said, his face wore an expression she had never seen before—he seemed rapt, absorbed. In describing it afterward, she said he appeared like a man in a trance. Is not this a clue to many pages in *Leaves of Grass?* It would almost seem that in writing his poems he was taken possession of by a force, genius, inspiration, or whatever it may be called, that he was powerless to resist. We all felt this strange power on first reading his book, and that his poetry both was and was not part of himself. So that (as sometimes happened afterward) when he would say things at variance with what he had written, Mr. A. would remark to him, half jokingly, "Why, Walt, you ought to read *Leaves of Grass*." After the interview I have just described, my mother always felt that she had seen him in the state in which many of the earlier poems were conceived.

I never took notes of his conversations, and can only recall the general impression they made upon me. I can remember an occasional expression or opinion, but nothing of any importance. My brother and I were starting out one morning to choose a parlor-carpet. Hearing of our errand he said, " What a good idea it would be to have the pattern of a carpet designed of leaves—nothing but leaves—all sizes, shapes, and colors, like the ground under the trees in autumn."

I met him once in the Brooklyn street cars, soon after an article appeared in "the Radical" entitled "A Woman's Estimate of Walt Whitman." He asked if I had read it. I answered that I had, and that I should think he would like to know the lady who wrote it. "No," he said, "that does not so much matter. I do not even know her name." After a pause, he added, "But it was a great comfort to me."

If I were asked what I considered Walt Whitman's leading characteristic, I should say—and it is an opinion formed upon an acquaintance of over twenty years—his *religious sentiment* or feeling. It pervades and dominates his life, and I think no one could be in his presence any length of time without being impressed by it. He is a born *exalté*. His is not that religion, or show of it, that is comprised in dogmas, churches, creeds, etc. These are of little or no consequence to him, but it is that habitual state of feeling in which the person regards everything in God's universe with wonder, reverence, perfect acceptance, and love. He has more of all this than any one I have ever met. The deeply earnest spirit with which he looks upon humanity and life is so utterly opposed to cynicism and persiflage, that these always chill and repel him. He himself laughs at nothing (in a contemptuous sense), looks down on nothing—on the contrary everything is beautiful and wonderful to him.

One day I called upon his mother in Brooklyn and found him there. When I was going home he said he would cross the ferry with me. On our journey we had to pass through one of the great markets of New York in order to reach the cars running to the upper part of the city. I was hurrying through, according to my usual custom, but he kept constantly stopping me to point out the beautiful combinations of color at the butchers' stalls, and other stands; but above all the fish excited in him quite an enthusiasm. He made me admire their beautiful shapes and delicate tints, and I learned from him that day a lesson I have never forgotten.

One evening in 1866, while he was stopping with us in New York, the tea
bell had been rung ten minutes or more when he came down from his room,
and we all gathered around the table. I remarked him as he entered the
room; there seemed to be a peculiar brightness and elation about him, an
almost irrepressible joyousness, which shone from his face and seemed to pervade his whole body. It was the more noticeable as his ordinary mood
was one of quiet, yet cheerful serenity. I knew he had been working at
a new edition of his book, and I hoped if he had an opportunity he would
say something to let us into the secret of his mysterious joy. Unfortunately
most of those at the table were occupied with some subject of conversation;
at every pause I waited eagerly for him to speak; but no, some one else
would begin again, until I grew almost wild with impatience and vexation.
He appeared to listen, and would even laugh at some of the remarks that
were made, yet he did not utter a single word during the meal; and his face
still wore that singular brightness and delight, as though he had partaken of
some divine elixir. His expression was so remarkable that I might have
doubted my own observation, had it not been noticed by another as well as
myself.

I never heard him allude directly but once to what has been so severely
condemned in his books. It happened in this way. He had come on from
Washington and was stopping with us at the time (it was in 1866), preparing the new edition of *Leaves of Grass* just spoken of. My mother and I
were busy sewing in the sitting-room when he came back from a two hours'
absence and threw himself on the lounge. He said he had been offered very
favorable terms by a publisher down town (we were living in the upper part
of New York at that time) if he would consent to leave out a few lines from
two of his pieces. " But I dare not do it," he said; " I dare not leave out or
alter what is so genuine, so indispensable, so lofty, so pure." Those were his
exact words. The intense, I might almost say religious, earnestness with
which they were uttered made an impression upon me that I shall never
forget.

Here is another authentic personal account out of those years
—say from 1854 to '60—taken from the New York "World"
of June 4th, 1882, and written by Thomas A. Gere:

Thirty years ago, while employed upon an East River steamboat, I became
acquainted with Walt Whitman, and the association has ever since been a
treasured one by myself and the rest of my companion boatmen. He came
among us simply as a sociable passenger, but his genial behavior soon made
him a most welcome visitor. We knew somewhat of his reputation as a man
of letters, but the fact made no great impression upon us, nor did he ever
attempt a display of his gifts or learning that would in the least make us feel
he was not " of us, and one of us," as he used to express it. In a charm-

ingly practical democratic manner he took great pains to teach many valuable things to a hard-handed band of men whose life had afforded little time for books. In later years I have realized that "Walt"—he would allow no other salutation from us—has done much gratuitous work as a teacher, and in looking back I also realize his excellence as an instructor. A careful choice of words and terse method of explaining a subject were truly peculiar to him —at least the faculty was marvellous to us. In our long watches—he would pass entire afternoons and even nights with us—he would discourse in a clear, conversational sort of way upon politics, literature, art, music or the drama, from a seemingly endless storing of knowledge. He certainly urged some of us into a desire for attainments that perhaps would not otherwise have been aroused.

"My boy," he would often say, after simply but eloquently treating some theme, "you must read more of this for yourself," and then generously put his library at the listener's service. I have seen a youth swabbing a steamboat's deck with Walt's Homer in his monkey-jacket pocket! At all times he was keenly inquisitive in matters that belonged to the river or boat. He had to have a reason for the actions of the pilot, engineer, fireman and even deck-hands. Besides, he would learn the details of everything on board, from the knotted end of a bucket-rope to the construction of the engine. "Tell me all about it, boys," he would say, "for these are the real things I cannot get out of books." I am inclined to think that such inquisitiveness must always have been an industrious habit with him, for his writings abound with apt technicalities.

Walt's appearance used to attract great attention from the passengers when he came on board the boat. He was quite six feet in height, with the frame of a gladiator, a flowing gray beard mingled with the hairs on his broad, slightly bared chest. In his well-laundried checked shirt-sleeves, with trousers frequently pushed into his boot-legs, his fine head covered with an immense slouched black or light felt hat, he would walk about with a naturally majestic stride, a massive model of ease and independence. I hardly think his style of dress in those days was meant to be eccentric; he was very antagonistic to all show or sham, and I fancy he merely attired himself in what was handy, clean, economical and comfortable. His marked appearance, however, obtained for him a variety of callings in the minds of passengers who did not know him. "Is he a retired sea captain?" some would ask; "an actor? a military officer? a clergyman? Had he been a smuggler, or in the slave trade?" To amuse Walt I frequently repeated these odd speculations upon him. He laughed until the tears ran when I once told him that a very confidential observer had assured me he was crazy!

What enjoyable nights they were when Walt would come to us after a long study at home or in some prominent New York library! He would, indeed, "loaf" and unbend to our great delight with rich, witty anecdotes and pleasant sarcasms upon some events and men of the day. At times he would be joined by some literary acquaintance, generally to our disgust, or perhaps I should say jealousy, for we fancied that in some way we rather owned Walt; but the long classical debates that would occur, and deep subjects that would be dug up, used to waste the night in a most exasperating degree.

Walt's musical ability was a very entertaining quality: he was devotedly fond of opera, and many were the pleasant scraps and airs with which he would enliven us in a round, manly voice, when passengers were few and those few likely to be asleep on the seats. Our best attention was given to his recitations. In my judgment few could excel his reading of stirring poems and brilliant Shakespearian passages. These things he vented evidently for his own practice or amusement. I have heard him proceed to a length of some soliloquy in " Hamlet," " Lear," " Coriolanus " and " Macbeth," and when he had stopped suddenly and said with intense dissatisfaction, " No! no! no! that's the way the bad actors would do it," he would start off again and recite the part most impressively.

It is believed and asserted that his works will yet rise to meritorious eminence. Of this I do not feel competent to speak. I did not know him as the " Gray-Maned Lion of Camden," or " America's Good Gray Poet," but simply as dear old Walt. T. A. G.

Walt Whitman kept on for some years, working probably half the time, (though his life those years was so leisurely and free, he averaged from six to seven hours regular labor every day from his thirteenth year to past fifty), making trips into the country, writing poems, and, above all, enjoying life as it has seldom been enjoyed—until the breaking out of the Secession War. That event, which affected the business and the feelings of every person in the country, had an extraordinary bearing upon him. His brother George had volunteered and gone to the front. One morning in the middle of December, 1862, just after the first Fredericksburg battle, they saw by the military news in the New York "Herald" that George was wounded, it was thought seriously. Walt Whitman at an hour's notice started for the army camp on the Rappahannock. He found his brother wounded in the face by a fragment of shell, but the hurt not serious and already healing. The poet stayed several weeks in camp, absorbing all the grim sights and experiences of actual campaigning (and nothing could have been gloomier or more bloody than the season following "first Fredericksburg") through the depth of winter, in the flimsy shelter-tents, and in the impromptu hospitals, where thousands lay wounded, helpless, dying. He then returned to Washington, in charge of some Brooklyn soldiers with amputated limbs or down with illness. He had no definite plans at that time, or for long afterwards; but attention to the Brooklyn friends led to nursing others, and he stayed on and on, gradually falling into the labor and occupation, with reference to the war, which would do the most good, and be most satisfactory to himself.

I have heard him say that he was as much astonished as any one at the success of that personal ministration in the army hospitals. To pay his way he began writing correspondence for the New York and other papers; his letters were accepted and quite handsomely remunerated. So he stayed at Washington month after month, engaged in the work of the hospitals, and from time to time visiting the battle-fields. His services seemed imperiously needed. At that period, indeed the gloomiest of the war, hundreds of the sick and wounded of both armies were literally perishing for the want of decent care. His work as now commenced and continued for two to three years has never been, and perhaps never will be fully told. Doubtless it best remains in the memories of the saved soldiers. In two extracts which follow presently, and perhaps still better by suggestion in W. D. O'Connor's "Carpenter,"* those three years are but outlined. A surgeon who throughout the war had charge of one of the largest army hospitals in Washington has told the present writer that (without personal acquaintance, or any other than professional interest) he watched for many months Walt Whitman's ministerings to the sick and wounded, and was satisfied that he saved many lives. I do not believe this statement exaggerated. I believe, knowing Walt Whitman as I do, and having some knowledge of medicine, that the man did possess an extraordinary power, by which he must have been able in many cases to turn the scale in favor of life, when without him

* The CARPENTER—A Christmas story—by the author of "The Ghost."—Putnam's Monthly Magazine, January, 1868.

the result would have been death. The following extract is from
a letter by John Swinton in the New York "Herald" of April
1st, 1876:

For nearly twenty years I have been on terms of affectionate intimacy with
Walt Whitman. I knew him in his splendid prime, when his familiar figure
was daily seen on Broadway, and when he was brooding over those extraordinary poems which have since been put into half a dozen languages, and
commanded the homage of many of the greatest minds in modern literature.
From then to the time of his paralysis I know of his life and deeds. Rich
in good works and in saddening trials, he has remained the same genuine man,
in whom the well-springs of poetry give perpetual freshness to the passing
years. His paralysis was the result of his exhausting labors among our sick
and wounded soldiers in the hospitals near Washington during the war. I
saw something of these labors when I was visiting the hospitals. I can testify, as
countless others can, that for at least three years the " Good Gray Poet " spent
a large portion of his time, day and night, in the hospitals, as nurse and
comforter of those who had been maimed or otherwise prostrated in the service of their country. I first heard of him among the sufferers on the Penin-
sula after a battle there. Subsequently I saw him, time and again, in the
Washington hospitals, or wending his way there with basket or haversack
on his arm, and the strength of beneficence suffusing his face. His devotion
surpassed the devotion of woman. It would take a volume to tell of his
kindness, tenderness, and thoughtfulness.

Never shall I forget one night when I accompanied him on his rounds
through a hospital, filled with those wounded young Americans whose heroism he has sung in deathless numbers. There were three rows of cots, and
each cot bore its man. When he appeared, in passing along, there was a
smile of affection and welcome on every face, however wan, and his presence
seemed to light up the place as it might be lit by the presence of the Son of
Love. From cot to cot they called him, often in tremulous tones or in whispers; they embraced him, they touched his hand, they gazed at him. To one he
gave a few words of cheer, for another he wrote a letter home, to others he gave
an orange, a few comfits, a cigar, a pipe and tobacco, a sheet of paper or a postage stamp, all of which and many other things were in his capacious haversack. From another he would receive a dying message for mother, wife, or
sweetheart; for another he would promise to go an errand; to another, some
special friend, very low, he would give a manly farewell kiss. He did the
things for them which no nurse or doctor could do, and he seemed to leave a
benediction at every cot as he passed along. The lights had gleamed for hours
in the hospital that night before he left it, and as he took his way towards the
door, you could hear the voice of many a stricken hero calling, " Walt, Walt,
Walt, come again! come again!"

His basket and store, filled with all sorts of odds and ends for the men, had been emptied. He had really little to give, but it seemed to me as though he gave more than other men.

Here also is a paragraph from the New York "Tribune," by G. S. McWatters, summer of 1880:

While walking in the neighborhood of New Rochelle, Westchester County, a few days ago, I observed a man at work in a field adjoining the road, and I opened a conversation with him. He had served in the Union Army during the Rebellion, and I had no trouble in inducing him to fight some of his battles over again. He gave me a graphic description of how he was badly wounded in the leg; how the doctors resolved to cut his leg off; his resistance to the proposed amputation, and his utter despair when he found he must lose his leg (as they said) to save his life. As a last resort, he determined to appeal to a man who visited the hospital about every alternate day. This man was a representative of the Sanitary Commission [this of course is a mistake], and he described him as a tall, well-built man with the face of an angel. He carried over his broad shoulders a well-filled haversack, containing about everything that would give a sick soldier comfort. In it were pens, ink and paper, thread, needles, buttons, cakes, candy, fruit, and above all, pipes and tobacco. This last article was in general demand. When he asked a poor fellow if he used tobacco and the answer was " no " he would express some kind words of commendation, but when the answer was " yes," he would produce a piece of plug and smilingly say, " Take it, my brave boy, and enjoy it." He wrote letters for those who were not able to write, and to those who could he would furnish the materials, and never forgot the postage stamp. His good-natured and sympathetic inquiry about their health and what changes had taken place since he last saw them, impressed every patient with the feeling that he was their personal friend. To this man Rafferty (that was my informant's name) made his last appeal to save his shattered leg. He was listened to with attention, a minute inquiry into his case, a pause, and after a few moments' thought the man replied, patting him on the head, " May your mind rest easy, my boy; they shan't take it off." Rafferty began to describe his feelings when he received this assurance, and though so many years have passed since then, his emotions mastered him, his voice trembled and thickened, his eyes filled with tears, he stopped for a moment and then blurted out, slapping his leg with his hand, " This is the leg that man saved for me." I asked the name of the Good Samaritan. He said he thought it was Whitcomb or something like that. I suggested it was just like Walt Whitman. The name seemed to rouse the old soldier within him; he did not wait for another word from me, but seized my hand in both of his, and cried, " That's the man, that's the name; do you know him?"

The following extract from a letter by a lady addressed to the present writer will help to show how Walt Whitman saved money to get little comforts for those hospital inmates ·

I remember calling upon him in Washington during the war, with Mr. T. He occupied a little room in the third or fourth story of a house where he could get the cheapest rent. He was just eating his breakfast; it was about 10 A.M.; he sat beside the fire, toasting a slice of bread on a jackknife, with a cup of tea without milk; a little sugar in a brown paper, and butter in some more brown paper. He was making his meal for the next eight hours. He was using all his means and time and energies for the sick and wounded in the hospitals.

Finally, the letter which follows—(one of hundreds that of course never dreamed of seeing print, recovered by me by a lucky accident), written by Walt Whitman himself to Mrs. Price, mother of the lady whose reminiscences are given some pages back—will help to throw light on this part of his life:

WASHINGTON, October 11th, 1863.

DEAR FRIEND: Your letters were both received, and were indeed welcome. Don't mind my not answering them promptly, for you know what a wretch I am about such things. But you must write just as often as you conveniently can. Tell me all about your folks, especially the girls, and about Mr. A. Of course you won't forget Arthur, and always when you write to him send my love. Tell me about Mrs. U. and the dear little rogues. Tell Mrs. B. she ought to be here, hospital matron, only it is a harder pull than folks anticipate. You wrote about Emma, her thinking she might and ought to come as nurse for the soldiers. Dear girl, I know it would be a blessed thing for the men to have her loving spirit and hand. But, my darling, it is a dreadful thing—you don't know these wounds, sickness, etc., the sad condition in which many of the men are brought here, and remain for days; sometimes the wounds full of crawling corruption, etc. Down in the field-hospitals in front they have no proper care (can't have), and after a battle go for many days unattended to.

Abby, I think often about you and the pleasant days, the visits I used to pay you, and how good it was always to be made so welcome. Oh, I wish I could come in this afternoon and have a good tea with you, and have three or four hours of mutual comfort, and rest and talk, and be all of us together again. Is Helen home and well? and what is she doing now? And you, my dear friend, how sorry I am to hear that your health is not rugged—but, dear Abby, you must not dwell on anticipations of the worst (but I know that is not your nature, or did not use to be). I hope this will find you feeling quite well and in good spirits—I feel so tremendously well myself—I will have to come and show myself to you, I think—I am so fat, good appetite, out considerably in the open air, and all red and tanned worse than ever. You see, therefore, that my life amid these sad and death-stricken hospitals has not told at all badly upon me, for I am this fall so running over with health I feel as if I ought to go on, on that account, working among all who are deprived of it—and O how gladly I would bestow upon them a liberal share of mine, dear Abby, if such a thing were possible.

I am continually moving around among the hospitals. One I go to oftenest these last three months is " Armory Square," as it is large, generally full of the worst wounds and sickness, and is among the least visited. To this or some other I never miss a day or evening. Above all, the poor boys' welcome simple kindness, loving affection (some are so fervent, so hungering for this)—poor fellows, how young they are, lying there with their pale faces, and that mute look in the eyes. Oh, how one gets to love them, often, particular cases, so suffering, so good, so manly and yet simple. Abby, you would all smile to see me among them—many of them like children. Ceremony is quite discarded— they suffer and get exhausted and so weary—not a few are on their dying beds —lots of them have grown to expect, as I leave at night, that we should kiss each other, sometimes quite a number; I have to go round. There is little petting in a soldier's life in the field, but, Abby, I know what is in their hearts, always waiting, though they may be unconscious of it themselves.

I have a place where I buy very nice home-made biscuits, sweet crackers, etc. Among others, one of my ways is to get a good lot of these, and for supper, go through a couple of wards and give a portion to each man—next day two wards more, and so on. Then each marked case needs something to itself. I spend my evenings altogether at the hospitals—my days often. I give little gifts of money in small sums, which I am enabled to do—all sorts of things, indeed, food, clothing, letter-stamps (I write lots of letters), now and then a good pair of crutches or a cane, etc. Then I read to them—the whole ward that can walk gathers around me and listens.

All this I tell you, my dear, because I know it will interest you. There is much else—many exceptions—those I leave out. I like Washington very well; I have three or four hours my own work every day copying, and in writing letters for the press, etc.; make enough to pay my way—live in an inexpensive manner anyhow. I like the mission I am at here, and as it is deeply holding me I shall continue.

[*On a second sheet*] October 15.

Well, Abby, I will send you enough to make up lost time. I ought to have finished and sent off the letter last Sunday, when it was written. I have been unusually busy. We are having new arrivals of wounded and sick now all the time—some very bad cases. I have found some good friends here, a few, but true as steel—W. D. O'C. and wife above all the rest. He is a clerk in the Treasury—she is a Yankee girl. Then C. W. E. in Paymaster's Depart-

ment. He is a Boston boy, too—their friendship and assistance have been
unswerving.

In the hospitals among these American soldiers from East and West, North
and South, I could not describe to you what mutual attachments, passing
deep and tender. Some have died, but the love for them lives as long as I
draw breath. These soldiers know how to love too, when once they have the
right person. It is wonderful. You see I am running off into the clouds (perhaps my element). Abby, I am writing this last note this afternoon in Major
H.'s office—he is away sick—I am here a good deal of the time alone—it is
a dark, rainy afternoon—we don't know what is going on down in front,
whether Meade is getting the worst of it, or not—(but the result of the big
elections permanently cheers us)—I believe fully in Lincoln—few know the
rocks and quicksands he has to steer through and over. I inclose you a note
Mrs. O'C. handed me to send you, written, I suppose, upon impulse. She is
a noble Massachusetts woman, is not very rugged in health—I am there very
much—her husband and I are great friends. Well, I must close—the rain is
pouring, the sky leaden, it is between 2 and 3—I am going to get some dinner
and then to the hospital. Good-by, dear friends; I send my love to all.

                                                              W. W.

Three unflinching years of work in that terrible suspense and
excitement of 1862–'5 changed Walt Whitman from a young to
an old man. Under the constant and intense moral strain to
which he was subjected (indicated in "A March in the Ranks
Hard-press'd," and especially in "The Wound-Dresser," in
"Drum Taps"), he eventually broke down. The doctors called
his complaint "hospital malaria," and perhaps it was; but that
splendid physique was sapped by labor, watching, and still
more by the emotions, dreads, deaths, uncertainties of three years,
before it was possible for hospital malaria or any similar cause to
overcome it. This illness (the first he ever had in his life) in the
hot summer of 1864, he never entirely recovered from—and never
will. He went North for a short time, and after getting apparently better, returned to his hospital work.

Some time before the close of the war, he was appointed
to a clerkship in the Department of the Interior; but was shortly
afterwards discharged by a new Secretary, Hon. James Harlan,
"because he was the author of *an indecent book.*" He was immediately given an equally good place (secured through
the good offices of W. D. O'Connor and J. Hubley Ashton) in

the office of Attorney-General James Speed. That dismissal brought out the pamphlet (to be given presently) called "The Good Gray Poet," which was adjudged at the time by Henry J. Raymond to be the most brilliant monogram in American literature. It is worth while to put on record here a brief memorandum of this dismissal. Walt Whitman at the period was dividing all his spare time between visits to the wounded and sick still left in several army hospitals at Washington, and composing the poem "When Lilacs Last in the Dooryard Bloom'd." The morning after he was dismissed, his friend, Mr. Ashton, (who had himself sat in the President's Cabinet, and who occupied a national legal position), drove down to the Patent Office and had a long interview with Secretary Harlan on the subject of the dismissal. The Assistant Secretary of the Interior, Judge Otto, was present, but took no part in the discussion. Mr. A. asked why Whitman was dismissed, whether he had been found inattentive to his duties or incompetent for them. Mr. Harlan said No, there was no complaint on those points; as far as he knew, W. was a competent and faithful clerk. Mr. A. said, "Then what is the reason?" Mr. Harlan answered, "Whitman is the author of *Leaves of Grass.*" Mr. A. said, "Is *that* the reason?" The Secretary said, "Yes, it is"—and then made a statement essentially to the following purport: He was exploring the Department after office hours, and in one of the rooms he found *Leaves of Grass.* He took it up and thought it so odd, that he carried it to his own office awhile, and examined it. There were marks by or upon the pieces all through the book. He found in some of these marked passages matter so outrageous that he determined to discharge the writer, etc. Mr. A. responded by a brief statement of the theory of *Leaves of Grass*—that any bad construction put upon the passages alluded to was not warranted either by the actual principle of the poems or the intentions of the author. Mr. Harlan said he couldn't help that—the author of *Leaves of Grass* was a free lover, etc. Mr. A. said, " Mr. Harlan, I *know* Walt Whitman personally and well, and if you will listen to me, I will tell you what his life has been and is." He then went on with quite a long narrative. Mr. Harlan finally said, "You have

4

changed my opinion of Mr. Whitman's personal character; but I shall adhere to my decision dismissing him." Mr. A. commenced some further remarks, when Mr. Harlan summarily said, "It's no use, Mr. A., I will not have the man who wrote *Leaves of Grass* in this Department, if the President himself were to order his reinstatement. I would resign myself sooner than put him back." Mr. Harlan then broke into a long and vehement tirade against the book and its writer, to which Mr. A. made no reply, but bowed and took his leave.

The following transient incidents and sketches of the man as he actually appeared on the streets of Washington from 1864 to '72, were jotted down at the time and on the spot:

An eye-witness and participator relates, in a letter to a friend, the following anecdote of Abraham Lincoln: It was in the winter-time, I think in '64, I went up to the White House with a friend of mine, an M. C., who had some business with the President. He had gone out, so we didn't stop; but coming down stairs, quite near the door, we met the President coming in, and we stept back into the East Room, and stood near the front windows, where my friend had a confab with him. It didn't last more than three or four minutes; but there was something about a letter which my friend had handed the President, and Mr. Lincoln had read it, and was holding it in his hand thinking it over, and looking out of the window, when Walt Whitman went by, on the White House walk in front, quite slow, with his hands in the breast-pockets of his overcoat, and a sizeable felt hat on, and his head pretty well up, just as I have often seen him on Broadway. Mr. Lincoln asked who that was, or something of the kind. I spoke up, mentioning the name, Walt Whitman, and said he was the author of *Leaves of Grass*. Mr. Lincoln didn't say anything, but took a good look, till Whitman was quite gone by. Then he says—(I can't give you his way of saying it, but it was quite emphatic and odd)—" Well," he says, " *he* looks like a MAN." He said it pretty loud, but in a sort of absent way, and with the emphasis on the words I have underscored. He didn't say any more, but began to talk again about the letter; and in a minute or so we went off.

From Burroughs's "Birds and Poets."

I give here a glimpse of him in Washington on a Pennsylvania Avenue and Navy Yard horse-car, toward the close of the war, one summer day at sundown. The car is crowded and suffocatingly hot, with many passengers on the rear platform, and among them a bearded, florid-faced man, elderly but agile, resting against the dash, by the side of the young conductor, and evidently his intimate friend. The man wears a broad-brim white hat. Among the jam inside, near the door, a young Englishwoman, of the working class, with two children, has had trouble all the way with the youngest, a strong, fat, fretful, bright babe of fourteen or fifteen months, who bids fair to worry the mother completely out, besides becoming a howling nuisance to everybody. As the car tugs around Capitol Hill the young one is more demoniac than ever, and the flushed and perspiring mother is just ready to burst into tears with weariness and vexation. The car stops at the top of the hill to let off most of the rear platform passengers, and the white-hatted man reaches inside and gently but firmly disengaging the babe from its stifling place in the mother's arms, takes it in his own, and out in the air. The astonished and excited child, partly in fear, partly in satisfaction at the change, stops its screaming, and as the man adjusts it more securely to his breast, plants its chubby hands against him, and pushing off as far as it can, gives a good long look squarely in his face; then, as if satisfied, snuggles down with its head on his neck, and in less than a minute is sound and peacefully asleep without another whimper, utterly fagged out. A square or so more, and the conductor, who has had an unusually hard and uninterrupted day's work, gets off for his first meal and relief since morning. And now the white-hatted man, holding the slumbering babe also, acts as conductor the rest of the distance, keeping his eye on the passengers inside, who have by this time thinned out greatly. He makes a very good conductor, too, pulling the bell to stop or go on as needed, and seems to enjoy the occupation. The babe mean-while rests its fat cheeks close on his neck and gray beard, one of his arms vigilantly surrounding it, while the other signals, from time to time, with the strap; and the flushed mother inside has a good half-hour to breathe, and cool, and recover herself.

From the Washington "Chronicle," May 9th, 1869.

On Pennsylvania Avenue or Seventh or Fourteenth Street, or perhaps of a Sunday along the suburban road toward Rock Creek, or across on Arlington Heights, or up the shores of the Potomac, you will meet moving along at a firm but moderate pace, a robust figure, six feet high, costumed in blue or gray, with drab hat, broad shirt collar, gray-white beard, full and curly, with face like a red apple, blue eyes, and a look of animal health more indicative of hunting or boating than the department office or author's desk. Indeed, the subject of our item, in his verse, his manners, and even in his philosophy, evidently draws from, and has reference to, the influences of sea and sky, and woods and prairies, with their laws, and man in his relations to them, while neither the conventional parlor nor library has cast its spells upon him.

From the New York "Evening Mail," Oct. 27th, 1870.

The papers here have all paragraphed Walt Whitman's return to town and to his desk in the Attorney-General's office, after quite a long vacation. His figure is daily to be seen here moving around in the open air, especially fine mornings and evenings, observing, listening to, or sociably talking with all sorts of people, policemen, drivers, market men, old women, the blacks, or dignitaries; or perhaps, giving some small alms to beggars, the maimed, or organ-grinders; or stopping to caress little children, of whom he is very fond. He takes deep interest in all the news, foreign and domestic. At the commencement of the present war in Europe he was strongly German, but is now the ardent friend of the French, and enthusiastically supports them and their Republic. Here at home he goes for general amnesty and oblivion to Secessionists. He speaks sharply of the tendency of the Republican party to concentrate all power in Congress, and make its legislation absolutely sovereign, as against the equal claims, in their spheres, of the Presidency, the Judiciary, and the single States.

Altogether, perhaps, "the good, gray poet" is rightly located here. Our wide spaces, great edifices, the breadth of our landscape, the ample vistas, the splendor of our skies, night and day, with the national character, the memories of Washington and Lincoln, and others that might be named, make our city, above all others, the one where he fitly belongs.

Walt Whitman is now in his fifty-second year, hearty and blooming, tall, with white beard and long hair. The older he gets the more cheerful and gay-hearted he grows.

From a letter in Burroughs's "Notes," Nov. 28th, 1870.

. . . . You ask for some particulars of my friend Whitman. You know I first fell in with him years ago in the army. We then lived awhile in the same tent, and now I occupy the adjoining room to his. I can, therefore, gratify your curiosity. He is a large-looking man. While in the market the other day with a party of us, we were all weighed; his weight was 200 pounds. But I will just start with him like with the day. He is fond of the sun, and at this season, soon as it is well up, shining in his room, he is out in its beams for a cold-water bath with hand and sponge, after a brisk use of the flesh-brush. Then blithely singing—his singing often pleasantly wakes me—he proceeds to finish his toilet, about which he is quite particular. Then forth for a walk in the open air, or perhaps some short exercise in the gymnasium. Then to breakfast—no sipping and nibbling—he demolishes meat, eggs, rolls, toast, roast potatoes, coffee, buckwheat cakes, at a terrible rate. Then walking moderately to his desk in the Attorney-General's office—a pleasant desk, with large south window at his left, looking away down the Potomac, and across to Virginia on one side.

He is at present in first-rate bodily health. Of his mind you must judge from his writings, as I have sent them to you. He is not what is called ceremonious or polite, but I have noticed invariably kind and tolerant with children, servants, laborers, and the illiterate. He gives freely to the poor, according to his means. He can be freezing in manner, and knows how to fend off bores. Sometimes he and I only—sometimes a larger party of us—go off on rambles of several miles out in the country, or over the hills; sometimes we go nights, when the moon is fine. On such occasions he contributes his part to the general fun. You might hear his voice, half in sport, declaiming some passage from a poem or play, and his song or laugh about as often as any, sounding in the open air.

Walt Whitman continued to live in Washington until 1873. He had toward the last a salary of $1600 a year. He exercised the strictest economy, almost parsimony, in his own personal living, spending probably less than a quarter of his income upon himself, putting by about one-third of the remainder, and using the rest, first for a dear relative at home, and then for needy persons and the inmates of the army hospitals, his visits to which he continued as long as they remained in the Capital. He always looked well, and the greater part of the time felt well, but his health was never at the stage of perfection and unconsciousness it had been before his illness in 1864, and he suffered occasional attacks of actual and sometimes severe sickness.

This condition of depressed vitality culminated in a paralytic seizure. He told me (one day in 1880) how it came on, almost or exactly in the following words: " On the night of "the 22d of February, 1873, I was in the Treasury building in " Washington ; outside it was raining, sleeting, and quite cold " and dark. The office was comfortable, and I had a good fire. "I was lazily reading Bulwer's ' What Will He Do With It ?' " But I did not feel well, and put aside the book several times. "I remained at the office until pretty late. My lodging-room " was about a hundred yards down the street. At last I got up " to go home. At the door of the Treasury one of the friendly " group of guards asked me what ailed me, and said I looked " quite ill. He proposed to let a man take his place while he " would convoy me home. I said, No, I can go well enough. " He again said he would go with me, but I again declined. " Then he went down the steps and stood at the door with his " lantern until I reached the house where I lived. I walked up " to my room and went to bed and to sleep—woke up about

"three or four o'clock and found that I could not move my left
"arm or leg—did not feel particularly uneasy about it—was in
"no pain and even did not seem to be very ill—thought it would
"pass off—went to sleep again and slept until daylight. Then,
"however, I found that I could not get up—could not move.
"After several hours, some friends came in, and they immedi-
"ately sent for a doctor—fortunately a very good one, Dr. W.
"B. Drinkard. He looked very grave—thought my condition
"markedly serious. I did not think so: I supposed the attack
"would pass off soon—but it did not."

And it never has passed off, and never will, although he has
regained the use of his limbs to a considerable degree. This
first attack kept him down for over two months, at the end of
which time he was growing perceptibly better, when, on 23d
May, the same year, his mother died somewhat suddenly. (In
Camden, New Jersey. He was present at her death-bed.) That
event was a terrible blow to him, and after its occurrence he
became much worse. He left Washington for good, and took
up his residence in Camden.

And now for several years, 1873, '74, '75, his life hung upon
a thread. Though he suffered at times severely, he never became
dejected or impatient. It was said by one of his friends that in
that combination of illness, poverty, and old age, Walt Whitman
has been more grand than in the full vigor of his manhood.
For along with illness, pain, and the burden of age, he soon had
to bear poverty also. A little while after he became incapacitated
by illness, he was discharged from his Government clerkship,
and everything like an income entirely ceased. As to the profits
of *Leaves of Grass*, they had never been much, and now two
men, in succession, in New York (T. O'K. and C. P. S.), in
whose hands the sale of the book, on commission, had been
placed, took advantage of his helplessness to embezzle the
amounts due—(they calculated that death would soon settle the
score and rub it out). So that, although I hardly ever heard him
speak of them, I know that during those four years Walt Whitman
had to bear the imminent prospect of death, great pain and suf-

Phototype, F. Gutekunst, Philada,

fering at times, poverty, his poetic enterprise a failure, and the face of the public either clouded in contempt or turned away with indifference. If a man can go through such a trial as this without despair or misanthropy—if he can maintain a good heart, can preserve absolute self-respect, and as absolutely the respect, love, and admiration of the few who thoroughly know him—then he has given proofs I should say of personal heroism of the first order. It was, perhaps, needed that Walt Whitman should afford such proofs; at all events he has afforded them. What he was, how he lived, kept himself up during those years, and how at the end partially recuperated, is so well set forth by himself in *Specimen Days*, that it would be mere impertinence for any one else to attempt to retell the tale. The illness his friends looked upon with so much dread has borne fruit in one of the sanest and sweetest of books, the brightest and halest "Diary of an Invalid" ever written—a book unique in being the expression of strength in infirmity—the wisdom of weakness—so bright and translucent, at once of the earth, earthy, and spiritual as of the sky and stars. Other books of the invalid's room require to be read with the blinds drawn down and the priest on the threshold; but this sick man's chamber is the lane, and by the creek or sea-shore—always with the fresh air and the open sky overhead.

CHAPTER II.

THE POET IN 1880.—PERSONNEL, ETC.

THIS chapter has been mainly written while Walt Whitman visited at the house of the writer in Canada, or while he and I were travelling together through the Provinces of Ontario or Quebec, or on the Lakes, or the St. Lawrence or Saguenay Rivers; and the greater part of it while we were in the same room.

First, as to his personal appearance, noted at the time. On the 31st of May, 1880, Walt Whitman was sixty-one years of age. At first sight he looked much older, so that he was often supposed to be seventy or even eighty. He is six feet in height, and quite straight. He weighs nearly two hundred pounds. His body and limbs are full-sized and well-proportioned. His head is large and rounded in every direction, the top a little higher than a semicircle from the front to the back would make it. Though his face and head give the appearance of being plentifully supplied with hair, the crown is moderately bald; on the sides and back the hair long, very fine, and nearly snow-white. The eyebrows are highly arched, so that it is a long distance from the eye to the centre of the eyebrow—(this is the facial feature that strikes one most at first sight). The eyes themselves are light blue, not large,—indeed, in proportion to the head and face they seemed to me rather small; they are dull and heavy, not expressive—what expression they have is kindness, composure, suavity. The eyelids are full, the upper commonly droops nearly half over the globe of the eye. The nose is broad, strong, and quite straight; it is full-sized, but not large in proportion to the rest of the face; it does not descend straight from the forehead, but dips down somewhat between the eyes with a long sweep. The mouth is full-sized, the lips full. The sides and

lower part of the face are covered with a fine white beard, which is long enough to come down a little way on the breast. The upper lip bears a heavy mustache. The ear is very large, especially long from above downwards, heavy, and remarkably handsome. I believe all the poet's senses are exceptionally acute, his hearing especially so; no sound or modulation of sound perceptible to others escapes him, and he seems to hear many things that to ordinary folk are inaudible. I have heard him speak of hearing the grass grow and the trees coming out in leaf. In the "Song of Myself" he mentions the "bustle of growing wheat." And as to scent, he says in *Specimen Days*, "There is a scent in everything, even the snow; no two places, hardly any two hours, anywhere, exactly alike. How different the odor of noon from midnight, winter from summer, or a windy spell from a still one." His cheeks are round and smooth. His face had no lines that expressed care, or weariness, or age—it was the white hair and beard, and his feebleness in walking (due to the paralysis) that made him appear old. The habitual expression of his face is repose, but there is a well-marked firmness and decision. I have never seen his look, even momentarily, express contempt, or any vicious feeling. I have never known him to sneer at any person or thing, or to manifest in any way or degree either alarm or apprehension, though he has in my presence been placed in circumstances that would have caused both in most men. His complexion is peculiar, a bright maroon tint, which, contrasting with his white hair and beard, makes an impression very striking. His body is not white like that of all others whom I have seen of the English or Teutonic stock—it is a delicate but well-marked rose-color. All his features are large and massive, but so proportioned as not to look heavy. His face is the noblest I have ever seen.

No description can give any idea of the extraordinary physical attractiveness of the man. I do not speak now of the affection of friends and of those who are much with him, but of the magnetism exercised by him upon people who merely see him for a few minutes or pass him on the street. An intimate friend of the author's, after knowing Walt Whitman a few days, said in a letter: "As for myself, it seems to me now that I have always known him and loved him." And in another letter, written from a town where the poet had been staying for a few days, the same person says: "Do you know, every one who met him here seems to love him."

The following is the experience of a person well known to the present writer. He called on Walt Whitman and spent an hour at his home in Camden, in the autumn of 1877. He had never seen the poet before, but he had been profoundly reading his works for some years. He said that Walt Whitman only spoke to him about a hundred words altogether, and these quite ordinary and commonplace; that he did not realize anything peculiar while with him, but shortly after leaving a state of mental exaltation set in, which he could only describe by comparing to slight intoxication by champagne, or to falling in love! And this exaltation, he said, lasted at least six weeks in a clearly marked degree, so that, for at least that length of time, he was plainly different from his ordinary self. Neither, he said, did it then or since pass away, though it ceased to be felt as something new and strange, but became a permanent element in his life, a strong and living force (as he described it), making for purity and happiness. I may add that this person's whole life has been changed by that contact (no doubt the previous reading of *Leaves of Grass* also), his temper, character, entire spiritual being, outer life, conversation, etc., elevated and purified in an extraordinary degree. He tells me that at first he used often to speak to friends and acquaintances of his feeling for Walt Whitman and the *Leaves*, but after a time he found that he could not make himself understood, and that some even thought his mental balance impaired. He gradually learned to keep silence upon the subject, but the feeling did not abate, nor its influence upon his life grow less.

Walt Whitman's dress was always extremely plain. He usually wore in pleasant weather a light-gray suit of good woollen cloth. The only thing peculiar about his dress was that he had no neck-tie at any time, and always wore shirts with very large turn-down collars, the button at the neck some five or six inches lower than usual, so that the throat and upper part of the breast were exposed. In all other respects he dressed in a substantial, neat, plain, common way. Everything he wore, and everything about him, was always scrupulously clean. His clothes might (and often did) show signs of wear, or they might be torn or have holes worn in them; but they never looked soiled. Indeed, an exquisite aroma of cleanliness has always been one of the special features of the man; it has always belonged to his clothes, his breath, his whole body, his eating and drinking, his conversation, and no one could know him for an hour without seeing that it penetrated his mind and life, and was in fact the expression of a purity which was physical as much as moral, and moral as much as physical.

Walt Whitman, in my talks with him at that time, always disclaimed any lofty intention in himself or his poems. If you accepted his explanations they were simple and commonplace. But when you came to think about these explanations, and to enter into the spirit of them, you found that the simple and commonplace with him included the ideal and the spiritual. So it may be said that neither he nor his writings are growths of the ideal from the real, but are the actual real lifted up into the ideal. With Walt Whitman, his body, his outward life, his inward spiritual existence and his poetry, were all one; in every respect each tallied the other, and any one of them could always be inferred from any other. He said to me one day (I forget now in what connection), " I have imagined a life which should be that " of the average man in average circumstances, and still grand, " heroic." There is no doubt that such an ideal has been constantly before his mind, and that all he has done, said, written, thought and felt, have been and are, from moment to moment, moulded upon it. His manner is curiously calm and self-contained. He seldom becomes excited in conversation, or at all events seldom shows excitement; he rarely raises his voice or uses any gestures. I never knew him to be in a bad temper. He seemed always pleased with those about him. He did not generally wait for a formal introduction; upon meeting any person for the first

time, he very likely stepped forward, held out his hand (either left
or right whichever happened to be disengaged), and the person
and he were acquainted at once.   People could not tell why they
liked him, they said there was "something attractive about him,"
that he "had a great deal of personal magnetism," or made some
other vague explanation that meant nothing.   One very clever
musical person, who spent a couple of days in my house while
Walt Whitman was there, said to me on going away, "I know
what it is, it is *his wonderful voice* that makes it so pleasant to be
with him."   I said, "Yes, perhaps it is, but where did his voice
get that charm?"

Though he would sometimes not touch a book for a week, he
generally spent a part (though not a large part) of each day in
reading.   Perhaps he would read on an average a couple of hours
a day.   He seldom read any book deliberately through, and
there was no more apparent system about his reading than in
anything else that he did, that is to say there was no system
about it at all.   If he sat in the library an hour, he would have
half a dozen to a dozen volumes about him, on the table, on
chairs and on the floor.   He seemed to read a few pages here
and a few there, and pass from place to place, from volume to
volume, doubtless pursuing some clue or thread of his own.   Sometimes (though very seldom) he would get sufficiently interested
in a volume to read it all.   I think he read almost if not quite
the whole of Renouf's "Egypt," and Brusch-bey's "Egypt," but
these cases were exceptional.   In his way of reading he dipped
into histories, essays, metaphysical, religious and scientific treatises, novels and poetry (though I think he read less poetry than
anything else).   He read no language but English, yet I believe
he knew a great deal more French, German and Spanish, than
he would own to.   But if you took his own word for it, he knew
very little indeed on any subject.

His favorite occupation seemed to be strolling or sauntering about
outdoors by himself, looking at the grass, the trees, the flowers,
the vistas of light, the varying aspects of the sky, and listening
to the birds, the crickets, the tree-frogs, the wind in the trees,
and all the hundreds of natural sounds and shows.   It was evident

that these things gave him a pleasure that ordinary people never experience. Until I knew the man, it had not occurred to me (though I am moderately fond of outdoor life myself and have read what most of the poets say on the subject) that any one could derive so much absolute happiness and ample fulfilment from these things, as he evidently did. He himself never spoke of all this pleasure. I dare say he hardly thought of it, but any one who watched him could see plainly that in his case it was real and deep.

He had a way of singing, generally in an undertone, wherever he was or whatever he was doing when alone. You would hear him the first thing in the morning while he was taking his bath and dressing (he would then perhaps sing out in full, ballads or martial songs), and a large part of the time that he sauntered outdoors during the day he sang, usually tunes without words, or a formless recitative. Sometimes he would recite poetry, generally I think from Shakespeare or Homer, once in a while from Bryant or others. His way of rendering poetry was peculiar but effective. I remember the "Midnight Visitor" from the French poet Murger, also Tennyson's "Ulysses," and Schiller's "Diver." *

---

* A letter from Camden, in the "Springfield Republican," July 23, 1875, says: The Camden mechanics and young men have a flourishing literary society here, called the "Walt Whitman Club;" and some weeks since, they gave a musical and other entertainment for the benefit of the poor fund, at which Whitman readily appeared as reader of one of his own poems. There was a crowded house, the report in the local paper saying, "Probably the best part of the audience drawn to the entertainment by a mixture of wonder and uncertainty what sort of a being Walt Whitman really was, and what sort of a thing one of his poems might prove to be." The report goes on to give the following account of his appearance and reading: A large, lame old man, six feet tall, dressed in a complete suit of English gray, hobbled slowly out to view, with the assistance of a stout buckthorn staff. Though ill from paralysis, the clear blue eyes, complexion of transparent red, and fulness of figure so well known to many New Yorkers and Washingtonians of the past 15 years, and in Camden and Philadelphia of late, all remain about the same. With his snowy hair and fleecy beard, and in a manner which singularly combined strong emphasis with the very realization of self-composure, simplicity and ease, Mr. Whitman, for it was he (though he might be taken at first sight for 75 or 80, he is in fact not yet 57), proceeded to read, sitting, his poem of the "Mystic Trumpeter." His voice is firm, magnetic, and with a certain peculiar quality we heard an admiring auditor call unaffectedness. Its range is baritone, merging into bass. He reads very leisurely, makes frequent pauses or gaps, enunciates with distinctness, and uses few gestures, but those very significant. Is he eloquent and dramatic? No, not in the conventional sense, as illustrated by the best known stars of the pulpit, court-room, or the stage—for the bent of his reading, in fact the whole idea of it, is evidently to first form an enormous mental fund, as it were, within the regions of the chest, and heart, and lungs—a

He spent very little time in writing. It is probable that he never did give much time to that occupation. He wrote very few private letters. While he was with us he would write a letter to a Canada paper, full of his travels, his condition and his latest doings and thoughts, and get fifty or a hundred copies and send them to his friends and relations, especially the girls and young folks, and make that do for correspondence. Almost all his writing was done with a pencil in a sort of loose book that he carried in his breast pocket. The book consisted of a few sheets of good white paper folded and fastened with a pin or two; he said he had tried all sorts of note-books and he liked that kind best. He has undoubtedly used up hundreds of such little books; his *Leaves of Grass,* his memoranda of the Secession War, and his writings to this day, including *Specimen Days,* were and are formed in that manner. The literary work that he did was done at all sorts of times, and generally on his knee, impromptu, and often outdoors. Even in a room with the usual conveniences for writing he did not use a table; he put a book on his knee, or held it in his left hand, laid his paper upon it and wrote so. His handwriting is clear and plain, every letter perfectly formed, and always to me characteristic of the man. His "copy" for the printers might look rather startling at first glance, full of crossings out, directions and interlineations, but compositors soon got used to it, and then wanted nothing better.

He was very fond of flowers (fortunately we had great plenty— acres of them), either wild or cultivated—would often gather and arrange an immense bouquet of them for the dinner-table, for the room where he sat, or for his bed-room—wore a bud or just-started rose or perhaps a geranium, pinned to the lapel of his coat a great part of the time—did not seem to have much preference for one kind over any other—liked all sorts. I think he admired lilacs and sunflowers just as much as roses. "The tall leaning of sunflowers on their stalks" seemed to have a fascina-

sort of interior battery—out of which, charged to the full with such emotional impetus only, and without ranting or any of the usual accessories or clap-trap of the actor or singer, he launches what he has to say, free of noise or strain, yet with a power that makes one almost tremble.

The Sobbing
of the Bells
Midnight Sept 19·20 1881

The sobbing of the bells,
The sudden death-news everywhere
The slumberers rouse
The rapport of the people,
(Full well they know that
    message in the darkness,
Full well return, respond
    within their breasts, their
    brains, the sad reverberations)
The passionate toll and clang,
City to city joining, sounding
    passing,
Those heart-beats of a Nation
    in the Night.

tion for him. Perhaps, indeed, no man who ever lived liked so many things and disliked so few as Walt Whitman. All natural objects seemed to have a charm for him; all sights and sounds, outdoors and indoors, seemed to please him. He appeared to like (and I believe he did like) all the men, women and children he saw (though I never knew him to say that he liked any one), but each who knew him felt that he liked him or her, and that he liked others also. He was here entirely natural and unconventional. When he did express a preference for any person (which was very seldom) he would indicate it in some indirect way; for instance, I have known him to say, "Good-bye, my love," to a young married lady he had only seen half a dozen times.

He was especially fond of children, and all children liked and trusted him at once. Often the little ones, tired out and fretful, the moment he took them up and caressed them, would cease crying, and perhaps go to sleep in his arms. One day in the summer of 1880, several ladies, the poet and myself, attended a picnic given to hundreds of poor children in London. During the day I lost sight of my friend for perhaps an hour, and when I found him again he was sitting in a quiet nook by the river side, with a rosy-faced child of four or five years' old, tired out and sound asleep in his lap.*

For young and old his touch had a charm that cannot be described, and if it could, the description would not be believed except by those who know him either personally or through *Leaves of Grass.* This charm (physiological more than psycholog-

---

* BURIAL OF LITTLE WALTER WHITMAN —Among the late mortality in Camden, from heat, to young children, Colonel George W. Whitman and wife lost their infant son and only child Walter, less than a year of age. The funeral was last Friday. In the middle of the room, in its white coffin, lay the dead babe, strewed with a profusion of fresh geranium leaves and some tuberoses. For over an hour all the young ones of the neighborhood kept coming silently in groups or couples or singly, quite a stream surrounding the coffin. Near the corpse, in a great chair, sat Walt Whitman, the poet, quite enveloped by children, holding one encircled by either arm, and a beautiful little girl on his lap. The little girl looked curiously at the spectacle, and then inquiringly up in the old man's face. "You don't know what it is, do you, my dear?" said he—adding, "We don't either." Of the children surrounding the coffin many were mere babes, and had to be lifted up to look. There was no sermon, no ceremony, everything natural and informal, but, perhaps, there never was a more silently eloquent, simple, solemn and touching sight.—*Philadelphia Ledger,* July 20, 1876.

ical), if understood, would explain the whole mystery of the man, and how he produced such effects not only upon the well, but among the sick and wounded.

It is certain also, perhaps contrary to what I have given, that there is another phase, and a very real one, to the basis of his character. An elderly gentleman I talked with (he is a portrait painter and a distant relative of the poet), who has been much with, and knew him, particularly through the years of his middle age and later (1845 to 1870), tells me that Walt Whitman, in the elements of his character, had deepest sternness and hauteur, not easily aroused, but coming forth at times, and then well understood by those who know him best as something not to be trifled with. The gentleman alluded to (he is a reader and thorough accepter of *Leaves of Grass*) agrees with me in my delineation of his benevolence, evenness, and tolerant optimism, yet insists that at the inner framework of the poet has always been, as he expresses it, "a combination of hot blood and fighting qualities." He says my outline applies more especially to his later years; that Walt Whitman has gradually brought to the front the attributes I dwell upon, and given them control. His theory is, in almost his own words, that there are two natures in Walt Whitman. The one is of immense suavity, self-control, a mysticism like the occasional fits of Socrates, and a pervading Christ-like benevolence, tenderness, and sympathy (the sentiment of the intaglio frontispiece portrait, which I showed him, and he said he had seen exactly that look in "the old man," and more than once, during 1863–'64, though he never observed it before or since). But these qualities, though he has enthroned them, and for many years governed his life by them, are duplicated by far sterner ones. No doubt he has mastered the latter, but he has them. How could Walt Whitman (said my interlocutor) have taken the attitude toward evil, and things evil, which is behind every page of his utterance in *Leaves of Grass*, from first to last—so different on that subject from every writer known, new or old—unless he enfolded all that evil within him? (To all of which I give place here as not essentially inconsistent—if true—with my own theory of the poet's nature, and also because I am determined to take the fullest view of him, and from all sides.)

In an article in the "Galaxy" for December, 1866, John Burroughs said :

Lethargic during an interview, passive and receptive, an admirable listener, never in a hurry, with the air of one who has plenty of leisure, always in perfect repose, simple and direct in manners, a lover of plain, common people, "meeter of savage and gentleman on equal terms," temperate, chaste, sweet-breath'd, tender and affectionate, of copious friendship, with a large, summery, paternal soul that shines in all his ways and looks, he is by no means the "rough" certain people have been so willing to believe. Fastidious as a high caste Brahmin in his food and personal neatness and cleanliness, well dressed, with a gray, open throat, a deep sympathetic voice, a kind, genial look, the impression he makes upon you is that of the best blood and breeding. He reminds one of the first men, the beginners; has a primitive, outdoor look—not so much from being in the open air as from the texture and quality of his make—a look as of the earth, the sea, or the mountains, and "is usually taken," says a late champion of his cause, "for some great mechanic, or stevedore, or seaman, or grand laborer of one kind or another." His physiognomy presents very marked features—features of the true antique pattern, almost obsolete in modern faces—seen in the strong, square bridge of his nose, his high arching brows, and the absence of all bulging in his forehead— a face approximating in type to the statued Greek. He does not mean intellect merely, but life; and one feels that he must arrive at his results rather by sympathy and absorption than by hard intellectual processes—by the effluence of power rather than by direct and total application of it.

In conclusion, I suppose I ought to say that there is another side to the picture, the indispensable exception that proves the rule. This man, the sight of whom excites such extraordinary affection, whose voice has for most of those who hear it such a wonderful charm, whose touch possesses a power which no words can express—in rare instances, this man, like the magnet, repels as well as attracts. As there are those who instinctively love him, so there are others, here and there, who instinctively dislike him. The furious assaults of the press during twenty-five years, the disgraceful action of Secretary Harlan in 1865, the continuous refusal of publishers to publish his poems, and of booksellers to sell them, the legal threats in 1882 of the Massachusetts Attorney-General, voiced by Boston's District Attorney Stevens—the cowardly throwing up of their contract by J. R. Osgood & Co.— persecution by the wretched Anthony Comstock and his pitiful "Society for the Suppression of Vice"—with all the prevalent doubt and freezing coldness of the literary classes and organs up to this hour—are fitting outcomes and illustrations of that other side. As his poetic utterances are so ridiculous to many, even his personal appearance, in not a few cases, arouses equally sarcastic remark. His large figure, his red face, his copious beard, his loose and free attire, his rolling and unusually ample shirt-collar, without neck-tie and always wide open at the throat, all meet at times (and not so seldom, either,) with jeers and explosive laughter. Pages and extracts in this volume (see Appendix) give many samples of incredible misapprehension and malignance toward the book *Leaves of Grass.* They could be fully tallied with records of equal rancor, foulness, and falsehood against Walt Whitman personally. That such exist, and will probably continue, is doubtless according to a morbid attribute of humanity, and one of its most mysterious laws. A Washington reviewer some years since said on this subject :

Walt Whitman personally is a study, affording the strongest lights and shades. With all his undoubted instincts of perfection, he by no means sets up for a saint, but is a full-blooded fellow, with a life showing past blunders and missteps, and a spirit not only tolerant toward weak and sinful mortals, but probably a secret leaning toward them.   Then he has not escaped the fate of personalities who rouse public attention, and canards, by originality and independence.   Perhaps, too, he has that affectation sometimes seen—a grim amusement in tacitly taunting and inviting them.   Singularly simple and plain, few men are so beloved as he—few have ever so magnetized; yet none afford more temptation to caricature or bogus anecdotes.   The late summing-up of a first-rate judge of human nature, that *personal knowledge* of him unerringly dissipates such fictions, is the best disposal of the whole matter.

CHAPTER III.

HIS CONVERSATION.

HE did not talk much. Sometimes, while remaining cheery and good-natured, he would speak very little all day. His conversation, when he did talk, was at all times easy and unconstrained. I never knew him to argue or dispute, and he never spoke about money. He always justified, sometimes playfully, sometimes quite seriously, those who spoke harshly of himself or his writings, and I often thought he even took pleasure in those sharp criticisms, slanders, and the opposition of enemies. He said that his critics were quite right, that behind what his friends saw he was not at all what he seemed, and that from the point of view of its foes, his book deserved all the hard things they could say of it—and that he himself undoubtedly deserved them and plenty more.

When I first knew Walt Whitman I used to think that he watched himself, and did not allow his tongue to give expression to feelings of fretfulness, antipathy, complaint, and remonstrance. It did not occur to me as possible that these mental states could be absent in him. After long observation, however, and talking to others who had known him many years, I satisfied myself that such absence or unconsciousness was entirely real.

His deep, clear, and earnest voice makes a good part, though not all, of the charm of the simplest things he says ; a voice not characteristic of any special nationality, accent, or dialect. If he said (as he sometimes would involuntarily on stepping to the door and looking out), "Oh, the beautiful sky!" or "Oh, the beautiful grass!" the words produced the effect of sweet music.

One evening he spoke quite freely of his British friends, Pro fessor Dowden, Addington Symonds, Tennyson (who had sent him a letter warmly inviting him over there to T.'s house), Professor Clifford, and other and younger ones. I remember his glowing words of esteem and affection for Mrs. Gilchrist, and also for Robert Buchanan (whose denunciations and scathing appeal in the London papers at the time of the poet's darkest persecution, sickness, and poverty, made such a flutter in 1876).*

He said one day when talking about some fine scenery, and the desire to go and see it (and he himself was very fond of new scenery), "After all, the great lesson is that no special natural "sights, not Alps, Niagara, Yosemitè, or anything else, is more "grand or more beautiful than the ordinary sunrise and sunset, "earth and sky, the common trees and grass." Properly understood, I believe this suggests the central teaching of his writings and life, namely, that the commonplace is the grandest of all things ; that the exceptional in any line is no finer, better, or more beautiful than the usual, and that what is really wanting is not that we should possess something we have not at present, but that our eyes should be opened to see and our hearts to feel what we all have.

On the evening of the 1st of August, 1880, as we were sitting together on the veranda of the "Hub House," among the Thousand Islands of the St. Lawrence, I said to Walt Whitman, "It seems to me surprising that you never married. Did you remain single of set purpose?" He said, "No, I have hardly "done anything in my life of set purpose, in the way you mean." After a minute, he added, "I suppose the chief reason why I "never married must have been an overmastering passion for "entire freedom, unconstraint ; I had an instinct against form- "ing ties that would bind me." I said, "Yes, it was the instinct of self-preservation. Had you married at the usual age, *Leaves of Grass* would never have been written."

---

* He who wanders through the solitudes of far-off Uist or lonely Donegal may often behold the Golden Eagle sick to death, worn with age or famine, or with both, passing with weary waft of wing from promontory to promontory, from peak to peak, pursued by a crowd of prosperous rooks and crows, which fall screaming back whenever the noble bird turns his indignant head, and which follow frantically once more, hooting behind him, whenever he wends again upon his way. The rook is a "recognized" bird ; the crow is perfectly "estab-lished." But for the Eagle, when he sails aloft in the splendor of his strength, who shall per-fectly discern and measure his flight?—Robert Buchanan, *London Daily News*, March 13, 1876.

The same evening we talked about the use of alcohol, and we agreed that as mankind advanced in a noble individuality they would give up stimulants of all kinds as being always in the long run a mistake and unprofitable. He said, "The capital argument "against alcohol, that which must eventually condemn its use, "is this, that it takes away all the reserved control, the power "of mastership, and therefore offends against that splendid "pride in himself or herself which is fundamental in every man "or woman worth anything."

One day talking about religious experiences, Walt Whitman said, "I never had any particular religious experiences—never "felt that I needed to be saved—never felt the need of spiritual "regeneration—never had any fear of hell, or distrust of the "scheme of the universe. I always felt that it was perfectly "right and for the best."

On the 9th of August we were together at the Falls of Mont-morenci, near the foot of the stairs. There had been a good deal of rain, the river was high, and the falls finer than usual. I said, "Now, Walt, put that in a poem just as it is; if that could be done it would be magnificent." He said, "All such things "need at least the third or fourth remove; in itself it would be "too much for nine out of every ten readers. Very few" (he said, a little mischievously, perhaps), "care for natural objects "themselves, rocks, rain, hail, wild animals, tangled forests, "weeds, mud, common Nature. They want her in a shape fit "for reading about in a rocking-chair, or as ornaments in china, "marble, or bronze. The real things are, far more than they "would own, disgusting, revolting to them. This" (he added, half quizzically) "may be a reason of the dislike of *Leaves of* "*Grass* by the majority."

Walt Whitman, however, never mentions *Leaves of Grass*, unless first spoken to on the subject; then he talks about it, and his purpose in writing it, as of any ordinary matter. I have never heard him myself say much on the subject, but I will give here some of his words taken from the "Springfield Republican," reported, I have reason to know, as they were said impromptu: " Well, I'll suggest to you what my poems have grown out of,

"since you want to know so bad. I understand as well as any
"one they are ambitious and egotistical, but I hope the founda-
"tions are far deeper. We have to-day no songs, no expressions
"from the poets' and artists' points of view, of science, of Ameri-
"can democracy, and of the modern. The typical war spirit of
"the antique world, and its heroes and leaders, have been fully
"depicted and preserved in Homer, and since. Rapt ecstasy and
"Oriental veneration are in the Bible; the literature of those
"qualities will never, can never, ascend any higher. The ages
"of feudalism and European chivalry, through their results and
"personalities, are in Shakespeare. But where is the work, where
"the poem, in which the entirely different but fully equal glories
"and practice of our own democratic times, of the scientific,
"the materialistic, are held in solution, fused in human person-
"ality and emotions, and fully expressed? If, for instance, by
"some vast, instantaneous convulsion, American civilization
"were lost, where is the poem, or imaginative work in any depart-
"ment, which, if saved from the wreck, would preserve the char-
"acteristics and memories of it to succeeding worlds of men?

"You speak of Shakespeare and the relative poetical demands
"and opportunities, then and now—my own included. Shake-
"speare had his boundless rich materials, all his types and char-
"acters, the main threads of his plots, fully ripened and waiting
"to be woven in. The feudal world had flourished for centuries—
"gave him the perfect king, the lord, all that is heroic and grace-
"ful and proud—gave him the exquisite transfigurations of caste,
"sifted and selected out of the huge masses, as if for him, choice
"specimens of proved and noble gentlemen, varied and romantic
"incidents of the military, social, political and ecclesiastical
"history of a thousand years, all ready to fall into his plots and
"pages. Then the time comes for the evening of feudalism. A
"new power has advanced, and the flush, the pomp, the accumu-
"lated materials of those ages take on the complex gorgeousness
"of sunset. At this point Shakespeare appears. By amazing
"opportuneness, his faculty, his power, the feudalistic demands
"on him, combine, and he is their poet. But for my poems, what
"have I? I have all to *make*—have really to fashion all, except

"my own intentions—have to constructively sing the ideal yet
"unformed America. Shakespeare sang the past, the formed;
"I project the unformed, the future—depend on the future, and
"have to make my own audience.

"Most of the great poets are impersonal; I am personal.
"They portray their endless characters, events, passions, love-
"plots, but seldom or never mention themselves. In my poems
"all concentrates in, radiates from, revolves around myself. I
"have but one central figure, the general human personality
"typified in myself. Only I am sure my book inevitably necessi-
"tates that its reader transpose him or herself into that central
"position, and become the actor, experiencer, himself or herself,
"of every page, every aspiration, every line."

In our family groups and sociable company, he was fond of
telling little funny stories, bringing in comical sayings, generally
trivial in themselves (sometimes quite venerable), deriving most
of their charm—and they were very amusing—from special apt-
ness to the case, and from his manner of telling them. In St.
Louis, where he was a half invalid, one winter, he was in the
habit of visiting, twice a week, the kindergarten schools, and
spending an hour at a time among the young children, who
gathered in swarms about him to listen to "The three Cats who
took a Walk," or some other juvenile story. Lingering with us
all at the table after tea was a favorite recreation with him. The
following are some examples of his dry anecdotes, generally told
to groups of little or larger children:

There was a very courageous but simple old woman, and some
chaps agreed upon a plan to frighten her. One of them dressed
up in black, with horns and tail, and made himself very frightful.
In this rig he appeared to the old woman at night and said in a
terrible voice, "Look at me!" The old lady calmly put on her
spectacles, looked him steadily all over and said, "Who are you?"
"I am the devil!" said he, in a deep voice. "You the devil,
are you?" said the old woman composedly; then calmly, after a
pause—"*poor creetur!*"

He was fond of the well-known story about a sailor shipwrecked upon a strange coast, who wandering inland after a long jaunt saw a gibbet holding a murderer's corpse, and immediately burst out, "Thank God, at last I am in a Christian land."

A dry expression of his, talking about some one was, "Well, he has the good sense to like me." He used to tell about some man who said, when it was alleged that a certain fact was historical, "Oh, it's in the history is it? then I *know* it must be a lie." He would often give the following as "the wise Frenchman's reason·" "Do you say it is impossible? then I am sure it will come to pass."

One day he said: "Among the gloomy and terrible sights of the Secession War were often extremely humorous occurrences. It was a sort of rule in many hospitals when certain that a patient would die, to give him almost whatever he wanted to eat or drink. Under these circumstances some of the men would ask for whisky, and drink it freely. One man, a rough Westerner, whose life was limited to a few hours, used to wake up in the night and call out to the watchman, 'Come, Bill, give me some whisky; you know we are going to die. Come, give me some whisky, quick!'"

He had many dry idioms from his old intimacy with omnibus drivers in New York and other cities. (He always "took to them" and they to him—and the same to this day; at Christmas, in Washington, Philadelphia, Camden, or where residing at the time, he has for years had a custom of dispensing to these drivers, on quite a large scale, presents of the strong warm buckskin gloves so serviceable in that occupation.) One little story was of an old Broadway driver, who, being interrogated about a certain unpopular new-comer, answered with a grin, "Oh, he's one o' them pie-eaters from Connecticut."

Walt Whitman was so invariably courteous and kind in his manner to every one, it might have been thought he could have easily been bored and imposed upon, but this was not at all the case. He had so much tact that he always found a way of escape. He had a horror of smart talkers, and particularly of being questioned or interrogated. He had a very dry manner of dismissing intruders, or correcting those who went too far—not surly, but a peculiar tone of the voice, and glance of the eye, and sometimes a good-natured anecdote. A gentleman said to him one evening at tea-time, "I should not think, Mr. Whitman, that you were at all an emotional man." "Well," he replied drily, "there is "an old farmer down in Jersey, who says nothing, but keeps up "a devil of a thinking; and there are others like him."

He once told me he had read a good many different translations of Homer, and that the one he liked best, after all, was Buckley's literal prose version. He did not care for either Lord Derby's or Bryant's. I was reading the "Iliad" one day as we sat on the veranda together, and I made some remark to the effect that it was praised on account of its age and scholarly associations rather than its intrinsic merit, and that if it was first published now, no one would care anything about it "Well," he said, "perhaps not, but not for the reason you say. See," he said— the subject seemed to inspirit him, for he rose and walked slowly up and down, leaning on his cane, occasionally pausing—"See "how broadly and simply it opens. An old priest comes, op- "pressed with grief, to the sea-shore. The beach stretches far "away, and the waves roll sounding in. The old man calls his "divine master, Apollo, not to permit the foul insults and inju- "ries put upon him by the leader of the Greeks. Almost at once "in the distance an immense shadowy form, tall as a tree, comes "striding over the mountains. On his back he carries his quiver "of arrows, and his long silver bow. Just think of it," he said, "so daring, so unlike the cultivated prettiness of our poets—so "grim, free, large. No, no," he continued, "don't make light "of the 'Iliad.' Think how hard it is for a modern, one of us, "to put himself in sympathy with those old Greeks, with their "associations." These are the words that he used, but to see them in print will convey only a faint impression of their effect, or of the man as he said them—the manner, the deep, rich melody of the finest voice I believe in the world.

He thinks much of Dr. John A. Carlyle's translation of Dante's "Inferno," has had the volume by him for many years, reads in it often, and told me he had learned very much from it, espe- cially in conciseness—"no surplus flesh," as he describes it.

He said very deliberately to me once that he believed he knew less, in certain respects, about *Leaves of Grass* than some of the readers of it; and I believe (strange as it may seem) that this is true. There are things in the book I am sure could never be fully appreciated from the author's point of view.

He said one day that he considered the most distinguishing feature of his own poetry to be " Its *modernness*—the taking up in " their own spirit of all that specially differentiates our era from " others, particularly our democratic tendencies."

Another time he said : " The unspoken meaning of *Leaves of* " *Grass*, never absent, yet not told out—the indefinable animus " behind every page, is a main part of the book. Something " entirely outside of literature, as hitherto written ; outside of art " in all departments. Takes hold of muscular democratic viril- " ities without wincing, and puts them in verse. This makes it " distasteful to technical critics and readers. I understand all " those shrinking objections," he said, " and consider them in " one sense right enough ; but there was something for me to " do, no matter how it hurt or offended ; and I have done it." He said further : " I don't at all ignore the old stock elements " and machinery of poetry, but instead of making them main " things, I keep them away in the background, or like the roots " of a flower or tree, out of sight. The emotional element, for " instance, is not brought to the front, not put in words " to any great extent, though it is underneath every page. " I have made my poetry out of actual, practical life, such as is " common to every man and woman, so that all have an equal " share in it. The old poets went on the assumption that there " was a selection needed. I make little or no selection, put in " common things, tools, trades, all that can happen or belongs to " mechanics, farmers, or the practical community. I have not " put in the language of politics, but I have put in the spirit ; " and in science, by intention at least, the most advanced points " are perpetually recognized and allowed for."

He said to me once, " I often have to be quite vehement with " my friends to convince them that I am not (and don't want to " be) singular, exceptional, or eminent. I am willing to think

"I represent vast averages, and the generic American masses—
"that I am their voice; but not that I should be in any sense
"considered an exception to ordinary men."

Another time he said, "I have always considered the writing
"and publication of *Leaves of Grass* an experiment. Time only
"can tell how it will turn out."

"Remember, the book arose," he said, another time, "out of
"my life in Brooklyn and New York from 1838 to 1853, absorb-
"ing a million people, for fifteen years, with an intimacy, an
"eagerness, an abandon, probably never equalled—land and
"water. I have told you how I used to spend many half nights
"with my friends the pilots on the Brooklyn ferry-boats. I some-
"times took the wheel and steered, until one night a boat I was
"steering nearly met with a bad accident. After that I would
"not touch the wheel any more."

Walt Whitman and Rev. Mr. R. had a long conversation on
the veranda one beautiful summer evening. Mr. R. wanted to
get at the sources and birth of *Leaves of Grass* from its author.
The latter spoke as he always does, without any *arrière pensée*.
Among other things, he said he had tried to do something that
would on the one hand give expression to deepest religious
thought and feeling, and on the other be in accord with the
last results of modern science. He said, "I do not know that
"I have succeeded, but at all events I have indicated what needs
"to be done—and some one else may accomplish the task."

Another day Mr. R. said, talking of Colonel Robert Ingersoll:
"He takes away what we have, and gives us nothing in its place
—is there any good or service in that?" He pressed Walt Whitman for an answer, to find out his opinion about Ingersoll's argument and about Christianity. Walt Whitman said at last: "Well,
"I think the main and final point about the whole or any of these
"things is—is it true?"

He several times spoke of President Lincoln, whom he considered the most markedly national, Western, native character
the United States has yet produced. He never had any particular intimacy with Mr. Lincoln, but (being a personal friend
of John Hay, confidential secretary) saw a good deal of L.—was

much at the White House (1863 and '64), and knew the President's character behind the scenes.   In after years he desired to keep the anniversary of Mr. Lincoln's death by a public lecture he had prepared (see *Specimen Days*), but he could get neither engagements, audiences, nor public interest,* and after delivering this lecture in 1879, '80, and '81, to small gatherings, he stopped it.

He said one Sunday morning after a previous merry evening: " God likes jokes and fun as well as He likes church-going and " prayers."   Once, after some conversation, he went on to speculate whether Luther was really as original and central a man as generally supposed, or whether circumstances ought not to be credited with a good deal that seemed to flow from him—and whether his Reformation was of such value to the world as most Protestants think.   He talked of great men generally, and how their apparent greatness is often due to the force of circumstances —often because it is convenient for history to use them as radiating points and illustrations of vast currents of ideas floating in the time, more than to any qualities inherent in themselves— and ended by discussing Renan's opinion of the relative greatness of Jesus, Jesus son of Sirach, and Hillel.

One evening he said he wondered whether modern poets might not best take the same " new departure" that Lord Bacon took in science, and emerge directly from Nature and its laws, and from things and facts themselves, not from what is said about them, or the stereotyped fancies, or abstract ideas of the beautiful, at second or third removes.

He once said no one but a medical man could realize the appropriateness (jeered at by the " Saturday Review," as proof positive that W. W. was no poet,) of his putting in the word " diarrhœa " in one of his hospital poems; a malady that stood third on the deadly list of camp diseases.   In the same connection, he said that several pieces in *Leaves of Grass* could only be

* In one of the principal cities of the United States, the 15th anniversary of President Lin_ coln's death (April 15, 1880) was commemorated by this public address.   The next morning the discriminating editor of the leading daily paper relegates all report of " the Death of Abraham Lincoln," as described and commented on by Walt Whitman, to a half-supercilious notice of five or six lines—and fills two columns of his journal with a lecture by a visiting English clergyman, on " the Evidential Value of the Acts of the Apostles "!

thoroughly understood by a physician, the mother of a family of children, or a genuine nurse.

He never spoke deprecatingly of any nationality or class of men, or time in the world's history, or feudalism, or against any trades or occupations—not even against any animals, insects, plants, or inanimate things—nor any of the laws of Nature, or any of the results of those laws, such as illness, deformity, or death. He never complains or grumbles either at the weather, pain, illness, or at anything else. He never in conversation, in any company, or under any circumstances, uses language that could be thought indelicate. (Of course, he has used language in his poems which has been thought indelicate, but none that is so.) In fact, I have never known of his uttering a word or a sentiment which might not be published without any prejudice to his fame. He never swears ; he could not very well, since as far as I know, he never speaks in anger, and apparently never is angry. (I know that he himself will emphatically contradict me —that he will refuse to accept this, and a great many more of my outlines, as a true portrait of himself, but I prefer to draw and color for myself.) He never exhibits fear, and I do not believe he ever feels it. His conversation, mainly toned low, is always agreeable and usually instructive. He never makes compliments —very seldom apologizes—uses the common forms of civility, such as " if you please," and " thank you," quite sparingly— usually makes a nod or a smile answer for them. He was, in my experience of him, not given to speculating on abstract questions (though I have heard others say that there were no subjects in which he so much delighted). He never gossips. He seldom talks about private people even to say something good of them, except to answer a question or remark, and then he always gives what he says a turn favorable to the person spoken of.

His conversation, speaking generally, is of current affairs, work of the day, political and historical news, European as well as American, a little of books, much of the aspects of Nature, as scenery, the stars, birds, flowers, and trees. He reads the news- papers regularly (I used to tell him that was the only vice he had);

he likes good descriptions and reminiscences. He does not, on the whole, talk much anyhow. His manner is invariably calm and simple, belongs to itself alone, and could not be fully described or conveyed. As before told, he is fond of singing to himself snatches of songs from the operas or oratorios, often a simple strain of recitative, a sort of musical murmur,—and he sings in that way a large part of the time when he is alone, especially when he is outdoors. He spends most of his time outdoors when the weather permits, and as a general thing he does not stay in for rain or snow, but I think likes them in turn as well as the sunshine. He recites poetry often to himself as well as to others, and he recites well, very well. He never recites his own poetry (he does not seem to know any of it). Yet he sometimes reads it, when asked by some one he wants to gratify, and he reads it well. I do not know whether or not he can be said to sing well; but whether he does or not, his voice is so agreeable that it is always a pleasure to hear him.

APPENDIX

TO PART I.

INTRODUCTORY LETTER

(NOW PREPARED, 1883, FOR THE PRESENT WORK) TO

THE GOOD GRAY POET (1865–'6),

BY

WILLIAM DOUGLAS O'CONNOR.

From a letter to R. M. B., by W. F., Mobile, Ala., March, 1883.

For twenty-seven years have

> A wild and many-weaponed throng
> Hung on the front, and flank, and rear

of *Leaves of Grass*, and the author has suffered two special public governmental insults for writing them. I hardly see how it could have happened any other way. But is it not a luckier fortune than eulogy would have been? It has developed in the poet himself an unflinching and sustained courage, fortitude, and perseverance without parallel in literature, and which will cast a peculiar and permanent glow over all his verse in the future. It has brought to his help a small minority of the most devoted and valiant champions that ever fought for man or cause. Best of all, it has formed that prefatory foreground and area specially needed in such cases, to test and try these most arrogant and relentless compositions. For, if *Leaves of Grass* succeed, they dethrone the old sovereigns, the long-settled poetic traditions of Asia and Europe, and compel Literature, perhaps Sociology and Politics, to a more revolutionary *renaissance*, a vaster stride, than any in the past.

(72)

MR. O'CONNOR'S LETTER, 1883.

WASHINGTON, D. C., U. S. A., February 22d, 1883.

DR. R. M. BUCKE, LONDON, ONTARIO, CANADA.

DEAR SIR:

It is nearly eighteen years since I published the impassioned protest against the mean and monstrous wrong done by the Hon. James Harlan to Walt Whitman, which you ask leave to reprint in your Appendix. The warmest friend of that old outburst might think of it as one might of the ring of flame he had seen Cotopaxi send with a blast into the tropic azure—a burning meteor thrown up to circle and shimmer for a moment in the upper air—then vanish. That it is to reappear and remain I shall owe to you. I thank you gratefully, but less for the kind personal honor your request does me, than for the opportunity you offer to make my otherwise ephemeral work a sharer in the enduring life assured to your volume. A pamphlet like mine, crude, extemporaneous, fragmentary, the birth of an exigency, the utterance evoked by outrage, the voice of an indignant heart, —is, no matter what its cause or purpose, the accident of an hour, and can ordinarily have but the hour's existence. This is sternly true of far better compositions of this class than mine. Who reads now the masterly "Labienus" of Rogeard? Who remembers those arrows of lightnings, the bright, barbed feuilletons of Paul Louis Courier? Even the shafts of the great sagittary, Rochefort, are already regathered into the black quiver of yesterday. But a book, with its long foreground of premeditation,—especially a book with such a subject, such an aim as yours, and written from your vantage-ground of science, and with your ardent intelligence and power,—can lay great bases for eternity. For my brochure to be linked to such a one is, therefore, a pledge of its perpetuity, and in this I feel cause for satisfaction. Not because of any merit I attach to pages of whose faults and deficiencies I am only too well aware, and which I wish I had had time and ability to make better, but because those pages hold the record of the one action of my life which I could wish might never be forgotten, even though it had brought upon me, and was still to bring, every misfortune and every dishonor. Long as I had revered Walt Whitman, and deeply as I had valued his book, I had never, up to the date of his expulsion from office, written a single line in his interest, considering, as I still consider, both him and his works subjects far beyond my powers. Even the twelve years of shameful persecution, ostracism, and insult, which followed the publication of his second edition, the exclusion of any specimen of his poetry from the anthologies of American song, the closing of the doors of all periodicals to his contributions, the insolent rejections of his work by the peddlers who call themselves publishers, the infamous calumnies invented and set in circulation by persons of repute respecting his personal conduct and character, the affectation of shuddering aversion practised in certain quarters at the sight of his face or the mention of his name, the showered misrepresentation and abuse of his poems by the reviewers and journalists,—even all this I witnessed and endured with as much composure as is compatible with scorn, knowing, in the noble words of Ellery Channing, that "who writes by fate the critics shall not kill, nor all the assassins of the great review," certain that, in the trumpet phrase of Leibnitz, "Another time shall come, worthier than ours, in which, hatreds being subdued, truth shall triumph," and that then Walt Whitman and his mighty volume would fail not of their meed of veneration. But when I saw the poetaster and the plagiary, the hypocrite and the prude, the eunuch and the fop, the poisoner and the blackguard, the snake and the hog, the gnat and the midge, all the creatures of the marsh and the copse, all the vermin of the kennel and the sewer, every monkey that mops and mows in the curule chair of Longinus fancying himself a critic, every chinch that poses on the triclinium of Horace imagining himself an author—when I saw the whole paltry and venomous swarm condense, as in some tale of enchantment, into a demon in the garb of an inquisitor;—when the Harlanunculi became resolved into the Harlan, and to moral animosity succeeded material consequences;—when I saw a man deprived of his employment, publicly degraded, and an official stigma set upon his name, simply and only because he had once, years before, published an honest book—and noted that among all our scholars and literati not one voice—not a single one—was raised even in the faintest deprecation of this dastardly outrage, welcomed instead with the silence that gives consent, and with gibes and guffaws of approval—then I felt that even for a writer so inexperienced and obscure as I, the hour of duty had arrived, and in the pages you reprint I did my best, as I have said in another place, to secure for the infamy of Mr. Harlan's action undying remembrance. It is because I did this—it is because, as Dr. Johnson says, I did what nobody else thought worth doing—that I am glad to have the record perpetuated in your volume. Let shame or credit follow, I care not which, nor have I ever cared. The man who tried to make an author suffer for his book I tried to brand! This is all the claim I make for my pamphlet, and that pamphlet is my act. I vaunt it and I stand by

I have spoken, you will remember, of the hour of Mr. Harlan's explorations in the Department, and I regret now that in the haste of the composition I did not more elaborately place this hour in amber. It was not enough that he chose to do a mean and monstrous action; the manner of his doing it was still meaner and more monstrous. The book had been for several years out of print. It was not in circulation. But in a drawer in the author's desk which stood in a room in the lower story of the Department building, there was a private copy filled with pencilled interlineations, erasures, annotations—the revisions which prepare a text for future publication. This copy was the one over which Mr. Harlan pored in the still hours which followed the closing of the official day in the Department. But it was in his own office, in an upper story, that he pursued these secret studies. The book was always in its place in the author's desk when he went home in the afternoon, and it was always there when he returned the next morning. It was in the interim that it was upstairs. Who was it that edged along the shadowy passages of the huge building from the Secretary's apartment—that quietly slipped down the dim stairway—that crept, crawled, stole, sneaked into the deserted room of his illustrious fellow-officer—that tiptoed up to the vacant desk—that put a furtive hand into the private drawer and drew out the private volume—that glided back with it to the office of the Secretary? When the hours of gloating were over, and the building was darker and dimmer under its few funereal gaslights, turned murkily low, who crept back down the dead-house corridors and stairways, with a volume in his hand, to the earlier visited apartment, stealthily replaced the volume in the desk, and softly slunk away? Was it Tartuffe disguised as Aminidab Sleek, or was it the rampant god Priapus masquerading as Paul Pry? Enough to know that these Department explorations and these sub-rosa examinations resulted in Mr. Harlan expelling Walt Whitman from his position for having once upon a time published a volume containing a little reference to some facts in universal physiology. This reference, it seems, shocked the Methodist virtue that had endured without flinching the daily conversation of Lincoln—Lincoln, under whom Mr. Harlan had accepted and held his Secretaryship—a President as soundly good and as frankly gross as Luther or Rabelais.

Mr. Harlan was the Secretary of the Department of the Interior. His charge included the public lands and the mines, the interests of the settlers and the diggers of ore, the fortune and fate of the red aborigines, the awards of the pensions and the tracts given in bounty to the soldiers and sailors, the promotion and safeguards of the myriad inventions through the issuance of their patents, the mighty task of the census when ordered, the care of the national insane and deaf and dumb, the supervision of vast territorial interests; in brief, an immense part of the ordinance, prosperity and development of the country. To execute the public business under his care, he had three thousand officers. As Secretary, his conduct of affairs could enhance the welfare of the nation ; as statesman, his recommendation could mould the future. From all this lofty ministerial function, he stooped to the meanness and shame of the pick-pry inquisition, and the brutal and insolent expulsion described—his victim a poet illustrious in the verdict of the fittest of two worlds.

When I dealt with this abominable action as it deserved—although I no more than recognized it in its obvious character as an audacious assault upon the liberty of letters, and a flagrant and enormous breach of administrative propriety—although I merely flung the light upon it in its avowed intentions and proportions, and properly refuted the pretences upon which it claimed to be justified, by plainly bringing into opposition the superb purity and grandeur of the poem it attacked, as certified by the noblest minds of two continents, and the simple and sublime life of the poet it persecuted, as known to many of his countrymen—it was of course quite natural and logical that all the leading literary and many of the other journals in this country, which for years had been devoted to the defamation of which Mr. Harlan's conduct was the bright consummate flower, should respond by alleging that I was making mountains out of molehills, that my censure and my eulogy were alike inordinate ; and that they should enter, as they did, into express extenuations and defences of the Secretary, coupled with their little sneers and scoffs at my vindication of the man he had wronged. You can judge of the force they brought to their task by the summary I offer of the points made upon me by the strongest article of all, the writer in this instance a prosperous and eminent man. By this literary magnate I was gravely reminded that Mr. Hawthorne lost his place in the Salem Custom House when the Whigs came into power, under our precious system of rotation in office, and hence in effect, that the Hon. Mr. Harlan's expulsion of Walt Whitman was quite a venial and normal act—as like the Whig dismissal of Hawthorne as one pea is like another pea. I was coldly informed that the gross wrong inflicted upon Mr. Whitman was "the mere loss of an office"—nothing more—nothing whatever ; and I was made to feel that I had the assurance upon the honor of a refrigerator. Furthermore, that this "mere loss of an office" furnished no proper occasion for such a denunciation of the outrage, and such an apotheosis of its object, as were given in my pamphlet. For cool ignoring of all the circumstances of the case as set forth in my indictment, and for the simple and absolute frigidity of its belittling of Mr. Harlan's damnable action, I think this article in comparison makes Wrangel Land in the height of the Arctic winter an image of all that is bland and warm. Beside it, the icy sepulchre itself would seem a summer resort for consumptives. It never occurs to the dry light of mind of this just and intelligent critic, taking him on his own chosen ground, that there would have been some difference between Hawthorne civilly dismissed from office because of a change of administration, and Hawthorne brutally expelled with ignominy, because he had celebrated (some think covertly justified), in the sombre and splendid pages of the " Scarlet Letter," the adultery of Arthur Dimmesdale and Hester Prynne. It never occurs to this icily brilliant reviewer that expulsion for such a cause would be necessary to establish parity between Hawthorne's case and Walt Whitman's—and of course he never so much as glances side-long at the consideration of the enormous uproar an expulsion on account of the " Scarlet Letter" would have created, though nobody knew this better than he. It never dawns for a moment on this prosperous and well-fed gentleman that to a poor man, hunted then by our literary ku-klux, almost outlawed at that time by the Kemper-county gang who carry out the shot-gun policy in our literature and journalism, " the mere loss of an office" might cut off the means of subsistence, and be no matter for whiffling away as a mere trifle. But why comment? Did he ever really think, or any of his tribe, that the expulsion of an author from a public employment on account of his book could be made to appear a small matter? While such as I are in the world, it can never be a small matter; it will always be a great matter, and among the greatest of great matters, in the lasting verdict of every man and woman who knows the relation of thought to life, of books to the fortunes of mankind. Suppose Chaucer had been ejected from his post of Comptroller of Customs under the third Edward, on account of some of that outrageous Gallo-Saxon license of conception and expression which so often wantons in his pages. Does any one fancy that our scholars and essayists, even at the distance of six centuries, would treat the incident coolly, or as of no import-ance? Suppose Defoe, on account of the broad pictures in " Moll Flanders," or the " Memoirs of a Cavalier," had been deprived of any one of his employ-ments under William or Anne. What sympathy or defence would the minister get that did it, from the biographers of the creator of " Robinson Crusoe "? Suppose Charles Lamb had been fired out of his clerkship in the India House, because of his defence of the fairy obscenities of Farquhar and Wycherly? Wouldn't there be heat in the blood of London in the Old World, and Boston in the New, over the record that such a thing had ever been done to sweet old Elia? Suppose Burns had been considered, in the holy name of virtue, chastity, decency, Christian civilization, morally unfit to measure Scotch malt forever, and turned out of his gaugership because of the ithyphallic audacities he showered on the Scotch Harlans in " Holy Willie's Prayer "! Wouldn't literature ring with the outrage? Yea, verily; and well do the literati know it, who tried to make out that Mr. Harlan's immortal disgrace was the merest bagatelle, and mocked at my pamphlet as one of the curiosi-ties of literature because it denounced his action on the scale of its proper magnitude.

Enough said, both of him and them. " A dog's obeyed in office," but the next one the humor of politics dresses up for a Secretary's chair, like Toby in a Punch and Judy show, will **think** seriously before he gives an order for the expulsion of an author on account of the book he had once published. The prospect both for Mr. Harlan and his literary apologists grows steadily worse as time goes on, and the character and value of Walt Whitman's book become established. This is no case of an abuse of power practised upon an author of the grade of Chaucer, or Defoe, or Lamb, or Burns. The gross wrong done by Mr. Harlan was done to a poet whom all time and every land will remember, and the dimensions of the insult and the outrage will be gauged by the measure of that universal and eternal fame. Whatever basis the contemptible scribblers of the day gave it, steadily crumbles. It is not in the nature of things, it is not in the control of the whole Dunciad, that the vast and sane affirmations, the simple and gorgeous beauty, the biblical and demiurgic power of *Leaves of Grass*, can continue to be themes for the ass reviewer's blattering bray. All the literati that ever hee-hawed from the rick in their prior existence, before the metempsychosis which placed them in the chairs of criticism to continue their symphonies, cannot drown the omni-prevalent voice of a work of genius. I remember a scene long ago in Faneuil Hall, when an attempt was made to silence a matchless orator, the incomparable Wendell Phillips, then in the prime of his indescribable forensic powers. He stood that evening in the full relief of his severe grace and beauty upon the lighted platform of the historic hall—from brow to foot all noble, like those knights of Venice Ruskin describes; the vast floor and galleries before and around him densely thronged; and central in the audience was a mob of stevedores and truckmen, the hired Alsatia of that class of merchants whose truckling servility to the Slave Power nourished in it the strength for rebellion, and at length brought on our Civil War. The moment the orator began, this swarm of hirelings became a roaring maëlstrom; they whirled around en masse without cessation in the middle of the concourse, yelling, howling, shouting, without a moment's intermission, and for some time the noise was deafening. But, gradually, amidst the tumult there was heard something marvellous. The orator had continued speaking with tranquil composure,—with his easy, almost careless grace,—with that memorable beauty of tone and demeanor veiling earnest feeling, as a Phidian vase might veil the Delphic fire within; and above the hoarse, unintermitted, tremendous uproar of the mob, in its preconcerted continuity, was heard his quiet voice! I never can forget the thrill it gave me. Not a word, not an accent was lost. Even the mob heard it, and strained their bull-throats to drown it. In vain. Paramount over all the clamor, that sweet and penetrating tone was heard, silverly asserting itself in even and uninterrupted flow, as clear and alien as the notes of the nightingale above the brawl of a flooded gorge; and it went on until it conquered wholly, and in silence, broken only by the sublime roar of acclamations, the splendid fountain of that eloquence was streaming upward in full silver flower. So dominant above the animal tumult of its defamers, so conquering and to conquer, is the voice of the book we champion. Over the clamor of the whole menagerie it is heard by the minds it has enlightened, the hearts it has comforted, the souls it has deeply stirred, and this voiceless multitude is the vanguard of the future.

Meanwhile the book has achieved the vantage-ground, hardly less valuable than its cordial recognition in certain quarters, of having been regularly bid for and issued by a business house, instead of being published, as previously, by its author only. It is an advance, which should, for the honor of our letters, be complemented by a corresponding change in the tone of criticism. But the welcome given the reappearance of the work proves, that, even after the lapse of twenty years, our reviews are in the same hands—that is to say, paws. The criticisms are, to be sure, somewhat improved since the former day when a filthy and malignant philistine in the London " Saturday Review " wrote that the author deserved to be scourged at the tail of the hangman's cart by the public executioner. Whoever seeks the missing link between the libidinous swell and the ferocious chimpanzee, might find it in this noble and decent criticaster. This amenity of criticism was prompted by the series of poems entitled " Children of Adam ;" and you know what physiologic dignity, what sanctities of purely human love and passion, what savor of natural sanity, what wealth of esoteric communication, what rapture of moral elevation, what adumbrations of holiness, are enshrined within those glorious verses, and give them their magnetic scope and fervor. They had the added honor some years afterward of causing one of Astor's gentlemen, who sometimes obscurely and feebly paddles in Castaly, to style their venerable author with fine scorn, " this swan of the sewers." I could retort upon Dr. Macnobody that he is a buzzard of the club-house kitchen, but this might be thought personal. Of the more recent notices it may be remarked that they are generally less poignant and more dull than their old prototypes. Some of them, as in the " Atlantic Monthly," show instinctively cordial perceptions quenched in abject cowardice. The review in the New York "Times," marked by great talent, is a singular example of stultification, the writer diplomatically annulling in one passage what he has just said in another, this process being pursued throughout with a mechanical uniformity which is simply comical. The one in the "Nation" is in artistic keeping with the tone of that chilly journal, and is otherwise only noticeable for its cold and brutal falsehoods. One of its indictments appears again in an article in " The Woman's Journal," signed with the initials of the Rev. Thomas Wentworth Higginson. The exceeding value of this accusation warrants its reproduction, and also its rescue from the oblivion of the anonymous. What, think you, is this weighty finding? Actually, now—really, now—Mr. Higginson avers that Walt Whitman ought to become the focal point of million-fingered scorn for having served in the hospitals! It appears that the old poet performed a pathetic, a sublime, an immortal service —he tended the wounded and dying soldiers throughout the whole war, and for years afterward, until the last hospital disappeared. O, but this was infamous! Shame on such "unmanly manhood," yells the Rev. Mr. Higginson! He should have personally "followed the drum," declares this soldier of the army of the Lord, himself a volunteer colonel. In bald words, instead of volunteering for the ghastly, the mournful, the perilous labors of those swarming infernos, the hospitals, Walt Whitman should have enlisted in the rank and file. From all which, I gather that Mr. Higginson would have cast a stone at Jean Valjean for going down without a musket into the barricades. I beg leave to tell this reverend militaire that if Longfellow had gone from Cambridge to serve in the hospitals, as Walt Whitman served, the land would have rung from end to end, and there would have been no objurgations on his not enlisting in the army, from the pen of the Rev. Thomas Wentworth Higginson. I also beg leave to tell him, since he brings personalities into fashion, that Walt Whitman's work of comfort and charity beside the cots of the Union and rebel soldiers, will last as long, and stand as fair, as the military bungling and blundering which distinguished this clergyman turned colonel, and evoked such agonized curses from his commanding officer at Port Royal. Better be a good nurse like Walt Whitman, than a nondescript warrior like the Rev. Col. Higginson.

The remainder of his article is quite taken up with an attack upon a few erotic verses in Oscar Wilde's poems, about which Mr. Higginson, as badly read as badly bred, says there is "nothing Greek," because they do not "suggest the sacred whiteness of an antique statue," although, as Mr. Higginson ought to know, there is a mass of literature, ranging from Aristophanes, Anacreon, Sappho, Longus, etc., to such as Mimnermus and Alcman, which they do suggest, and which Mr. Higginson could hardly describe as having "nothing Greek," but which could give Mr. Wilde a good many points in erotic composition, if that has anything to do with making him Hellenic. On the strength of these poetic audacities of Mr. Wilde, the Rev. Mr. Higginson lumps him in with Walt Whitman for reprobation, holding them both up in contrast with Sir Philip Sidney, whom he appears to consider the proper model of a poet, and calls (quoting Fulke Greville, I suppose), "a brave example of virtue and religion." I read this effusion with infinite amusement. Is it credible that the Rev. Mr. Higginson has never seen the "Astrophel and Stella" of that very Sir Philip Sidney he vaunts so roundly? He puts on the face of Nightgall the jailor, Sorrocold the torturer, Mauger the headsman, Mawworm the gospeller, and Moddles the weeper, all in one—he is dark, cruel, implacable, denunciatory, and disconsolate, all together—over the terrible fact that "the poems of Wilde and Whitman lie in ladies' boudoirs." Does he think that the "Astrophel and Stella" of Sir Philip Sidney is the sort of poem that ought preferably to "lie in ladies' boudoirs"? This work, a galaxy of songs and sonnets, some of them exquisite, was inspired, be it remembered, by a married woman, Lady Rich, who figures in it as Stella, and is addressed by Sidney as Astrophel. The husband, Lord Rich, is repeatedly mentioned in terms of the utmost contumely and insult. In one of the songs (the second) the fourth stanza of which is specially lascivious, the poet limns in glowing terms the lovely wife sleeping, steals a voluptuous kiss, and blames himself for not having taken the extremest advantage of her slumber! In another song (the fourth) there is protracted and vehement amorous solicitation for her person to be yielded to him, ending with a strain of whimpering dejection because of her refusal! The eighth song is in a similar style. In the fifty-second sonnet he fables a contest between Virtue and Love for the possession of Stella, which he pro- poses to settle by letting Virtue have the lady on the condition that her volup- tuous body be yielded to Love and him! In the tenth song his thought dwells in gloating anticipation of carnal enjoyment with her, and runs and revels in a rosy riot of amorous images, prolonged through half a hundred lines! These are specimens of the staple of the poetry this virtuous clergyman would seem to choose for the accompaniment of ladies' boudoirs! Ah, Mr. Higginson! it will take the effacing memories of Zutphen—it will take some of the immortal water the dying Sidney yielded from his flask to the parched lips of the wounded soldier, to wash away, for some of us, from the fame of one of the last of England's chevaliers, the stain of these disgraceful poems— poems which dishonor the wife while they insult the husband, and whose author is nevertheless your chosen exemplar of manly excellence—brought forward to shame by contrast Oscar Wilde for the sin of publishing a few verses far less bold than the verses of the Rev. Dr. Donne, or the " Venus and Adonis " of Shakespeare—brought forward also to darken Walt Whitman be- cause in a few of his lines he has celebrated with grave simplicity the noble amative impulse great Nature feels forever through all her immensity! So much for the criticism wherewith the Rev. Mr. Higginson decorates " The Woman's Journal."

As for the review in the " New York Tribune," it would seem to have been written, as Sir Walter Scott says " Amadis de Gaul " was written, in a brothel. The writer leads off by saying that the poems have " been read behind the door;" that " they have been vaunted extravagantly by a band of extravagant disciples, and the possessors of the books have kept them locked up from the family;" which makes you think that the critic is simply, as the Hon. Thomas H. Benton called Pettee, " a great liar and a dirty dog," until, reading further, you find him declaring that the book, which he has already elegantly called "the slop-bucket of Walt Whitman," has for a principle "a belief in the preciousness of filth," is " entirely bestial," full of " nastiness and animal insensibility to shame," and that the chief question it raises " is whether anybody, even a poet, ought to take off his trousers in the market- place; " which makes you at once set down the reviewer as indubitably, in the phrase of the moralist Hawkesworth, " a lewd young fellow," and " a great liar and a dirty dog " besides. The whole article is thoroughly obscene. It is characterized throughout by what might be called the indecent exposure of the mind, and is a disgrace to even its author and to the journal in which it appears.

Better and worse than the stuff these scurrilous dreams are made of is an article by Mr. Clarence Cook, in the "International Review," which I have read with mingled feelings of regret and indignation. It is almost incredible to find this gentleman, who ought by his intellectual connections to be better informed, and who should have education enough to know the truth without information, asserting and assuming through his whole essay that *Leaves of Grass* is a derivation from the writings of Emerson. He says that the prose preface to the original edition of the poem shows "where the author came from intellectually;" that "Mr. Whitman had been for a long time milking the New England transcendentalists," and that "most of it is an echo of Emerson himself, minus his music and his wit." Furthermore, that Walt Whitman in his poetry "does nothing more than enlarge and exaggerate the 'Nature' and the first volume of 'Essays,' of his master." It was long ago published authentically in Mr. Conway's widely copied and circulated article, what is the fact, that Walt Whitman had never read Emerson at all until after the publication of his first edition; and he was quite as innocent of any knowledge of the papers in the "Dial," despite the preface which Mr. Cook fancies an echo of Emerson and Concord. But he *had* read Kant, Schelling, Fichte, and Hegel, as Mr. Cook, if he had taken the trouble to read the book he was reviewing, could have seen plainly, and the thought of that giant quaternion, which, in fact, is rather an expression of what is in the minds of all men in our age, than anything that has been communicated to them by the four philosophers, is precisely the thought of which Mr. Emerson, in this country, like Cousin in France, is, in his writings, without any derogation to his own proper originality, the carrier or interpreter; so that all the indebtedness Mr. Cook oracularly fancies, is referable to the German source both minds had drunk from, though in Walt Whitman's case it is easy to see that his own powerful and sensitive genius, naturally in rapport with the thought of his age, far better accounts for the ideas of his book than any acquaintance with the well-heads of modern philosophy. This ridiculous notion of *Leaves of Grass* as a sort of rowdy amplification of Emerson, began twenty years ago with some amusing persiflage in "Putnam's Magazine"—the harmless fancy of my old friend Mr. George William Curtis, who sometimes softly, sweetly, slips into ad captandums with irresponsible indolent grace. It was taken up again, and enforced, not at all harmlessly, but with malicious iteration, by Mr. Bayard Taylor, in a series of gratuitous and inappropriate editorials, published seven years ago in the "New York Tribune," with the object of breaking down a certain movement in behalf of Mr. Whitman, and it gave me then, in conjunction with some of his other representations, a new idea of what might be meant by the old saying that "a tailor is the ninth part of a man." Now it comes up again, with the pertinacity of wood-wax or the Canada thistle, among a lot of similar superstitions, in this "International Review" article, making me think of the Spanish proverb, "God sends meat, but the devil sends cooks." The meat is *Leaves of Grass*, and the æsthetic Clarence being *cuisinier*, a nice dish he makes of it, with his bogus recipes! Did it ever occur to any of these gentlemen who derive Walt Whitman's thought from Emerson's, to compare the two in their palpable and tremendous dissimilarities? Where, for one instance out of a hundred, is the pantheistic doctrine in the *Leaves*, which is the constant assertion and implication in the Essays? Where, for another instance, do you find in Emerson the haughty and rejoicing faith in the immortality of the personal soul, which peals from end to end of *Leaves of Grass* like the trumpet of the resurrection? It would be well for Mr. Clarence Cook's reputation as a critic, if the utter sciolism his dealing with this branch of his subject betrays, had no worse concomitants. But he goes on, and dropping into apologies in a friendly way, he slips in as their basis a string of defamations regarding the noble frankness of those passages of the book in which Emerson found "the courage of treatment which so delights us, and which large perception only can inspire." In the face of this imprimatur he has the Himalayan effrontery to represent that Emerson was originally "in the marble purity of his mind" very much shocked at these passages. "At first," says Mr. Cook, "he could not see the wood-god for his phallus." I beg to compliment Mr. Cook on the marble purity of this image, which does not, however, precisely remind one of the marble faun, nor of the good satyr the poet heard playing his flute in the heart of the twilight on Mount Janiculum.

But Mr. Cook's metaphors concern me less than his calumnies, and I would really like to know what evidence he has that Emerson was ever, first or last, shocked at Walt Whitman's volume. For in proof of his bold assertion he advances not one word. "Later," he continues, "Emerson wrote a letter to Whitman, in which he said, ' I greet you at the beginning of a great career '—" and the ice being thin here, he deftly skates away into an old worn-out impertinence about Mr. Whitman's "breach of confidence," as he calls it, in printing this sentence from a communication not confidential "in letters of gold on the back of a new edition of his book," as it certainly deserved to be printed, and as Mr. Whitman had an unquestionable right to print it. But this letter of Emerson's in which he expressed his cool, deliberate judgment of *Leaves of Grass*, and told precisely how it affected him, what was it, and why did he not bring it forward? Here it is, and I invite you and your readers to decide whether it bears out, by any expression or implication, Mr. Clarence Cook's misrepresentations:

" I am not blind to the worth of the wonderful gift of *Leaves of Grass*. I
" find it the most extraordinary piece of wit and wisdom that America has yet
" contributed. I am very happy in reading it, as great power makes us happy.
" It meets the demand I am always making of what seemed the sterile and

"stingy nature, as if too much handiwork, or too much lymph in the tem-
"perament, were making our Western wits fat and mean.

"I give you joy of your free and brave thought. I have great joy in it.
"I find incomparable things said incomparably well, as they must be. I find
"the courage of treatment which so delights us, and which large perception
"only can inspire.

"I greet you at the beginning of a great career, which yet must have had
"a long foreground somewhere, for such a start. I rubbed my eyes a little
"to see if this sunbeam were no illusion; but the solid sense of the book is a
"sober certainty. It has the best merits, namely, of fortifying and encour-
"aging."

This was Mr. Emerson's judgment on *Leaves of Grass,* and never, to his
undying honor, did he retract it. I call your attention to its scope, its absolute comprehensiveness. If there was anything in the book of which he dis-
approved he had the plain opportunity to say so, and it was his imperative
duty to say so. On the contrary, he gives the poem—he gives the very edition
of it Mr. Cook says had shocked him—the most unreserved, the most unqual-
ified, the most unbounded approval. He calls it the most extraordinary piece
of intellect and wisdom America has yet contributed; he congratulates the
author on the liberty and valor of his thought; and he finds especial delight
in the courage of treatment which marks the whole performance, and which, he
says, and Walt Whitman's critics would do well to remember, large perception
only can inspire. This is the proof Mr. Cook shies from supplying, of the
way *Leaves of Grass* "shocked" Mr. Emerson! He has no other, for the
sentence he ascribes to Mr. Emerson as his judgment upon the book or its
author—"Strange that a man with the brain of a god should have a snout
like a hog"—was never uttered by Emerson at all. In a matter of this importance I insist upon the purity of the text, and Mr. Cook has reported this
flashing moment of the wise wrong. The *mot* as it was really uttered ran
thus, "Strange that a man should have the brain of a god and the snout of
a hog," and in this shape it was said of Walt Whitman by Mr. E. P. Whipple
in 1855 or thereabouts, and reported to me, with great glee, fresh from his
lips, by one of his dear friends, who afterwards ran away with the trust funds
and beggared the widow and the orphan—a natural consequence of his delight
in such sarcasms. The habit of murder, De Quincey warns us, inevitably
leads to procrastination and Sabbath-breaking, and a man who admires Mr.
Whipple's wit may be expected, sooner or later, to make off with the cash of
the community. I will only remark upon this particular *jeu d'esprit* that in
its vitreous brilliancy, and the perfect moral absurdity of its antithesis, to say
nothing of the falsehood of its application, it is entirely worthy of its true
author, and I leave Mr. Cook to its continued enjoyment. But I assure him
that his success in the correct ascription of epigram is not such as to inspire
me with an unfaltering trust that Wendell Phillips uttered the pleasantry he

attributes in turn to him. When I gratefully remember that Mr. Phillips wrote me that he placed Walt Whitman's "Democratic Vistas" in equal honor on the same shelf with his beloved Tocqueville, and when I recall with equal gratitude the glowing and ample welcome he gave my pamphlet defence of the slandered poet, I have little reason to assume on Mr. Cook's authority that that clear and generous voice expressed even the light disparagement the reviewer puts into currency. Still, Mr. Cook may claim something from my bounty, and I will give him this as a donation. Let me suppose that Mr. Phillips, in his own enchanting fashion, really did say of *Leaves of Grass*, as our gossip reports him—"here be all sorts of leaves except fig leaves"—but added with a graver modulation, "including those of the Tree of Life, whose leaves are for the healing of the nations"! That this is the true version, though a guess, I will venture my last obolus, and go in debt to Charon!

Of Mr. Cook's remaining "International" excursions in criticism, it is not necessary to say anything. When he declares the poem destitute of beauty and proportion, and absolutely wanting in art, I might remind him that Ruskin, who is a tolerable authority in these respects, having forgotten considerably more of æsthetic law than Mr. Cook ever knew, has recently, if the public journals say truly, uttered a eulogium upon *Leaves of Grass*, which hardly sustains this weighty dictum. When he charges as the "worst fault of all" in the book "its absolute want of humor," I might venture to suggest that, although the rich mirthful temperament of the author, which all who know him know well, is evident enough in the opulent cheerfulness and the mellow tone of his work, *Leaves of Grass* is not, as Mr. Cook appears to fancy, an attempt at comedy, nor can it be considered the "worst fault of all" that we do not split our sides with laughter over the book of Isaiah. When he pronounces the work utterly "without taste," I could retort upon him that there are only ten baskets of taste let down from heaven for each generation, and he and nimble men like him have always got them all, which is probably the reason why none of the great geniuses in poetry ever had any, from Aristophanes to Molière, or from Æschylus to Victor Hugo. But there is only one point upon which I care to offer a serious comment. In speaking of the first issue of *Leaves of Grass*, Mr. Cook says that in it was expressed "scorn of the conventions of society by one who never knew them, and was as ignorant of society as a Digger Indian." When I came upon this stroke of ignorant insolence I felt my blood stir, and Mr. Cook owes it to my forbearance if I do not make him feel what resources the English language has for the chastisement of offences of this description. What does he mean by publishing as a species of Yahoo a man who all his life has been the honor and ornament of society as good as Mr. Cook ever entered? whose high spiritual cultivation is as apparent in his personal manners as in his poetry; and who never, even in thought, could be guilty of such insufferable low-breeding as this sentence of his critic displays? I remember, years ago, the eminent son of the most eminent man in New England, at the very top of the highest and most exclusive Boston society, coming from his first interview with Walt Whitman, whom he had met with distrust and prejudice, and all we could get from him as to what had passed was the abstracted, iterated rejoinder, the expression of his prevailing impression—"He is a perfect gentleman." In his young manhood Walt Whitman was an intimate friend of Bryant, his companion in many long country rambles. He was a welcome guest, when I first knew him, at some of the best and wealthiest houses in New York. It was the same when he was with us here. It was the same when he was with me once in Providence. It was the same during his recent visit to Boston. It was the same when he was with you in Canada. Yet Mr. Cook prates of his ignorance of society and its conventions, and matches him, in reference, with the very lowest western savage. I used to think Mr. Clarence Cook, when I slightly knew him many years ago, a gentleman, although a somewhat superfine one, but one would think he desired to forfeit all claim to such consideration. He says, in the latter part of his article, that for much that Walt Whitman has written it would not be easy to repay him with grateful words. It is a sorry way to show gratitude, this reproduction of stale and shallow figments, most of them denied and refuted time and again; and this utterance of as brutal a personal insult, couched in utter falsehood, as one man could well offer to another.

Such, up to this date, is the best specimen we can offer in America of a review of *Leaves of Grass* in its new edition. Let me show you, in this connection, the kind of knave a literary editor can be. The New York "Tribune" reprinted this article of Clarence Cook's, in which, it is just to Mr. Cook to say, he had imbedded several paragraphs favorable in some degree to the work and its author; one praising its original typographical appearance, the poet's own get-up; another eulogizing some of the poems by name; and notably another, from which I give the following sentences: "It would be a "thousand pities were the author judged by the few passages, perhaps not two "pages in all, where his frankness pushes him to say things that are only "coarse because they are said. Of indecency, of essential grossness, there is "in the book really nothing. It is easy to believe the author as pure-minded, "as incapable of doing or thinking evil, as any best man among us who would "blush to be seen in his shirt-sleeves by a woman." These favorable paragraphs, the one quoted from being in direct opposition to the obscene review previously published in the "Tribune," its literary editor suppressed in reproducing the article, sending it out thus shorn to a million of readers. The animus is evident. Such is the treatment received by the grandest book of poetry uttered in the English tongue for over two centuries. And it *is* grand! Well might Emerson greet its author at the beginning of a great career! Nothing equal to it has appeared in Celto-Saxon literature since Shakespeare.

I mean what I say, and I have considered my words. It is the first poetic work in the English language since Shakespeare—let them deny it who dare —that sounds the trumpet for a new advance; that is not merely original but aboriginal; that pours forth the afflatus for another movement; that is in its theory and purpose a new departure. "Solitary, singing in the West," the poet himself says, "I strike up for a New World."

Consider the cardinal poets since the age of Elizabeth. We all know the absolute high level, below that Elizabethan mountain range, constituted by Milton. Great and noble as he is, he is not even the poet of that Puritanism whose harsh spell left him, like the prince in the Arabian story, half breathing flesh and half marble. The lofty mood of Ann Hutchinson and Sir Harry Vane is not expressed in his poetry. What is Pope? The philosophy of Bolingbroke felicitously arrayed in facile iambics—a theism fit, as Heine says, to be the religion of watch-makers; a popular paraphrase, almost a court disguise, of Homer; some splendid intercolumniations of polished urban satire; these are his masterpieces. What is Dryden? A masterly satiric talent without a conscience. What is Walter Scott? In his verse, only a superb story-teller. In Wordsworth we have a strong but circumscribed intelligence. Once only, in his noble ode upon Immortality, he rose and broadened into the serene region of the great ideas. Below that, he is great only in a true perception of some common things—a stalk of celandine, a village rustic, a mountain cloud. But his kosmos is Westmoreland, and he is radically the centaur of the parson. In Burns there are true songs, wild gleams, immortal pulses, arrested by an early death. In Keats death also soon stopped that copious rich flowering into English verse of the Greek rose and asphodel. What leader of the nations might not the all-noble Byron have become, had he but lived to make ripe the continental promise which appears in the broad European picturings, the magnanimous intellections, the clarion blasts of rebellion, that fill "Childe Harold"; which appear still clearer in "Don Juan," whose fearless stripping of the veil from the monstrous hypocrisy of society, whose aggrandizement of humanity and liberty, and whose mines of liberal and revolutionary epigram, give it the rank of one of the greatest poems ever inspired by the pure moral sentiment! And Shelley—had he but grown to maturity, and gathered force and become intimate with rude life, what fire upon the altar of what gods would not have been pale beside that which sparkles in the ashes of his lines! If Tennyson had continued as he began, the loyal outgrowth of Shelley and Byron, the developed poet of "Maud," of "Clara Vere de Vere," of "Ulysses" and "Locksley Hall" . . . but he soon learned that kind hearts are less than coronets, and simple faith than Norman blood;—he shrank back into aristocracy;—and now at the last analysis, what is he? An ethereal delight of poesy; no less; no more. I speak only of Celto-Saxon poetry, not of the mighty births of the French romantic movement. In my own country, in the United States, that poetry, aside from *Leaves of Grass*, has not appeared in a single racy specimen. The only possible exception, though in a minor key, is the weird and lovely lyric verse of Edgar Poe, perfectly distinctive, shrining a strange mythology of personal love and sorrow, and having its roots in certain parts of our southern life. But poetry such as his only influences, it does not emancipate or lead. Not one of our poets has had broad or deep aims. Longfellow, with exquisite literary grace and human benignity, yields only centos and distillations. Whittier makes local ballads. Emerson has produced a handful of mystic jewels, rose diamonds and white, a virtuoso's joy, like the gems of Andrew Marvell or Vaughan. Bryant's fame rests on " Thanatopsis," a thing of faithless beauty, though a joy forever, but which internal evidence shows stolen, and which might have been written in Sherwood Forest, or by Omar Khayyam, so little does it smack of any particular soil. In fine, the last supreme performance in poetry, before any of the poets I have named, was Elizabethan. The last full signal for a great march—for an exodus out of old conventions, old dogmas, old ideas, old theories, was Shakespeare.

What is Shakespeare's new departure? It is this: He is the first poet that ever devoted the drama to the physiology of the human passions—the chief problem, Bacon says, of moral philosophy; the knowledge that philosopher proclaimed wanting in the antique past; the condition indispensable, he declares, to the human advancement. That initial body of natural history demanded by Bacon has been supplied by Shakespeare, in the interest of the human race. This is his cardinal distinction as a poet; this makes his greatness and his glory.

An old and valued friend of mine, whose opinions are entitled to deep respect, has lately said that the Greek dramatists, especially Æschylus, excel Shakespeare in their treatment of the passions. I am sorry not to be able to think this true. Indeed, it seems to me it would be far nearer the truth to say that the Greek dramatists, in their colossal spectacular operas, never treated the passions at all. Much wisdom, much deep lore, much lofty morality, much fearful history, much dread theology, and questioning of that theology, expressed in tremendous passionate situation, these tragedies have indeed, but this is their whole staple. No one can better feel its majesty than I, nor can any one more than I appreciate the sublimity of the appalling thunder-crash of fatal circumstance which bursts forth in pealing reverberations against that drama's religious and legendary depth of gloom, or the stupendous power of what must have been its lovely and mournful groupings, its horrible and magnificent dénouements, its strange and supra-mortal living tableaux, as of gigantic animated sculpture, moving to breath-suspending music. But I affirm that never in a single instance did the Greek poets devote their tragedies to the exhibition of the passions in their evolution—in their circumstantial development from grade to grade of action—such as we see in " Hamlet," in " Othello," in " Lear." Indeed, the very conditions of their drama precluded such an exhibition. The theatre of Athens was built to accommodate thirty thousand spectators. To such a concourse the tragedy of "Macbeth," even with Kemble and Siddons in the chief parts, would have seemed a play of dwarfs—the tragic expression unseen, the gestures those of puppets, the voices almost lost, the sense incoherent, in the vastness of that stage and auditorium. In such a space nothing but a form of drama, of the nature of a spectacular opera, conceived in a gigantic mould, and suggesting the superhuman, would have been possible. Instead of the subtle passional metaphysics which Shakespeare, availing himself of the limits of the modern stage, can make dramatically evident—better still, can make by language alone even more evident to the solitary student of his pages—the Greek dramatist had to substitute such conceptions, ideas, conclusions, as might be broadly expressed in imposing stage effects, with adjuncts of scenic action and music. Hence actions rather than passions; hence a succession of tableaux; a tremendous, significant, sombre, sounding show. Hence upon the vast Athenian stage only two interlocutors at a time upon the scene, besides the choruses—Æschylus bayed at as an audacious innovator for introducing three; the stature of these actors raised to a supra-mortal height by the cothurnus; their size increased by voluminous draperies; their faces discharged of all but the one expression, by the awful and petrific mask; their voices augmented to thunderous or silver-shrilling tones by the brazen trumpet of the mouth-piece; and the verses of the tragedy intoned and sung by the duo or trio of histrions, or by the pealing voices of the choirs, ranged in dramatic sympathy with their action. In fact, if we can imagine an appalling and mysterious legend played by titanic statues of dreadful bronze and marble against a scene of eld, those statues become animate and vocal and resembling little that is human, we can gain some idea of the impression of a Greek tragedy. Something of its fearful and beauteous weirdness is suggested by that eerie line of Cowper, where, musing in his garden, he sees "a statue walk." Except to the evocation of the soul this form of supreme art is forever gone; the superb, the terrible, the enchanting spectacle, the astounding accumulation of catastrophes, the piled-up agonies, the marble loveliness, the celestial pathos, the horrent grandeurs, the Corybantic dances, the Eolian music, once ocular and auricular to the Greek audience, and surcharged with meaning not of this world, made evident through the senses to the souls of the auditors—all this can only be dimly recovered by the imagination; and of the august Greek tragedies (such as remain to us) we have nothing but the meagre and almost unintelligible librettos, no more to us than the librettos of great modern operas, except—a formidable exception indeed—that, unlike the librettos of "William Tell," of "Don Giovanni," of "Il Puritani," or the rest, they were written by mighty poets and in the pentecostal language of poetry. Still, they are but librettos, the broken fiery lines of a dying firework of Promethean fire, the *caput mortuum*, the mere skeleton, the vacant framework of what was once in its enacting an orbicular and living drama,

8

vital, glowing, sublime and enormous, the work of men like gods. As librettos—mere outlines which the representations are needed to complete—they cannot fairly be brought into comparison with the text of Shakespeare, a text as full to the reader as to the play-goer—fuller, indeed, so long as Shakespeare can be butchered to make a schoolboy's holiday by the gang of Barnums who run the modern stage, and mangle his dramas, and disembowel his meaning, with that brutish indifference to art and truth and human progress, which is fed by sole regard for fat receipts at the ticket-office. But, completed by the exercise of the conceptive power, the dry though mighty bones of these librettos, again clothed with their terrible and magnificent life, the Greek drama (although Æschylus has unquestionable features of resemblance) differs radically in form and motive from the drama of Shakespeare, and is intrinsically removed from comparison. I think Aristotle gives the full account of it when he says that its object was to move the soul with pity and terror; and the criticism that has been justly given in censure upon Aristotle as a philosopher in regard to his treatment of the human passions, namely, that he only considers the rhetorical or artificial means whereby they may be excited, and neglects to compile their natural history, may be made in no spirit of censure, but in simple descriptiveness, in regard to the Greek tragedies, inasmuch as their authors only regarded in their composition the means of exciting the passions of those who were to behold them played, and attempted in the works themselves no analysis or synthesis of any of the passions—not one. This undertaking was reserved for Shakespeare, and I affirm that the entire novelty of the conception and the scientific accuracy and massive comprehensiveness, as well as the supreme power and beauty of its execution, constitute his special and distinctive greatness as a poet. The main scope and purpose of the Shakespeare drama are definitely given by Lord Bacon in connection with his assertion that the compilation of the natural history of the human passions is the first duty of philosophy, and that it is particularly the province of poetry. In this connection he describes the Shakespearean work perfectly. Therein, he says, " we may find painted forth " with great life how passions are kindled and incited; how pacified and " refrained; and how again contained from act and further degree; how they " disclose themselves; how they work; how they vary; how they gather and " fortify; how they are inwrapped one within another; and how they do " fight and encounter one with another; and other the like particulars." " That is to say," remarks Dr. Kuno Fischer, quoting this passage : " Bacon " desires nothing less than a natural history of the passions; the *very thing* " *that Shakespeare has produced.* Is not," he says further, " the inexhaustible " theme of Shakespeare's poetry the history and course of human passion ? " In the treatment of this special theme, is not Shakespeare the greatest of " all poets, nay, is he not unique among them all ?" Strange, I must remark, in passing, that the illustrious Kantian (and the observation applies to Gervinus as well) should have gone so far in this matter, and not taken the step that would seem inevitable! But the fact remains, admitted on all sides, its significance only remaining unperceived—Shakespeare is the poet of that particular knowledge of human nature which Bacon declares necessary " in order " that the precepts concerning the culture and cure of the mind may be " rightly concluded upon;" and no matter what the myriad-figured, many-millioned play of the imagination which attends his work—no matter how profuse and rich the pageant, wherein kings, lords, prelates, gentlemen, clowns, fairies, ghosts, trades, employments, wars, elements, cities, landscapes, antique and modern shows, appear in uni-multiplex projection, and form in ensemble the immense profile of Europe from the view-point of the Elizabethan age—no matter how ample the pour of learning, wisdom, apothegm, axiom, wit, humor, literary felicity, dazzling metaphor, noble imagery, classic allusion, every verbal grace and grandeur, as from a cornucopia heaped with constellations—no matter how deep the summer of his verse, the purpose to present the physiology of the human passions runs through it all; and his drama stands the perfect suppliance of an immense defect in ancient philosophy, and the foremost division of that scientific movement of his time for the relief of the human estate, the extension of the empire of man over Nature, the transformation of the world into Paradise, which still continues, and which we call Baconian. His main purpose does not, of course, prevent the inclusion of collateral purposes, only less vast—parables of a new philosophy, as in the " Tempest " and the " Midsummer Night's Dream;" special solutions of political problems, as in " Coriolanus " and " Julius Cæsar;" in one instance a complete epic of the Wars of the Roses—the series of historical plays which Bacon calls "history made visible." But the main purpose remains other than the special purposes of these.

To the historical plays, with their high-stomached lords, their dragon rancors, their stormy feudal splendor, I think Walt Whitman gives undue weight in his estimate of Shakespeare's world. He seems to derive from them his powerful generalization of Shakespeare as the poet of Feudalism. This would be true of Walter Scott, a man sounder and healthier in his moral nature than in his intellect, and who saw the horrible grandeur of the feudal past through a glamour of beauty: it would be measurably true of Tennyson; I doubt if it is true of Shakespeare. Certainly " King John," " Richard the Second," " Richard the Third" and the rest, do not affect the mind with the winsome charm of " Ivanhoe" or " The Talisman." Their atmosphere is one of barbarous and tumultuous gloom, and they do not make us love the times they limn. They seem simply and rudely historical in their motive, as aiming to give in the rough a tableau of warring dynasties, and carry to me a lurking sense of being in aid of some ulterior design, probably well enough understood in that age, which perhaps time and criticism will reveal. The literature of the Middle Ages, issued under the jealous eye of a military despotism, is extremely insidious; often needs to be read between the lines; and there is deep suggestion in Bacon's saying that "we ought to be much beholden to Machiavel, who writes what men do, and not what they ought to do." In Machiavel himself what dark nobility, when in "The Prince"—that hideous masterpiece—at the utter cost of his fair fame, at the price of giving his very name to become a byword among men—he teaches the tyrant so minutely, and with such perfect candor, all the arts by which a free people may be subjugated, that the people become masters of the trick too! "The ostent evanescent" has its application to much of the great literature of those times—at least to the penetrating eye that finds the ostent of that literature deceitful; and it is impossible to believe that the greatest of the Elizabethan men could have sought to indoctrinate the ages with the love of feudalism which his own drama in its entirety, if the view taken of it herein be true, certainly and subtly saps and mines. The only supreme tyrant is Ignorance. To destroy this, as the Shakespeare drama assists to destroy it—to destroy this by teaching man the science of his own nature—is to deliberately forelay for the destruction of the whole Olympus of lesser tyrants, feudal and other, of which Ignorance is the Jove. If I sought to express the Shakespeare drama in the image of a person, I would not choose the eidolon of any feudal emperor. My choice would be a man like Francis Bacon—so majestic in his presence, Osborne, his contemporary, says of him, that he awed all men upon occasion into reverence, and yet, continues Osborne, so much one of the commonalty that he could pass from talk with a lord about his hawks and hounds to out-cant a London chirurgeon in his slang, so that all sorts of men thought him one of themselves; Francis Bacon, wise with all the lore of all the ages, the companion and counsellor of princes, the familiar of gypsies and tinkers and sailors as well; deep-eyed with long insight into the minds of men of every degree; master of multiform experiences; travelled, elegant, courtly, august, intrepid, loyal, gentle, compassionate, sorrowful, beautiful; clothed from fondness for sumptuous apparel in purple three-piled velvet, rich laces and the hat with plumes, yet loving—another anecdote tells of him—to ride with bared head, in the warm and perfumed rains of spring, that he might feel upon him, he said, the universal spirit of the world! Such would be the image of the man I would choose to express the Shakespeare drama— an image, by the way, not much like the infamous caricature made of him by that brilliant thimble-rigging Scotch scoundrel, Macaulay, with the noble and honorable object of spiting Basil Montagu.

Still, let it be distinctly admitted, although the imputation of feudalism may be rejected, the point of view in the Shakespeare drama is always that of the court. The court perfume streams, like a necessity of authorship, less from choice than circumstance, through all this mighty and beneficent creation. For the plebeian point of view, maintained unconsciously throughout, despite the learning, despite the patrician themes or characters chosen, despite even the voluptuous dainty elegance and charm of some of the lyrics and epigrams, contrast the works of Ben Jonson. The son of the bricklayer appears through-out, and it is the bricklayer's son of the mournful age of Elizabeth and James, before the people was born. Strange grace of chance if, in that age, the patrician spirit, which may easily be the natural birthright of any farmer or mechanic now—at least in this country—should have animated one as lowly born as Shakespeare, so as to tincture all his works with an odor, clinging as the musk of Nepaul! But the fact cannot be unperceived—the outlook of the Shakespeare drama is from the court; the sympathy, though universal, is from the social above, never from the below; the implied life of the author is that of the gently born and bred, not of the tradesman or the laborer. In every page we feel the superior social grade. It is the best spirit of the best Elizabethan noble. One would say the author was a lord. Truly—but a lord as Buddha was a prince.

The times have gone by when the court was the generalization of the nation, and the typical man, either as person or poet, was necessarily of the aristocracy. The change has come to pass which the great Elizabethan men darkly toiled to accomplish, in an age when the new was stirring in the old the dawn of which appeared for a little while a few years after they had passed away, in the Commonweal of Vane and Hampden, which Cromwell quenched in cloud. In every country in Christendom the people has been born, and in this has come to sovereignty. That democratic sovereignty, a political fact here to-day, will be a social fact here to-morrow, and of that fact in its present and its future, and of that New World which is the arena of its evolution, Walt Whitman is the poet, and *Leaves of Grass* is the poem. The very resist-ance to the work, as when a foreign journal denounced "its rank republican insolence," proves its democratic scope and character; the very criticism of its foes, who "cannot dispraise but in a sort of praise," supports its claim. Next in the order of intellectual succession to Shakespeare, its author appears in his typical mechanic's garb, as the portrait in the book shows him, a work-man sprung from a race of workmen, a representative poet of the people; such here specifically, and collaterally throughout the world. "The people—the poor," says a recent reviewer, sympathetically defining. Alas! no: the poor are not the people! "The poor," says Victor Hugo, "are the mourn-ful commencement of the people!" The people are the inhabitants of the country when political organization has secured for them the power of the sceptre, and social organization has endowed them with the opulence of the crown. From power and wealth in equitable distribution results the great spiritual patrician race worthy to be called the people. That race in its mighty infancy is here—a baby Hercules, who in its cradle has strangled monsters, and whose manhood and the labors of whose manhood are to come.

I have gazed for years into this grand orb of poetry; I have mused upon its wild elegance and splendor, its tranquil and candid reproduction of things gross and delicate as they are in the sphere of the great Pan, its august masculine and feminine ideals, its teeming shows of historic and current life, its magic changing palingenesis of the populous cities, the diversified landscapes, the picturesque solitudes, the genrè male and female figures, the infinite fauna and flora, the skies, mountains, streams, prairies of our Continental West, all recreated here in their several idiosyncrasies, under every diversity of times and seasons, vital and magnetic, a scenic whole exhaling delicious natural odors, swept by free winds, alive and moving in harmony to the marching measures, the glorious rolling music of a rhythmus, caught, one might divine, from the movements, copious and unequal, of the surf sweeping in forever upon the beaches where the poet wandered as a child. I have brooded long upon it all, and I have compared it with the famous poems of the supreme men of all ages, and found it in no wise inferior to the best, as many besides me have felt, and the near future will declare; but I should shrink, faint-hearted in my conscious inferiority, from any effort at its adequate interpretation. It spreads before us all, a superb cosmorama of the West, populous, colossal and golden, under the ascending race of the rejoicing sun. Who am I that I should unfold the mystic reminiscences of this Universal Poem, reveal its oracular suggestions, comment upon its sublime annunciations, interpret its prophetic voices, declare anything of what it is to every reader with an awakened soul?

Sometimes I think it might be considered the poem of embodiment. It indicates the august kosmic fact of numberless material entities held in cohesion by spirit, which in time loosens and departs. In a more restricted consideration, it appears as the poem of the embodied human soul. Other writers have celebrated the body, others the spirit, until we feel them almost in disconnection. Take, as opposing poles, Rabelais and Shelley. In Rabelais there is a creation, gross, enormous, carnal, full-blown, laughing, obscene, alimentative, bibulous, excrementitious, loathsome and magnificent. It is the fearful apotheosis of the flesh, the monstrous apocalypse of the abdomen become lord paramount—man submerged in his lusts and appetites. The conception could only have proceeded from a mighty intellect and a great moral nature. In Shelley there is evolved an image, phantasmal, super-celestial, inessential, divinely wan and lovely, the ghost become consubstantial with a music unearthly and wandering, a shape of woven perfume, an odic force grown palely visible, a perceived pneuma, an apprehended essence, an ethereal apparition, the presence of the violet-breathing night-wind of the spring. The eidolon of his poetry is as incredible in its beauty as in its utter removal from carnality. It is like a dream of the soul remembered in a dream. Its extreme sublimation will forever make it incomprehensible to any but the most imaginative minds—to aught but the clairvoyant sense that comes into rapport with thought clinging to the dim boundaries of the world: and Shelley can never have the fame his genius deserves, so far is his work removed from the reality and passion of our lives. His merits as a poet are inexpressible. Not least among them is the altogether new ideal of woman, radiant, heroic, noble, and exalté, which appears in his pages. His poetry suggests in its furthest rapt remove from realization, almost from apprehension, the unbodied soul. The athletic spirituality of *Leaves of Grass* has no kinship to the spirit of the " Gargantua," and it is far nearer to the divine afflatus of the " Epipsychidion." But the creation of the book is its author's own—as original as *sui generis*— and that creation is, within the limits of the present reference, the strongest, amplest, most definite projection of the soul incarnate—of the representative human being—which has ever been thrown into literature. In it the spirit and the flesh appear as a unit, in perfect equilibrium, in the mutual interpenetration and consubstantiality appropriate to the ideal Adam. Were humanity to disappear from the globe, and this poem alone to remain, the being of another species than ours, finding it among the ruins, could recover from its pages full knowledge of what manner of man had inhabited here, as surely as Lamarck or Owen from the fossil vestiges can reconstruct the vanished mastodon. The great affirmation which pervades the whole conception is the veracity of consciousness. Let us bow down before this supreme word ! Behind it there is nothing. It indicates the true finality, and in it is the entire proof of life. To be aware is all. To be aware is to be. Memory—the personal past—is consciousness retained : anticipation—the personal future— is consciousness projected. It is this divine fact that the poet, as he himself says, sings in so many ecstatic songs, and out of it has emerged his transcendent conception of the incarnate soul—the human creature, male or female, the female equal to the male—the being, dual and unitary at once, like the globe of two hemispheres—the insulated identity, type of all human identities, the woman, the man. A creature of substantial body, parts and passions ; divine in every organ and attribute, not one of which is to be omitted or contemned in celebration, since each and all are intermutual in their adaptation, as they must be in an organic whole ; infinite and omnigenous in character, without origin and without end, and grown and growing through sympathy by the accrument of myriad experiences ; shaped, propelled, developed alike by good and evil, as under the mechanical law of the composition of rival forces, effects are resultant ; prepared for in the earthly advent by all the cyclic preparations of the globe, and continued in endless course by all the operations of things ; eternal in personal identity, the phases at once merged and retained, as infancy is both lost and kept in childhood, childhood in youth, youth in maturity, and so on forever ; fathomless, abysmal, immense and interminable as Nature, to which he or she is related as a constant vital influence forever influenced ; representative, at any given stage of his or her evolution, of the innumerable lower beings, progressing to that level, to sink in turn that level, and continue on ; representative, in the best estate, of the intrinsic spiritual greatness and majesty of each and all of the rest through whatever the pitiable, grotesque or vile disguises of appearance incident to the processes of transformation; heir to an omnific personal destiny which is alike the destiny of each and all; governed through all the nature by the egoistic pride, and by love and the necessity for love, as by two paramount vital springs; conscious at the summit of the highest knowledge of the eternal mystery in which all beings must remain to each, and of the eternal mystery one must be to one's-self; and, from that lofty summit, joyous, haughty, transfigured in the sense of the democratic constitution of the Universe, in which all between the worm and the god are equal, being all organically necessary to the whole, and of which perpetual ascension, perpetual transfer and promotion, is the law. Such, in my apprehension, and in a crude, didactic account of it, is this majestic conception, which, in the poet's work, is expressed in a thousand magnetic and eloquent sentences, in a thousand vivid and wondrous verbal pictures, and with a power of alto-relievo statement and illustration which the fancy-dealers in letters can never deal in. It is far enough removed from the conception wherewith Mr. Harlan's Messiah, Wesley, startled England, when he defined man as "half brute and half devil." The body is the temple of the Holy Ghost, says the rapt apostle; and of this text Walt Whitman's book is, within the limitations of this view of it, the ample, the electric, the robust and un-rivalled commentary. As such it offers a new foundation for our philosophy, our politics, our life, above all for our religion—a religion to be greater than the world has ever seen, and worthy of these shores.

To others better equipped for the grateful labor, I will leave it to descant upon what is correlated to the conception I have so imperfectly touched—the matchless presentation of the representative man and woman of this country. In Shakespeare there are no ideals in the sense of exemplars of human excellence, or if so to any degree, it is in artistic and moral subordination to what seems his main aim, namely, to create types or models showing the operation of the perturbations or tempests of the mind. In *Leaves of Grass* the ideals are distinct, and nothing could be more resplendent or commanding. They will haunt the imagination of this country, they will haunt the imagination of the world, until they are realized in "the life that shall be copious, vehement, spiritual, bold," which the poet prophesies—in "the great individuals, fluid as Nature, chaste, affectionate, compassionate, fully armed"—in "the breeds of the most perfect mothers"—"the myriads of youths, beautiful, gigantic, sweet-blooded"—"the race of splendid and savage old men"—"the hundred millions of superb persons," which appear in his sublime annuncia-tion as belonging to the future of America. Women have especial cause to be grateful to Walt Whitman. The noblest ideal of woman ever contributed appears in his pages. His supreme presentation of her in the natural privi-lege of her motherhood—in her all-enclosing, all-determining and divine maternity, is of more than any former majesty, and is unparalleled in philo-sophic depth and truth, as it is in august and tender beauty. I would fain dwell upon this feature of his book, as I would upon the crowded and splendid cartoon of the United States, in all their diversified truth of essence and appearance, in all their multiplicity and variety of life, which his pages offer broadly to contemplation. There are few national works which have so fully imaged the distinctive form of a land and its people. Homer has given to the ages a wondrous picture of the old Pelasgic civilization; Rome, when the city was the world, glows in the tragic light of dying liberty and virtue in the mighty pages of Juvenal; amidst the great fulgurations of the laughter of Rabelais, we see the gross swarming life of old Paris and Touraine; and France, as in the magic mirror of Agrippa, in all the horror and grandeur of the feudal past, the revolutionary combat and the anguish of the present, the superb promise of the future, and in the supreme glory of compassion which streams from the poet's own mighty heart, lives in the poetry, the drama, the romance of the illustrious Victor Hugo; but in what poem have all the things which make up the show of a people's life appeared with such comprehensive and vivid reality, such national distinctiveness and such strength of charm, as in *Leaves of Grass?* Above all, the wonder of it is, to me, the marvel that what was thought commonplace and prosaic is restored in the book to the superbest poetry by the revelation of its intrinsic significance—by the establishment of its mystical relation. The common objects as well as the most beautiful and striking—the ordinary events and incidents as well as those of the greater series—the rude, plain, simple, unlettered people, as well as the elevated and heroic—all appear in the poem in an equality of consideration, unrobbed of the deep interior value which truly belongs to every figure, to every object and emblem in the divine procession of life. Such mighty and democratic handling of a theme, without rejection or evasion, reveals the great master, just as the true sculptor is seen, when, after you have gazed at a number of the stone dolls which adorn our Capitol, in which the fact of the genrè costume is commouly sought to be dodged by the artifice of a marmoreal cloak, you turn to David's noble bronze of Jefferson, in which the grace, the strength, the fire, the life of the figure are fused into every detail of the frankly rendered old colonial garb. The great master is equally revealed in the poems of the war for the Union, around which the orbit of the book is now arranged. Of these poems it may be said that they alone of all the song born from that struggle are in the true key. Apart from their clear, fresh and vital picturing—the sad and stormy truth and color of their scenery—they are surcharged with the peculiar tragic pathos which civil war must always inspire in hearts deeply noble, and will be accepted in all our latitudes, North and South alike, since they can be read without unmanly exultation by the victor, and without humiliation by the vanquished. The word "Reconciliation" spans them all:

Word over all, beautiful as the sky;
Beautiful that war and all its deeds of carnage must in time be utterly lost,
That the hands of the sisters Death and Night incessantly softly wash again, and ever again,
    this soiled world;

For my enemy is dead, a man divine as myself is dead,
I look where he lies white-faced and still in the coffin—I draw near,
Bend down and touch lightly with my lips the white face in the coffin.

A few years ago there was an old man in this city, an eminent officer of the government, formerly a judge, with whom I sometimes conversed, and the idol of whose thought and life was Jefferson. He set great value upon *Leaves of Grass*, but the works and life of the author of the Declaration of Independence made his central theme, of which he never wearied, nor, indeed, made others weary, he discoursed upon it so eloquently well. He has passed from among us; but I can still see in memory, his old, wrinkled, earnest, smiling face, and dark, sunken eyes tinged around with black, and hear his low, eager voice, as with the ardor of a boy he unrolled his dissertation upon some sentence of the sage of Monticello, or, kindling into some magian gloss upon his text, ﹐ɔretold in a sort of measured ecstasy the complete ultimate triumph of the democ⌄atic principle, and the transfiguration of government and society in the operation of the ideas of his master. But always as the climax of his rapt argument, or at the close of any stage thereof, before it mounted to a higher proposition, he would say, bending his old head forward, his voice trembling with intensity, his face glowing into a deeper wizard smile, his dark eyes shining in their swarthy circles—" and here," he would exclaim, " here is where our glorious Walt comes in and confirms Jefferson!" No description could convey a sense of the tone of utter satisfaction and triumph in which he announced his prophet confirmed by his poet, nor of the tremulous fervor, the supreme unction with which the words " our glorious Walt" were uttered. I take the remembrance of those words, as I would a wild flower from the kind old scholar's grave, and lay it on our poet's book as my latest offering, worth more than the little tribute I have ever brought, or all that I could ever bring. " Our glorious Willy" was the phrase the author of the " Faery Queen" threw, like a star, upon the name of Shakespeare, in the days when the term " a willy" was simply a euphuism for " a poet," and no more. " Our glorious Walt," the utterance of lips that fondly loved the name of Jefferson, and yielded the words in homage to the bard who has carried into literature earth's greatest dream, is at least an honor equal to that Spenser gave, and goes to an object no less worthy of such honor. For to have conceived and written *Leaves of Grass*—to have been of the old heroic strain of which such books alone are born—to have surcharged the pages with their world of noble and passionate life—to have done all this, to have dared all this, to have suffered for all this—is to be the true brother of Shakespeare.

Pardon my imperfect contribution to your volume. You know how hastily I have written, using the little time left by the pressing tasks of the Life-Saving Service. And with cordial wishes for the success of your book,

Believe me, Dear Sir,

Faithfully yours,

WILLIAM DOUGLAS O'CONNOR.

THE GOOD GRAY POET

A VINDICATION.

WASHINGTON, D. C., Sept. 2, 1865.

NINE weeks have elapsed since the commission of an outrage, to which I have not till now been able to give my attention, but which, in the interest of the sacred cause of free letters, and in that alone, I never meant should pass without its proper and enduring brand.

For years past, thousands of people in New York, in Brooklyn, in Boston, in New Orleans, and latterly in Washington, have seen, even as I saw two hours ago, tallying, one might say, the streets of our American cities, and fit to have for his background and accessories their streaming populations and ample and rich façades, a man of striking masculine beauty—a poet—powerful and venerable in appearance; large, calm, superbly formed; oftenest clad in the careless, rough, and always picturesque costume of the common people; resembling, and generally taken by strangers for some great mechanic or stevedore, or seaman, or grand laborer of one kind or another; and passing slowly in this guise, with nonchalant and haughty step along the pavement, with the sunlight and shadows falling around him. The dark sombrero he usually wears was, when I saw him just now, the day being warm, held for the moment in his hand; rich light an artist would have chosen, lay upon his uncovered head, majestic, large, Homeric, and set upon his strong shoulders with the grandeur of ancient sculpture. I marked the countenance, serene, proud, cheerful, florid, grave; the brow seamed with noble wrinkles; the features, massive and handsome, with firm blue eyes; the eyebrows and eyelids especially showing that fulness of arch seldom seen save in the antique busts; the flowing hair and fleecy beard, both very gray, and tempering with a look of age the youthful aspect of one who is but forty-five; the simplicity and purity of his dress, cheap and plain, but spotless, from snowy falling collar to burnished boot, and exhaling faint fragrance; the whole form surrounded with manliness as with a nimbus, and breathing, in its perfect health and vigor, the august charm of the strong.

We who have looked upon this figure, or listened to that clear, cheerful, vibrating voice, might thrill to think, could we but transcend our age, that we had been thus near to one of the greatest of the sons of men. But Dante stirs no deep pulse, unless it be of hate, as he walks the streets of Florence; that shabby, one-armed soldier, just out of jail and hardly noticed, though he

has amused Europe, is Michael Cervantes; that son of a vine-dresser, whom
Athens laughs at as an eccentric genius, before it is thought worth-while to
roar him into exile, is the century-shaking Æschylus; that phantom whom
the wits of the seventeenth century think not worth extraordinary notice, and
the wits of the eighteenth century, spluttering with laughter, call a barbarian,
is Shakespeare; that earth-soiled, vice-stained ploughman, with the noble
heart and sweet bright eyes, abominated by the good and patronized by the
gentry, subject now of anniversary banquets by gentlemen who, could they
wander backward from those annual hiccups into time, would never help his
life or keep his company—is Robert Burns; and this man, whose grave, perhaps, the next century will cover with passionate and splendid honors, goes
regarded with careless curiosity or phlegmatic composure by his own age.
Yet, perhaps, in a few hearts he has waked that deep thrill due to the passage
of the sublime.   I heard lately, with sad pleasure,* of the letter introducing a
friend, filled with noble courtesy, and dictated by the reverence for genius,
which a distinguished English nobleman, a stranger, sent to this American
bard.   Nothing deepens my respect for the beautiful intellect of the scholar
Alcott, like the bold sentence "Greater than Plato," which he once uttered
upon him.   I hold it the surest proof of Thoreau's insight, that after a conversation, seeing how he incarnated the immense and new spirit of the age,
and was the compend of America, he came away to speak the electric sentence,
" He is Democracy !"   I treasure to my latest hour, with swelling heart and
springing tears, the remembrance that Abraham Lincoln, seeing him for the
first time from the window of the east room of the White House as he passed
slowly by, and gazing at him long with that deep eye which read men, said,
in the quaint, sweet tone, which those who have spoken with him will remember,
and with a significant emphasis which the type can hardly convey, " Well, *he*
looks like a MAN !"   Sublime tributes, great-words; but none too high for
their object, the author of *Leaves of Grass*, Walt Whitman, of Brooklyn.

On the 30th of June last, this true American man and author was dismissed,
under circumstances of peculiar wrong, from a clerkship he had held for six
months in the Department of the Interior.   His dismissal was the act of the
Hon. James Harlan, the Secretary of the Department, formerly a Methodist
clergyman, and president of a Western college.

Upon the interrogation of an eminent officer of the Government, at whose
instance the appointment had, under a former Secretary, been made, Mr. Harlan averred that Walt Whitman had been in no way remiss in the discharge
of his duties, but that, on the contrary, so far as he could learn, his conduct had
been most exemplary.   Indeed, during the few months of his tenure of office,

---

* Pleasure a mean lie saddened.   Stopping en route at Cambridge, the bearer of this letter
was informed by one of its most distinguished resident authors, that Walt Whitman was
" nothing but a low New York rowdy," " a common street blackguard," and he accordingly
did not venture to present the letter.

he had been promoted. The sole and only cause of his dismissal, Mr. Harlan said, was that he had written the book of poetry entitled *Leaves of Grass.* This book Mr. Harlan characterized as " full of indecent passages." The author, he said, was " a very bad man," a " free lover." Argument being had upon these propositions, Mr. Harlan was, as regards the book, utterly unable to maintain his assertions, and, as regards the author, was forced to own that his opinion of him had been changed. Nevertheless, after this substantial admission of his injustice, he absolutely refused to revoke his action. Of course, under no circumstances would Walt Whitman, the proudest man that lives, have consented to again enter into office under Mr. Harlan ; but the demand for his reinstatement was as honorable to the gentleman who made it as the refusal to accede to it was discreditable to the Secretary.

The closing feature of this transaction, and one which was a direct consequence of Mr. Harlan's course, was its remission to the scurrilous, and in some instances libellous, comment of a portion of the press. To sum up, an author, solely and only for the publication, ten years ago, of an honest book, which no intelligent and candid person can regard as hurtful to morality, was expelled from office by the Secretary, and held up to public contumely by the newspapers. It only remains to be added here, that the Hon. James Harlan is the gentleman who, upon assuming the control of the Department, published a manifesto, announcing that it was thenceforth to be governed " upon the principles of Christian civilization."

This act of expulsion, and all that it encloses, is the outrage to which I referred in my opening paragraph.

I have had the honor, which I esteem a very high one, to know Walt Whitman intimately for several years, and am conversant with the details of his life and history. Scores and scores of persons, who know him well, can confirm my own report of him, and I have therefore no hesitation in saying that the scandalous assertions of Mr. Harlan, derived from whom I know not, as to his being a bad man, a free lover, etc., belong to the category of those calumnies at which, as Napoleon said, innocence itself is confounded. A better man in all respects, or one more irreproachable in his relations to the other sex, lives not upon this earth. His is the great goodness, the great chastity of spiritual strength and sanity. I do not believe that from the hour of his infancy, when Lafayette held him in his arms, to the present hour, in which he bends over the last wounded and dying of the war, any one can say aught of him, which does not consort with the largest and truest manliness. I am perfectly aware of the miserable lies which have been put into circulation respecting him, of which the story of his dishonoring an invitation to dine with Emerson, by appearing at the table of the Astor House in a red shirt; and with the manners of a rowdy, is a mild specimen. I know too the inferences drawn by wretched fools, who, because they have seen him riding upon the top of an omnibus; or at Pfaff's restaurant; or dressed in rough clothes suitable for his purposes, and only remarkable because the wearer was a man of genius; or mixing freely and lovingly, like Lucretius, like Rabelais, like Francis Bacon, like Rembrandt, like all great students of the world, with low and equivocal and dissolute persons, as well as with those of a different character, must needs set him down as a brute, a scallawag, and a criminal. Mr. Harlan's allegations are of a piece with these. If I could associate the title with a really great person, or if the name of man were not radically superior, I should say that for solid nobleness of character, for native elegance and delicacy of soul, for a courtesy which is the very passion of thoughtful kindness and forbearance, for his tender and paternal respect and manly honor for woman, for love and heroism carried into the pettiest details of life, and for a large and homely beauty of manners, which makes the civilities of parlors fantastic and puerile in comparison, Walt Whitman deserves to be considered the grandest gentleman that treads this continent. I know well the habits and tendencies of his life. They are all simple, sane, domestic, worthy of him as one of an estimable family and a member of society. He is a tender and faithful son, a good brother, a loyal friend, an ardent and devoted citizen. He has been a laborer, working successively as a farmer, a carpenter, a printer. He has been a stalwart editor of the Republican party, and often, in that powerful and nervous prose of which he is master, done yeoman's service for the great cause of human liberty and the imperial conception of the indivisible Union. He has been a visitor of prisons, a protector of fugitive slaves, a constant voluntary nurse, night and day, at the hospitals, from the beginning of the war to the present time; a brother and friend through life to the neglected and the forgotten, the poor, the degraded, the criminal, the outcast, turning away from no man for his guilt, nor woman for her vileness. His is the strongest and truest compassion I have ever known. I remember here the anecdote told me by a witness, of his meeting in a by-street in Boston a poor ruffian, one whom he had known well as an innocent child, now a fullgrown youth, vicious far beyond his years, flying to Canada from the pursuit of the police, his sin-trampled features bearing marks of the recent bloody brawl in New York, in which, as he supposed, he had killed some one; and having heard his hurried story, freely confided to him, Walt Whitman, separated not from the bad even by his own goodness, with well I know what tender and tranquil feeling for the ruined being, and with a love which makes me think of that love of God which deserts not any creature, quietly at parting, after assisting him from his means, held him for a moment, with his arm around his neck, and, bending to the face, horrible and battered and prematurely old, kissed him on the cheek, and the poor hunted wretch, perhaps for the first time in his low life, receiving a token of love and compassion like a touch from beyond the sun, hastened away in deep dejection, sobbing and in tears. It reminds me of the anecdotes Victor Hugo, in his portraiture of Bishop Myriel, tells, under a thin veil of fiction, of Charles Miolles, the good Bishop of Digne.　I know not what talisman Walt Whitman carries, unless it be an unexcluding friendliness and goodness which is felt upon his approach like magnetism; but I know that in the subterranean life of cities, among the worst roughs, he goes safely; and I could recite instances where hands that, in mere wantonness of ferocity, assault anybody, raised against him, have of their own accord been lowered almost as quickly, or, in some cases, have been dragged promptly down by others; this, too, I'mean, when he and the assaulting gang were mutual strangers.　I have seen singular evidence of the mysterious quality which not only guards him, but draws to him with intuition, rapid as light, simple and rude people, as to their natural mate and friend.　I remember, as I passed the White House with him one evening, the startled feeling with which I saw a soldier on guard there—a stranger to us both, and with something in his action that curiously proved that he was a stranger—suddenly bring his musket to the " present " in military salute to him, quickly mingling with this respect due to his colonel, a gesture of greeting with the right hand as to a comrade, grinning, meanwhile, good fellow, with shy, spontaneous affection and deference, his ruddy, broad face glowing in the flare of the lampions.　I remember, on another occasion, as I crossed the street with him, the driver of a street-car, a stranger, stopping the conveyance, and inviting him to get on and ride with him.　Adventures of this kind are frequent, and " I took a fancy to you," or " You look like one of my style," is the common explanation he gets upon their occurrence.　It would be impossible to exaggerate the personal adhesion and strong, simple affection given him, in numerous instances on sight, by multitudes of plain persons, sailors, mechanics, drivers, soldiers, farmers, sempstresses, old people of the past generation, mothers of families— those powerful, unlettered persons, among whom, as he says in his book, he has gone freely, and who never in most cases even suspect as an author him whom they love as a man, and who loves them in return.

His intellectual influence upon many young men and women—spirits of the morning sort, not willing to belong to that intellectual colony of Great Britain which our literary classes compose, nor helplessly tied, like them, to the old forms—I note as kindred to that of Socrates upon the youth of ancient Attica, or Raleigh upon the gallant young England of his day.　It is a power at once liberating, instructing, and inspiring.—His conversation is a university! Those who have heard him in some roused hour, when the full afflatus of his spirit moved him, will agree with me that the grandeur of talk was accomplished.　He is known as a passionate lover and powerful critic of the great music and of art.　He is deeply cultured by some of the best books, especially those of the Bible, which he prefers above all other great literature, but principally by contact and communion with things themselves, which literature can only mirror and celebrate.　He has travelled through most of the United States, intent on comprehending and absorbing the genius and history of his

country, that he might do his best to start a literature worthy of her, sprung
from her own polity, and tallying her own unexampled magnificence among
the nations. To the same end, he has been a long, patient, and laborious
student of life, mixing intimately with all varieties of experience and men,
with curiosity and with love. He has given his thought, his life, to this beautiful ambition, and, still young, he has grown gray in its service. He has
never married; like Giordano Bruno, he has made Thought in the service of
his fellow-creatures his *bella donna*, his best beloved, his bride. His patriotism is boundless. It is no intellectual sentiment; it is a personal passion.
He performs with scrupulous fidelity and zeal the duties of a citizen. For
eighteen years, not missing once, his ballot has dropped on every national and
local election day, and his influence has been ardently given for the good
cause. Of all men I know, his life is most in the life of the nation. I remember, when the first draft was ordered, at a time when he was already performing an arduous and perilous duty as a volunteer attendant upon the
wounded in the field—a duty which cost him the only illness he ever had in
his life, and a very severe and dangerous illness it was, the result of poison
absorbed in his devotion to the worst cases of hospital gangrene, and when it
would have been the easiest thing in the world to evade duty, for though then
only forty-two or three years old, and subject to the draft, he looked a hale
sixty, and no enrolling officer would have paused for an instant before his
gray hair—I remember, I say, how anxious and careful he was to get his
name put on the enrolment lists, that he might stand his chance for martial
service. This, too, at a time when so many gentlemen were skulking, dodg-
ing, agonizing for substitutes, and practising every conceivable device to escape
military duty. What music of speech, though Cicero's own—what scarlet
and gold superlatives could adorn or dignify this simple, antique trait of
private heroism?—I recall his love for little children, for the young, and for
very old persons, as if the dawn and the evening twilight of life awakened
his deepest tenderness. I recall the affection for him of numbers of young
men, and invariably of all good women. Who, knowing him, does not regard him as a man of the highest spiritual culture? I have never known one
of greater and deeper religious feeling. To call one like him good seems an
impertinence. In our sweet country phrase, he is one of God's men. And
as I write these hurried and broken memoranda—as his strength and sweetness of nature, his moral health, his rich humor, his gentleness, his serenity,
his charity, his simple-heartedness, his courage, his deep and varied knowledge of life and men, his calm wisdom, his singular and beautiful boy-inno-
cence, his personal majesty, his rough scorn of mean actions, his magnetic
and exterminating anger on due occasions—all that I have seen and heard of
him, the testimony of associates, the anecdotes of friends, the remembrance
of hours with him that should be immortal, the traits, lineaments, incidents of
his life and being—as they come crowding into memory—his seems to me a

character which only the heroic pen of Plutarch could record, and which Socrates himself might emulate or envy.

This is the man whom Mr. Harlan charges with having written a bad book. I might ask, How long is it since bad books have been the flower of good lives? How long is it since grape-vines produced thorns or fig-trees thistles? But Mr. Harlan says the book is bad because it is " full of indecent passages." This allegation has been brought against *Leaves of Grass* before. It has been sounded long and strong by many of the literary journals of both continents. As criticism it is legitimate. I may contemn the mind or deplore the moral life in which such a criticism has its source; still, as criticism it has a right to existence. But Mr. Harlan, passing the limits of opinion, inaugurates punishment. He joins the band of the hostile verdict; he incarnates their judgment; then, detaching himself, he proceeds to a solitary and signal vengeance. As far as he can have it so, this author, for having written his book, shall starve. He shall starve, and his name shall receive a brand. This is the essence of Mr. Harlan's action. It is a dark and serious step to take. Upon what grounds is it taken?

I have carefully counted out from Walt Whitman's poetry the lines, perfectly moral to me, whether viewed in themselves or in the light of their sublime intentions and purport, but upon which ignorant and indecent persons of respectability base their sweeping condemnation of the whole work. Taking *Leaves of Grass*, and the recent small volume, " Drum-Taps " (which was in Mr. Harlan's possession), there are in the whole about nine thousand lines or verses. From these, including matter which I can hardly imagine objectionable to any one, but counting everything which the most malignant virtue could shrink from, I have culled eighty lines. Eighty lines out of nine thousand! It is a less proportion than one finds in Shakespeare. Upon this so slender basis rests the whole crazy fabric of American and European slander and the brutal lever of the Secretary.

Now, what by competent authority is the admitted character of the book in which these lines occur? For, though it is more than probable that Mr. Harlan never heard of the work till the hour of his explorations in the Department, the intellectual hemispheres of Great Britain and America have rung with it from side to side. It has received as extensive a critical notice, I suppose, as has ever been given to a volume. Had it been received only with indifference or derision, I should not have been surprised. In an age in which few breathe the atmosphere of the grand literature—which forgets the superb books and thinks Bulwer moral, and Dickens great, and Thackeray a real satirist—which gives to Macaulay the laurel due to Herodotus, and to Tennyson the crown reserved for Homer, and in which the chairs of criticism seem abandoned to squirts, and pedagogues, and monks—a mighty poet has little to expect from the literary press save unconcern and mockery. But even under these hard conditions the tremendous force of this poet has achieved a relative conquest, and the tone of the press denotes his book as not merely great, but illustrious. Even the copious torrents of abuse which have been lavished upon it have, in numerous instances, taken the form of tribute to its august and mysterious power, being in fact identical with that still vomited upon Montaigne and Juvenal. On the other hand, eulogy, very lofty and from the highest sources, has spanned it with sunbows. Emerson, our noblest scholar, a name to which Christendom does reverence, a critic of piercing insight and full comprehension, has pronounced it "the most extraordinary piece of wit and wisdom that America has yet contributed." How that austere and rare spirit, Thoreau, regarded it may be partly seen by his last posthumous volume. He thought of it, I have heard, with measureless esteem, ranking it with the vast and gorgeous conceptions of the Oriental bards. It has been reported to me that unpublished letters, received in this country from some of Europe's greatest, announce a similar verdict. The "North American Review," unquestionably the highest organ of American letters, in the course of a eulogistic notice of the work, remarking upon the passages which Mr. Harlan has treated as if they were novel in literature, observes: "There is not anything, perhaps (in the book), which modern usage would stamp as more indelicate than are some passages in Homer. There is not a word in it meant to attract readers by its grossness as there is in half the literature of the last century, which holds its place unchallenged on the tables of our drawing-rooms." The London "Dispatch," in a review written by the Rev. W. J. Fox, one of the most distinguished clergymen in England, after commending the poems for "their strength of expression, their fervor, their hearty wholesomeness, their originality and freshness, their singular harmony," etc., says that, "in the unhesitating frankness of a man who dares to call simplest things by their plain names, conveying also a large sense of the beautiful," there is involved "a clearer conception of what manly modesty really is than in anything we have in all conventional forms of word, deed, or act, so far known of," and concludes by declaring that "the author will soon make his way into the confidence of his readers, and his poems in time will become a pregnant text-book, from which quotations as sterling as the minted gold will be taken and applied to every form of the inner and the outer life." The London "Leader," one of the foremost of the British literary journals, in a review which more nearly approaches perception of the true character and purport of the book than any I have seen, has the following sentences:

"Mr. Emerson recognized the first issue of the *Leaves*, and hastened to welcome the author, then totally unknown. Among other things, said Emerson to the new avatar, 'I greet you at the beginning of a great career which yet *must have had a long foreground somewhere for such a start.*' The last clause was, however, overlooked entirely by the critics, who treated the new author as one self-educated, yet in the rough, unpolished, and owing nothing to instruction. The authority for so treating the author was derived from himself, who thus described in one of his poems, his person, character, and name, having omitted the last from the title-page,

> 'Walt Whitman, an American, one of the roughs, a kosmos,
> Disorderly, fleshy, and sensual,'—

and in various other passages confessed to all the vices, as well as the virtues, of man.   All this, with intentional wrong-headedness, was attributed by the sapient reviewers to the individual writer, and not to the subjective-hero supposed to be writing.   Notwithstanding the word 'kosmos,' the writer was taken to be an ignorant man.   Emerson perceived at once that there had been a long foreground somewhere or somehow;—not so they.   Every page teems with knowledge, with information; but they saw it not, because it did not answer their purpose to see it. .   The poem in which the word 'kósmos' appears explains in fact the whole mystery—nay, the word itself explains it.   The poem is nominally upon himself, but really includes everybody.   It begins:

> 'I celebrate myself,
> And what I assume, you shall assume;
> For every atom belonging to me, as good belongs to you.'

In a word, Walt Whitman *represents the kosmical man—he is the* ADAMUS *of the Nineteenth century—not an individual, but* MANKIND.   As such, in celebrating himself, he proceeds to celebrate universal humanity in its attributes, and accordingly commences his dithyramb with the five senses, beginning with that of smell.   Afterwards, he deals with the intellectual, rational, and moral powers, showing throughout his treatment an intimate acquaintance with Kant's transcendental method, and perhaps including in his development the whole of the German school, down to Hegel—at any rate as interpreted by Cousin and others in France and Emerson in the United States.   He certainly includes Fichte, for he mentions the egotist as the only true philosopher, and consistently identifies himself not only with every man, but with the universe and its Maker; and it is in doing so that the strength of his description consists.   It is from such an ideal elevation that he looks down on Good and Evil, regards them as equal, and extends to them the like measure of equity. . . .   Instead, therefore, of regarding these *Leaves of Grass* as a marvel, they seem to us as the most natural product of the American soil.   They are certainly filled with an American spirit, breathe the American air, and assert the fullest American freedom."   The passages characterized by the Secretary as "indecent" are, adds the "Leader," "only so many instances adduced in support of a philosophical principle, not meant for obscenity, but for scientific examples, introduced, as they might be in any legal, medical, or philosophical book, for the purpose of instruction."

I could multiply these excerpts; but here are sufficient specimens of the competent judgments of eminent scholars and divines, testifying to the intel- ⌐ lectual and moral grandeur of this work.   Let it be remembered that there is nothing in the book that in one form or another is not contained in all great poetic or universal literature.   It has nothing either in quantity or quality so offensive as everybody knows is in Shakespeare.   All that this poet has done is to mention, without levity, without low language, very seriously, often devoutly, always simply, certain facts in the natural history of man and of life, and sometimes, assuming their sanctity, to use them in illustration or imagery. Far more questionable mention and use of these facts are common to the greatest literature. Shall the presence in a book of eighty lines, similar in character to what every great and noble poetic book contains, be sufficient to shove it below even the lewd writings of Petronius Arbiter, the dirty dramas of Shirley, or the scrofulous fiction of Louvet de Couvray? to lump it in with the anonymous lascivious trash spawned in holes and sold in corners, too witless and disgusting for any notice but that of the police—and to entitle its author to treatment such as only the nameless wretches of the very sewers of authorship ought to receive?

If, rising to the utmost cruelty of conception, I can dare add to the calamities of genius a misery so degrading and extreme as to imagine the great authors of the world condemned to clerkships under Mr. Harlan, I can at least mitigate that dream of wretchedness and insult by adding the fancy of their fate under the action of his principles. Let me suppose them there, and he still magnifying the calling of the Secretary into that of literary headsman. He opens the great book of Genesis. Everywhere "indecent passages." The mother hushes the child, and bids him skip as he reads aloud that first great history. It cannot be read aloud in "drawing-rooms" by "gentlemen" and "ladies." The freest use of language, the plainest terms, frank mention of forbidden subjects; the story of Onan, of Hagar and Sarai, of Lot and his daughters, of Isaac, Rebekah, and Abimelech, of Jacob and Leah, of Reuben and Bilhah; of Potiphar's wife and Joseph; tabooed allusion and statement everywhere; no veils, no euphemism, no delicacy, no meal in the mouth anywhere. Out with Moses! The cloven splendor on that awful brow shall not save him.

Mr. Harlan takes up the Iliad and the Odyssey. The loves of Jupiter and Juno, the dalliance of Achilles and Patroclus with their women; the perfectly frank, undraped reality of Greek life and manners naively shown without regard to the feelings of Christian civilizees—horrible! Out with Homer!

Here is Lucretius: Mr. Harlan opens the "De Rerum Natura," and reads the vast, benign, majestic lines, sad with the shadow of the intelligible universe upon them; sublime with the tragic problems of the Infinite; august with their noble love and compassion for mankind. But what is this? "Ut quasi transactis soepe omnibus rebus," etc. And this: "Morè ferarum quadrupedumque magis ritu." And this: "Nam mulier prohibet se consipere atque repugnat," etc. And this: "Quod petiere, premunt arcte, faciuntque dolorem," etc. Enough. Fine language, fine illustrations, fine precepts, pretty decency! Out with Lucretius! Out with the chief poet of the Tiber side!

Here is Æschylus; a dark magnificence of cloud, all rough with burning gold, which thunders and drips blood! The Greek Shakespeare. The gorgeous and terrible Æschylus! What is this in the "Prometheus" about Jove and Iŏ? What sort of detail is that which, at the distance of ten years, I remember amazed Mr. Buckley as he translated the Agamemnon? What kind of talk is this in the " Choephori," in " The Suppliants," and in the fragments of the comic drama of " The Argians "? Out with Æschylus!

Here is the sublime book of Ezekiel. All the Hebrew grandeur at its fullest is there. But look at this blurt of coarse words, hurled direct as the prophet-mouth can hurl them—this familiar reference to functions and organs voted out of language—this bread for human lips baked with ordure—these details of the scortatory loves of Aholah and Aholibah. Enough. Dismiss this dreadful majesty of Hebrew poetry. He has no "taste." He is " indecent." Out with Ezekiel!

Here is Dante. Open the tremendous pages of the " Inferno." What is this about the she-wolf Can Grande will kill? What picture is this of strumpet Thais?—ending with the lines:

> "Taida è, la puttana che rispose
> Al drudo suo, quando disse: Ho io grazie
> Grandi appo te? Anzi meravigliose."

What is this also in the eighteenth canto?

> "Quivi venimmo, e quindi giù nel fosso
> Vidi gente attuffata in uno sterco
> Che dagli uman privati parea mosso:
> E mentre ch' io là giù con l'occhio cerco,
> Vidi un col capo si di merda lordo,
> Che non parea s'era laico o cherco."

What is this line at the end of the twenty-first canto, which even John Carlyle flinches from translating, but which Dante did not flinch from writing?

> "Ed egli avea del cul fatto trombetta."

And look at these lines in the twenty-eighth canto ·

> "Già reggia, per mezzul perdere o lulla
> Com' io vidi un, cosi non si pertugia
> Rotto dal mento insin dove si trulla."

That will do. Dante, too, has " indecent passages." Out with Dante!

Here is the book of Job: the vast Arabian landscape, the picturesque pastoral details of Arabian life, the last tragic immensity of Oriental sorrow, the whole overarching sky of Oriental piety, are here. But here also the inevitable " indecency." Instead of the virtuous fiction of the tansy bed, Job actually has the indelicacy to state how man is born—even mentions the belly; talks about the gendering of bulls, and the miscarriage of cows; uses rank idioms; and in the thirty-first chapter especially, indulges in a strain of thought and expression which it is amazing does not bring down upon him, even at this late date, the avalanches of our lofty and pure reviews. Here is certainly " an immoral poet." Out with Job!

Here is Plutarch, prince of biographers, and Herodotus, flower of historians. What have we now? Traits of character not to be mentioned, incidents of conduct, accounts of manners, minute details of customs, which our modern historical dandies would never venture upon recording. Out with Plutarch and Herodotus!

Here is Tacitus. What statement of crimes that ought not to be hinted? Does the man gloat over such things? What dreadful kisses are these of Agrippina to Nero—the mother to the son? Out with Tacitus! And since there are books that ought to be publicly burned,* by all means let the stern grandeur of that rhetoric be lost in flame.

Here is Shakespeare: "indecent passages" everywhere—every drama, every poem thickly inlaid with them; all that men do displayed, sexual acts treated lightly, jested about, mentioned obscenely; the language never bolted; slang, gross puns, lewd words, in profusion. Out with Shakespeare!

Here is the Canticle of Canticles: beautiful, voluptuous poem of love literally, whatever be its mystic significance; glowing with the color, odorous with the spices, melodious with the voices of the East; sacred and exquisite and pure with the burning chastity of passion, which completes and exceeds the snowy chastity of virgins. This to me, but what to the Secretary? Can he endure that the female form should stand thus in a poem, disrobed, unveiled, bathed in erotic splendor? Look at these voluptuous details, this expression of desire, this amorous tone and glow, this consecration and perfume lavished upon the sensual. No! Out with Solomon!

Here is Isaiah. The grand thunder-roll of that righteousness, like the lion-roar of Jehovah above the guilty world, utters coarse words. Amidst the bolted lightnings of that sublime denunciation, coarse thoughts, indelicate figures, indecent allusions, flash upon the sight, like gross imagery in a midnight landscape. Out with Isaiah!

Here is Montaigne. Open those great, those virtuous pages of the unflinching reporter of man; the soul all truth and daylight, all candor, probity, sincerity, reality, eyesight. A few glances will suffice. Cant and vice and sniffle have groaned over these pages before. Out with Montaigne!

Here is Hafiz, the Anacreon of Persia, but more; a banquet of wine in a garden of roses, the nightingales singing, the laughing revellers high with festal joy; but a heavenly flame burns on every brow; a tone not of this sphere is in all the music, all the laughter, all the songs; a light of the Infinite trembles over every chalice and rests on every flower; and all the garden is divine. Still when Hafiz cries out, " Bring me wine, and bring the famed

---

* Mr. Harlan had said that *Leaves of Grass* ought to be publicly burned.

veiled beauty, the Princess of the brothel," etc., or issues similar orders, Mr. Harlan, whose virtue does not understand or endure such metaphors, must deal sternly with this kosmic man of Persia.　Out with Hafiz!

Here is Virgil, ornate and splendid poet of old Rome; a master with a greater pupil, Alighieri—a bard above whose ashes Boccaccio kneels a trader and arises a soldier of mankind.　But he must lose those fadeless chaplets, the undying green of a noble fame; for here in the " Æneid " is " Dixerat; et niveis hinc atque hinc Diva lacertis," etc., and here in the " Georgics " is " Quo rapiat sitiens Venerem, interiusque recondat," etc., and there are other verses like these.　Out with Virgil!

Here is Swedenborg.　Open this poem in prose, the " Conjugial Love," to me, a temple, though in ruins; the sacred fane, clothed in mist, filled with moonlight, of a great though broken mind.　What spittle of critic epithets stains all here?　" Lewd," " sensual," " lecherous," " coarse," " licentious," etc. Of course these judgments are final.　There is no appeal from the tobacco-juice of an expectorating and disdainful virtue.　Out with Swedenborg!

Here is Goethe : the horrified squealing of prudes is not yet silent over pages of " Wilhelm Meister : " that high and chaste book, the " Elective Affinities," still pumps up oaths from clergymen : Walpurgis has hardly ceased its uproar over Faust.　Out with Goethe!

Here is Byron : grand, dark poet; a great spirit—a soul like the ocean; generous lover of America; fiery trumpet of liberty; a sword for the human cause in Greece; a torch for the human mind in " Cain ; " a life that redeemed its every fault by taking a side, which was the human side; tempest of scorn in his first poem, tempest of scorn and laughter in his last poem, only against the things that wrong man; vast bud of the Infinite that Death alone prevented from its vaster flower; immense, seminal, electrical, dazzling Byron. But Beppo—O! But Don Juan—O, fie! Not to mention the Countess Guiccioli—ah, me! Prepare quickly the yellow envelope, and out with Byron!

Here is Cervantes : open " Don Quixote," paragon of romances, highest result of Spain, best and sufficient reason for her life among the nations, a laughing novel which is a weeping poem.　But talk such as this of Sancho Panza and Tummas Cecial under the cork trees, and these coarse stories and bawdy words, and this free and gross comedy—is it to be endured?　Out with Cervantes!

Here is another, a sun of literature, moving in a vast orbit with dazzling plenitudes of power and beauty; the one only modern European poet and novelist worthy to rank with the first; permanent among the fleeting; a demigod of letters among the pigmies; a soul of the antique strength and sadness, worthy to stand as the representative of the high thought and hopes of the Nineteenth century—Victor Hugo.　Now open " Les Misèrables."· See the great passages which the American translator softens and the English translator tears away.　Open this other book of his, " William Shakespeare," a book with only one grave fault, the omission of the words "a Poem" from the title-page; a book which is the courageous arch, the comprehending sky of criticism, but which no American publisher will dare to issue, or if he does will expurgate. Out with Hugo, of course!

Here is Juvenal, terrible and splendid fountain of all satire; inspiration of all just censure; exemplar of all noble rage at baseness; satirist and moralist sublimed into the poet; the scowl of the unclouded noon above the low streets of folly and of sin. But what he withers, he also shows. The sun-stroke of his poetry reveals what it kills. Juvenal tells all. His fidelity of exposure is frightful. Mr. Harlan would make short work of him. Out with Juvenal!

Open the divine "Apocalypse." What words are these among the thunderings and lightnings and voices? Is this a poem to be read aloud in parlors? (for such appears to be the test of propriety and purity). At least, John might have been a little more choice in language. Some of these texts are "indecent." Yes, indeed! John must go!

Here is Spenser. Encyclopædic poet of the ideal chivalry. It is all there. Amadis, Esplandian, Tirante the White, Palmerin of England, all those Paladin romances were but the leaves; this is the flower. A lost dream of valor, chastity, courtesy, glory—a dream that marks an age of human history—glimmers here, far in these depths, and makes this unexplored obscurity divine. "But is the 'Faëry Queen' such a book as you would wish to put into the hands of a lady?" What a question! Has it not been expurgated? Out with Spenser!

Here is another, a true soldier of the human emancipation; one who smites amid uproars of laughter; the master of Titanic farce; a whirlwind and earthquake of derision—Rabelais. A nice one for Mr. Harlan! One glimpse at the chapter which explains why the miles lengthen as you leave Paris, or at the details of the birth and nurture of Gargantua, will suffice. Out with Rabelais—out with the great jester of France, as Lord Bacon calls him!

And here is Lord Bacon himself, in one of whose pages you may read,* done from the Latin by Spedding into a magnificent golden thunder of English, the absolute defence of the free spirit of the great authors, coupled with stern rebuke to the spirit that would pick and choose, as dastard and effeminate. Out with Lord Bacon!

Not him only, not these only, not only the writers are under the ban. Here is Phidias, gorgeous sculptor in gold and ivory, giant dreamer of the Infinite in marble; but he will not use the fig-leaf. Here is Rembrandt, who paints the Holland landscape, the Jew, the beggar, the burgher, in lights and glooms of Eternity; and his pictures have been called "indecent." Here is Mozart, his music rich with the sumptuous color of all sunsets; and it has been called "sensual." Here is Michael Angelo, who makes art tremble with a new and

---

* *Novum Organum;* Aphorism CXX.

strange afflatus, and gives Europe novel and sublime forms that tower above the centuries, and accost the Greek; and his works have been called " bestial " ! Out with them all!

Now, except Virgil, for vassalage to literary models, and for grave and sad falsehood to liberty; except Goethe for his lack of the final ecstacy of self-surrender which completes a poet, and for coldness to the great mother, one's country; except Spenser for his remoteness, and Byron for his immaturity, and there is not one of those I have named that does not belong to the first order of human intellect. But no need to make discriminations here; they are all great; they have all striven ; they have all served. Moses, Homer, Lucretius, Æschylus, Ezekiel, Dante, Job, Plutarch, Herodotus, Tacitus, Shakespeare, Solomon, Isaiah, Montaigne, Hafiz, Virgil, Swedenborg, Goethe, Byron, Cervantes, Hugo, Juvenal, John, Spenser, Rabelais, Bacon, Phidias, Rembrandt, Mozart, Angelo—these are among the demi-gods of human thought; the souls that have loved and suffered for the race; the light-bringers, the teachers, the lawgivers, the consolers, the liberators, the inspired inspirers of mankind ; the noble and gracious beings who, in the service of humanity, have borne every cross and earned every crown. There is not one of them that is not sacred in the eyes of thoughtful men. But not one of them do the rotten taste and morals of the Nineteenth century spare. Not one of them is qualified to render work for bread under this Secretary ! Do I err? Do I exaggerate? I write without access to the books I mention (it is fitting that this piece of insolent barbarism should have been committed in almost the only important American city which is without a public library !)—and with the exception of three or four volumes which I happen to have by me, I am obliged to rely for my statements on the memory of youthful readings, eight or ten years ago. But name me one book of the first order in which such passages as I refer to do not occur! Tell me who can—what poet of the first grade escapes this brand " immoral," or this spittle " indecent " ?

If the great books are not, in the point under consideration, in the same moral category as *Leaves of Grass*, then why, either in translation or in the originals, either by a bold softening which dissolves the author's meaning, or by absolute excision, are they nearly all expurgated? Answer me that. By one process or the other, Brizeux, Cary, Wright, Cayley, Carlyle, everybody, expurgates Dante ; Langhorne and others expurgate Plutarch ; Potter and others expurgate Æschylus; Gifford, Anthon and others expurgate Juvenal; Creech, Watson and others expurgate Lucretius; Bowdler and others expurgate Shakespeare; Nott (I believe it is) expurgates Hafiz; Wraxall and Wilbour expurgate Hugo; Kirkland, Hart and others expurgate Spenser; somebody expurgates Virgil; somebody expurgates Byron; the Oxford scholars dilute Tacitus; Lord Derby expurgates Homer, besides making him as ridiculous as the plucked cock of Diogenes in translation; several hands expurgate Goethe; and Archbishop Tillotson in design expurgates Moses,

Ezekiel, Solomon, Isaiah, St. John, and all the others—a job which Dr. Noah Webster executes, but, thank God, cannot popularize. What book is spared? Nothing but a chain of circumstances, which one might fancy divinely ordained, saves us the relatively unmutilated Bible. Nearly every other great book bleeds. When one is not expurgated, the balance is restored by its being cordially abused. Thanks to the splendid conscience and courage of Mr. Wight, we can read Montaigne in English without the omission of a single word. Thanks also to Smollett, Motteux and others, Cervantes has gone untouched, and we have not as yet a family Rabelais. Neither have we as yet a family Mankind nor a family Universe; but this is an oversight which will, doubtless, be repaired in time. God's works will also, doubtless, be expurgated whenever it is possible. Why not? One step to this end is taken in the expurgation of Genius, which is His second manifestation, as Nature is His first! Go on, gentlemen! You will yet have things as " moral " as you desire!

I am aware that as far as his opinion, not his act, is concerned, Mr. Harlan, however unintelligently, represents to some extent the shallow conclusions of his age, and I know it will be said that if the great books contain these passages, they ought to be expurgated. It is not my design to endeavor to put a quart into people who only hold a gill, nor would I waste time in endeavoring to convert a large class of persons whom I once heard Walt Whitman describe, with his usual Titanic richness and strength of phrase, as " the immutable granitic pudding-heads of the world." But there is a better class than these; and I am filled with measureless amazement, that persons of high intelligence, living to the age of maturity, do not perceive, at least, the immense and priceless scientific and human *uses* of such passages, and the consequent necessity, transcending and quashing all minor considerations, of having them where they are. But look at these sad sentences—a complete and felicitous statement of the whole modern doctrine—in the pages of a man I love and revere: " The literature of three centuries ago is not decent to be read; we expurgate it. Within a hundred years, woman has become a reader, and for that reason, as much as, or more than, anything else, literature has sprung to a higher level. No need now to expurgate all you read." He goes on to argue that literature in the next century will be richer than in the classic epochs, because woman will contribute to it as an author— her contribution, I infer, to be of the kind that will not need expurgating. These, I repeat, are sad sentences. If they are true, Bowdler is right to expurgate Shakespeare, and Noah Webster the Bible. But no, they are not true! I welcome woman into art; but when she comes there grandly, she will not come either as expurgator or creator of emasculate or partial forms. Woman, grand in art, is Rosa Bonheur, painting with fearless pencil the surly, sublime Jovian bull, equipped for masculine use; painting the powerful, ramping stallion in his amorous pride; not weakly nor meanly flinching from the full celebration of what God has made. Woman, grand in art, will come creating in forms, however novel, the absolute, the permanent, the real, the evil and the good, as Æschylus, as Cervantes, as Shakespeare before her; with sex, with truth, with universality, without omissions or concealments. And woman, as the ideal reader of literature, is not the indelicate prude, flushing and squealing over some frank page; it is that high and beautiful soul, Marie de Gournay, devoutly absorbing the work of her master Montaigne, finding it all great, greatly comprehending, greatly accepting it all; fronting its license and grossness without any of the livid shuddering of Puritans, and looking on the book in the same universal and kindly spirit as its author looked upon the world. Woman reading otherwise than thus—shrinking from Apuleius, from Rabelais, from Aristophanes, from Shakespeare, from even Wycherley, or Petronius, or Aretin, or Shirley—is less than man, is not ideal, not strong, not nobly good, but petty, and effeminate, and mean. And not for her, nor by her, nor by man, do I assent to the expurgation of the great books. Literature cannot spring to a higher level than theirs. Alas! it has sprung to a lower.

The level of the great books is the Infinite, the Absolute. To contain all, by containing the premise, the truth, the idea and feeling of all, to tally the universe by profusion, variety, reality, mystery, enclosure, power, terror, beauty, service; to be great to the utmost conceivability of greatness—what higher level than this can literature spring to? Up on the highest summit stand such works, never to be surpassed, never to be supplanted. Their indecency is not that of the vulgar; their vulgarity is not that of the low. Their evil, if it be evil, is not there for nothing—it serves; at the base of it is Love. Every poet of the highest quality is, in the masterly coinage of the author of *Leaves of Grass*, a kosmos. His work, like himself, is a second world, full of contrarieties, strangely harmonized, and moral indeed, but only as the world is moral. Shakespeare is all good, Rabelais is all good, Montaigne is all good, not because all the thoughts, the words, the manifestations are so, but because at the core, and permeating all, is an ethic intention—a love which, through mysterious, indirect, subtle, seemingly absurd, often terrible and repulsive, means, seeks to uplift, and never to degrade. It is the spirit in which authorship is pursued, as Augustus Schlegel has said, that makes it either an infamy or a virtue; and the spirit of the great authors, no matter what their letter, is one with that which pervades the Creation. In mighty love, with implements of pain and pleasure, of good and evil, Nature develops man; genius also, in mighty love, with implements of pain and pleasure, of good and evil, develops man; no matter what the means, that is the end.

Tell me not, then, of the indecent passages of the great poets! The world, which is the poem of God, is full of indecent passages! "Shall there be evil "in a city and the Lord hath not done it?" shouts Amos. "I form the light,

" and create darkness; I make peace, and create evil; I, the Lord, do all these
" things," thunders Isaiah. " This," says Coleridge, " is the deep abyss of the
" mystery of God." Ay, and the profound of the mystery of genius also!
Evil is part of the economy of genius, as it is part of the economy of Deity.
Gentle reviewers endeavor to find excuses for the freedoms of geniuses. " It
is to prove that they were above conventionalities." " It is referable to the
age." " The age permitted a degree of coarseness," etc. " Shakespeare's
indecencies are the result of his age." Oh, Ossa on Pelion, mount piled
on mount, of error and folly! What has genius, spirit of the absolute and
the eternal, to do with the definitions of position, or conventionalities, or
the age? Genius puts indecencies into its works, because God puts them
into His world. Whatever the special reason in each case, this is the
general reason in all cases. They are here, because they are there. That is
the eternal why.—No; Alphonso of Castile thought that, if he had been con-
sulted at the Creation, he could have given a few hints to the Almighty. Not
I. I play Alphonso neither to genius nor to God.

What is this poem, for the giving of which to America and the world, and
for that alone, its author has been dismissed with ignominy from a Government
office? It is a poem which Schiller might have hailed as the noblest specimen
of naïve literature, worthy of a place beside Homer. It is, in the first place,
a work purely and entirely American, autochthonic, sprung from our own soil;
no savor of Europe nor of the past, nor of any other literature in it; a vast
carol of our own land, and of its Present and Future; the strong and haughty
psalm of the Republic. There is not one other book, I care not whose, of
which this can be said. I weigh my words and have considered well. Every
other book by an American author implies, both in form and substance, I cannot even say the European, but the British mind. The shadow of Temple Bar
and Arthur's Seat lies dark on all our letters. Intellectually, we are still a de-
pendency of Great Britain, and one word—colonial—comprehends and stamps
our literature. In no literary form, except our newspapers, has there been
anything distinctively American. I note our best books—the works of Jefferson, the romances of Brockden Brown, the speeches of Webster, Everett's
rhetoric, the divinity of Channing, some of Cooper's novels, the writings of
Theodore Parker, the poetry of Bryant, the masterly law arguments of Ly-
sander Spooner, the miscellanies of Margaret Fuller, the histories of Hil-
dreth, Bancroft and Motley, Ticknor's "History of Spanish Literature,"
Judd's " Margaret," the political treatises of Calhoun, the rich, benignant
poems of Longfellow, the ballads of Whittier, the delicate songs of Philip
Pendleton Cooke, the weird poetry of Edgar Poe, the wizard tales of Hawthorne, Irving's " Knickerbocker," Delia Bacon's splendid sibyllic book on
Shakespeare, the political economy of Carey, the prison letters and immortal
speech of John Brown, the lofty patrician eloquence of Wendell Phillips, and

those diamonds of the first water, the great clear essays and greater poems of Emerson. This literature has often commanding merits, and much of it is very precious to me; but in respect to its national character, all that can be said is that it is tinged, more or less deeply, with America; and the foreign model, the foreign standards, the foreign ideas, dominate over it all.

At most, our best books were but struggling beams; behold in *Leaves of Grass* the immense and absolute sunrise! It is all our own! The nation is in it! In form a series of chants, in substance it is an epic of America. It is distinctively and utterly American. Without model, without imitation, without reminiscence, it is evolved entirely from our own polity and popular life. Look at what it celebrates and contains! hardly to be enumerated without sometimes using the powerful, wondrous phrases of its author, so indissoluble are they with the things described. The essences, the events, the objects of America; the myriad varied landscapes; the teeming and giant cities; the generous and turbulent populations; the prairie solitudes, the vast pastoral plateaus; the Mississippi; the land dense with villages and farms; the habits, manners, customs; the enormous diversity of temperatures; the immense geography; the red aborigines passing away, "charging the water and the land with names;" the early settlements; the sudden uprising and defiance of the Revolution; the august figure of Washington; the formation and sacredness of the Constitution; the pouring in of the emigrants; the million-masted harbors; the general opulence and comfort; the fisheries, and whaling, and gold-digging, and manufactures, and agriculture; the dazzling movement of new States, rushing to be great; Nevada rising, Dakota rising, Colorado rising; the tumultuous civilization around and beyond the Rocky Mountains, thundering and spreading; the Union impregnable; feudalism in all its forms forever tracked and assaulted; liberty deathless on these shores; the noble and free character of the people; the equality of male and female; the ardor, the fierceness, the friendship, the dignity, the enterprise, the affection, the courage, the love of music, the passion for personal freedom; the mercy and justice and compassion of the people; the popular faults and vices and crimes; the deference of the President to the private citizen; the image of Christ forever deepening in the public mind as the brother of despised and rejected persons; the promise and wild song of the future; the vision of the Federal Mother, seated with more than antique majesty in the midst of her many children; the pouring glories of the hereafter; the vistas of splendor, incessant and branching; the tremendous elements, breeds, adjustments of America— with all these, with more, with everything transcendent, amazing, and new, undimmed by the pale cast of thought, and with the very color and brawn of actual life, the whole gigantic epic of our continental being unwinds in all its magnificent reality in these pages. To understand Greece, study the "Iliad" and "Odyssey;" study *Leaves of Grass* to understand America. Her democracy is there. Would you have a text-book of democracy? The writings of

Jefferson are good; De Tocqueville is better; but the great poet always contains historian and philosopher—and to know the comprehending spirit of this country, you shall question these insulted pages.

Yet this vast and patriotic celebration and presentation of all that is our own, is but a part of this tremendous volume. Here in addition is thrown in poetic form, a philosophy of life, rich, subtle, composite, ample, adequate to these great shores. Here are presented superb types of models of manly and womanly character for the future of this country, athletic, large, naïve, free, dauntless, haughty, loving, nobly carnal, nobly spiritual, equal in body and soul, acceptive and tolerant as Nature, generous, cosmopolitan, above all, religious. Here are erected standards, drawn from the circumstances of our case, by which not merely our literature, but all our performance, our politics, art, behavior, love, conversation, dress, society, everything belonging to our lives and their conduct, will be shaped and recreated. A powerful afflatus from the Infinite has given this book life. A voice which is the manliest of human voices sounds through it all. In it is the strong spirit which will surely mould our future. Mark my words: its sentences will yet clinch the arguments of statesmen; its precepts will be the laws of the people! From the beams of this seminal sun will be generated, with tropical luxuriance, the myriad new forms of thought and life in America. And in view of the national character and national purpose of this work—in view of its vigorous re-enforcement and service to all that we hold most precious—I make the claim here, that so far from defaming and persecuting its author, the attitude of an American statesman or public officer towards him should be to the highest degree friendly and sustaining.

Beyond his country, too, this poet serves the world. He refutes by his example the saying of Goethe, one of those which stain that noble fame with baseness, that a great poet cannot be patriotic; and he dilates to a universal use which redoubles the splendors of his volume, and makes it dear to all that is human. I am not its authorized interpreter, and can only state, at the risk of imperfect expression and perhaps error, what its meanings and purpose seem to me. But I see that, in his general intention, the author has aimed to express that most common but wondrous thing—that strange assemblage of soul, body, intellect—beautiful, mystical, terrible, limited, boundless, ill-assorted, contradictory, yet singularly harmonized—a Human Being, a single, separate identity—a Man—himself; but himself typically, and in his universal being. This he has done with perfect candor, including the bodily attributes and organs as necessary component parts of the creation. Every thinking person should see the value and use of such a presentation of human nature as this. I also see—and it is from these parts of the book that much of the misunderstanding and offence arises—that this poet seeks in subtle ways to rescue from the keeping of blackguards and debauchees, to which it has been abandoned, and to redeem to noble thought and use, the great element of amativeness or sexuality, with all its acts and organs. Sometimes by direct assertion, sometimes by implication, he rejects the prevailing admission that this element is vile; declares its natural or normal manifestation to be sacred and unworthy shame; awards it an equal but not superior sanctity with the other elements that compose man; and illustrates his doctrine and sets his example by applying this element, with all that pertains to it, to use as part of the imagery of poetry. Then, besides, diffused like an atmosphere throughout the poem, tincturing all its quality, and giving it that sacerdotal and prophetic character which makes it a sort of American Bible, is the pronounced and ever-recurring assertion of the divinity of all things. In a spirit like that of the Egyptian priesthood, who wore the dung-beetle in gold on their crests, perhaps as a symbol of the sacredness of even the lowest forms of life, the poet celebrates all the Creation as noble and holy—the meanest and lowest parts of it, as well as the most lofty; all equally projections of the Infinite; all emanations of the creative life of God. Perpetual hymns break from him in praise of the divineness of the universe; he sees a halo around every shape, however low; and life in all its forms inspires a rapture of worship.

How some persons can think a book of this sort bad, is clearer to me than it used to be. Swedenborg says that to the devils, perfumes are stinks. I happen to know that some of the vilest abuse *Leaves of Grass* has received, has come from men of the lowest possible moral life. It is not so easy to understand how some persons of culture and judgment can fail to perceive its literary greatness. Making fair allowance for faults, which no great work, from " Hamlet " to the world itself, is perhaps without, the book, in form as in substance, seems to me a masterpiece. Never in literature has there been more absolute conceptive or presentative power. The forms and shows of things are bodied forth so that one may say they become visible, and are alive. Here, in its grandest, freest use, is the English language, from its lowest compass to the top of the key; from the powerful, rank idiom of the streets and fields to the last subtlety of academic speech—ample, various, telling, luxuriant, pictorial, final, conquering; absorbing from other languages to its own purposes their choicest terms; its rich and daring composite defying grammar; its most incontestable and splendid triumphs achieved, as Jefferson notes of the superb Latin of Tacitus, in haughty scorn of the rules of grammarians. Another singular excellence is the metre—entirely novel, free, flexible, melodious, corresponsive to the thought; its noble proportions and cadences reminding of winds and waves, and the vast elemental sounds and motions of Nature, and having an equal variety and liberty. I have heard this brought into disparaging comparison with the metres of Tennyson; the poetry also disparaged in the same connection. I hardly know what to think of people who can talk in this way. To say nothing of the preference, the mere parallel is only less ludicrous and arbitrary than would be one between Moore and Isaiah. Tennyson is an exquisite and sumptuous poet of the third, perhaps the fourth order, as certainly below Milton and Virgil as Milton and Virgil are certainly below Æschylus and Homer. His full-fluted verbal music, which is one of his chief merits, is of an extraordinary beauty. But in this respect the comparison between him and Walt Whitman is that between melody and harmony—between a song by Franz Abt or Schubert and a symphony by Beethoven. Speaking generally, and not with exact justice to either, the words of Tennyson, irrespective of their sense, make music to the ear, while the sense of Walt Whitman's words makes a loftier music in the mind. For a music, perfect and vast, subtle and more than auricular—woven not alone from the verbal sounds and rhythmic cadences, but educed by the thought and feeling of the verse from the reader's soul by the power of a spell few hold—I know of nothing superior to " By the Bivouac's fitful flame," the " Ashes of Soldiers," the " Spirit whose Work is done," the prelude to " Drum Taps," that most mournful and noble of all love songs, ' Out of the Rolling Ocean, the Crowd," or " Out of the Cradle endlessly Rocking," " Elemental Drifts," the entire section entitled " Song of Myself," the hymn commencing " Splendor of Falling Day," or the great salute to the French Revolution of '93, entitled " France." If these are not examples of great structural harmony as well as of the highest poetry, there are none in literature. And if all these were wanting, there is a poem in the volume which, if the author had never written another line, would be sufficient to place him among the chief poets of the world. I do not refer to " Chanting the Square Deific," though that also would be sufficient, in its incomparable breadth and grandeur of conception and execution, to establish the highest poetic reputation, but to the strain commemorating the death of the beloved President, commencing " When lilacs last in the dooryard bloomed," a poem whose rich and sacred beauty and rapture of tender religious passion, spreading aloft into the sublime, leave it unique and solitary in literature, and will make it the chosen and immortal hymn of Death forever. Emperors might well elect to die, could their memories be surrounded with such a requiem, which, next to the grief and love of the people, is the grandest and the only grand funeral music poured around Lincoln's bier.

In the face of works like these, testimony of the presence on earth of a mighty soul, I am thunderstruck at the low tone of the current criticism. Even from eminent persons, who ought to know how to measure literature, and who are friendly to this author, I hear, mingled with inadequate praises, the self-same censures—the very epithets even which Voltaire not more ridiculously passed on Shakespeare. Take care, gentlemen! What you, like Voltaire, take for rudeness, chaos, barbarism, lack of form, may be the sacred and magnificent wildness of a virgin world of poetry, all unlike these fine and ordered Tennysonian rose-gardens which are your ideal, but excelling these as the globe excels the parterre. I, at any rate, am not deceived. I see how swiftly the smart, bright conventional standards of modern criticism would assign Isaiah or Ezekiel to the limbo of abortions. I see of how limited worth are the wit and scholarship of these "Saturday Reviews" and "London Examiners," with their *doppelgangers* on this side of the Atlantic, by the treatment some poetic masterpiece of China or Hindustan receives when it falls into their hands for judgment. Anything not cast in modern conventional forms, any novel or amazing beauty, strikes them as comic. Read Mr. Buckley's notes, even at this late day, on a poet so incredibly great as Æschylus. Read an Æschylus illustrated by reference to Nicholas Nickleby, Mrs. Bombazine, and Mantalini, and censured in contemptuous, jocular or flippant annotations—this, too, by an Oxford scholar of rank and merit. No wonder *Leaves of Grass* goes underrated or unperceived. Modern criticism is Voltaire estimating the Apocalypse as "dirt," and roaring with laughter over the leaves of Ezekiel. Why? Because this poetry has not the court tread, the perfume, the royal purple of Racine—only its own wild and formless incomparable sublimity. Voltaire was an immense and noble person; only it was not part of his greatness to be able to see that other greatness which transcends common sense as the Infinite transcends the Finite. These children of Voltaire, also, who make the choirs of modern criticism, have great merits. But to justly estimate poetry of the first order is not one of them. "Shakespeare's 'Tempest' or 'Midsummer Night's Dream,' or any "such damned nonsense as that," said one of this school to me a month ago. " Look at that perpendicular grocery sign-board, the letters all fantastic and reading from top to bottom, a mere oddity: that is *Leaves of Grass*," said another, a person of eminence. No, gentlemen! you and I differ. I see, very clearly, the nature of a work like this, the warmest praise of which, not to mention your blame, has been meagre and insufficient to the last degree, and which centuries must ponder before they can sufficiently honor. You have had your say; let me have at least the beginning of mine: Nothing that America had before in literature rose above construction; this is a creation. Idle, and worse than idle, is any attempt to place this author either among or below the poets of the day. They are but singers; he is a bard. In him you have one of that mighty brotherhood who, more than statesmen, mould the future; who, as Fletcher of Saltoun said, when they make the songs of a nation, it matters not who makes the laws. I class him boldly, and the future will confirm my judgment, among the great creative minds of the world. By a quality almost incommunicable, which makes its possessor, no matter what his diversity or imperfections, equal with the Supremes of art, and by the very structure of his mind, he belongs there. His place is beside Shakespeare, Æschylus, Cervantes, Dante, Homer, Isaiah—the bards of the last ascent, the brothers of the radiant summit. And if any man think this estimate extravagant, I leave him, as Lord Bacon says, to the gravity of that judgment, and pass on. Enough for me to pronounce this book grandly good and supremely great. Clamor, on the score of its morality, is nothing but a form of turpitude; denial of its greatness is nothing but an insanity; and the roar of Sodom and the laughter of Bedlam shall not, by a hair's breadth, swerve my verdict.

As for those passages which have been so strangely interpreted, I have to say that nothing but the horrible inanity of prudery, to which civilization has become subject, and which affects even many good persons, could cloud and distort their palpable innocence and nobleness. What chance has an author to a reasonable interpretation of such utterances in an age when squeamishness, the Siamese twin-brother of indelicacy, is throned as the censor of all life? Look at the nearest, the commonest, and homeliest evidences of the abysm into which we have fallen. Here in my knowledge is an estimable family which, when the baby playing on the floor kicked up its skirts, I have repeatedly seen rush *en masse* to pull down the immodest petticoat. Here is a lady whose shame of her body is such that she will not disrobe in the presence of one of her own sex, and thinks it horrible to sleep at night without being swaddled in half her garments. Everywhere you see women perpetually glancing to be sure their skirts are quite down; twisting their heads over their shoulders, like some of the damned in Dante, to get a rear view; drawing in their feet if so much as a toe happens to protrude beyond the hem of the gown, and in various ways betraying a morbid consciousness which is more offensive than positive immodesty. When I went to the hospital, I saw one of those pretty and good girls, who in muslin and ribbons ornament the wards, and are called "nurses," pick up her skirts and skurry away, flushing hectic, with averted face, because as she passed a cot the poor fellow who lay there happened, in his uneasy turnings, to thrust part of a manly leg from beneath the coverlet. I once heard Emerson severely censured in a private company, five or six persons present, and I the only dissenting voice, because in one of his essays he had used the word "spermatic." When Tennyson published the "Idyls of the King," some of the journals in both America and England, and several persons in my own hearing, censured the weird and magnificent "Vivien," one of his finest poems, as "immoral", and "vulgar." When Charles Sumner, in the debate on Louisiana, characterized the new-formed State as "a seven months' child, begotten by the bayonet, in criminal conjunction with the spirit of caste"—a stroke of absolute genius—he was censured by the public prints, and reminded that there were ladies in the gallery! Lately the "London Observer," one of the most eminent of the British journals, in a long and labored editorial on the bathing at Margate, denounced the British wives and matrons in the severest terms for sitting on the beach when men were bathing in "slight bathing-dresses" (it was not even pretended that the men were nude)—and even went the length of demanding of the civil authorities that they should invoke the interference of Parliament to stop this scandal! These are fair minor specimens of the prudery, worse than vice, but also the concomitant of the most shocking vice, which

prevails everywhere. Its travesty is the dressing in pantalettes the "limbs" |
of the piano; its insolent tragi-comedy is the expulsion of Shakespeare from |
office because he writes "indecent passages"; its tragedy is the myriad results
of wrong, and crime, and ruin, carried into all the details of every relation
of life.

A civilization in which such things as I have mentioned can be thought or
done is guilty to the core. It is not purity, it is impurity, which calls clothes
more decent than the nakèd body—thus inanely conferring upon the work of
the tailor or milliner a modesty denied to the work of God. It is not innocent but guilty thought which attaches shame, secrecy, baseness, and horror
to great and august parts and functions of humanity. The tacit admission
everywhere prevalent that portions of the human physiology are base; that
the amative feelings and acts of the sexes, even when hallowed by marriage,
are connected with a low sensuality; and that these, with such subjects or occurrences as the conception and birth of children, are to be absconded from,
blushed at, concealed, ignored, withheld from education, and in every way
treated as if they belonged to the category of sins against Nature, is not only
in itself a contemptible insanity, but a main source of unspeakable personal
and social evil. From the morbid state of mind which such a theory and
practice must induce are spawned a thousand guilty actions of every description and degree. There is no occurrence in the vast and diversified
range of sexual evil, from the first lewd thought in the mind of the budding
child, the very suspicion of which makes the parent tremble, down to the
last ghastly and bloody spasm of lust which rends its hapless victim in some
suburban woodland, that is not fed mainly from this mystery and mother of
abominations, to whose care civilization has remitted the entire subject.
The poet who, in the spirit of that divine utility which marked the first
great bards and will mark the last, seeks to make literature remediate to an
estate like this, works in the best interests of his country and his fellow-
beings, and deserves their gratitude. This is what Walt Whitman has done.
Directly and indirectly, in forms as various as the minds he seeks to influence;
in frank opposition to the great sexual falsehood by which we are ruled and
ruined, he has thrown into civilization a conception intended to be slowly and
insensibly absorbed, and to ultimately appear in results of good—the conception of the individual as a divine democracy of essences, powers, attributes,
functions, organs—all equal, all sacred, all consecrate to noble use; the sexual
part the same as the rest, no more a subject for mystery, or shame, or secrecy,
than the intellectual, or the manual, or the alimentary, or the locomotive part
—divinely commonplace as head, or hand, or stomach, or foot; and, though
sacred, to be regarded as so ordinary that it shall be employed the same as
any other part, for the purposes of literature—an idea which he exemplifies in
his poetry by a metaphorical use which it is a deep disgrace to any intellect to
misunderstand. This is his lesson. This is one of the central ideas which

rule the myriad teeming play of his volume, and interpret it as a law of Nature interprets the complex play of facts which proceeds from it. This, then, is not license, but thought. It may be erroneous, it may be chimerical, it may be ineffectual; but it is thought, serious and solemn thought, on a most difficult and deeply immersed question—thought emanating from the deep source of a great love and care for men, and seeking nothing but a pure human welfare. When, therefore, any persons undertake to outrage and injure its author for having given it to the world, it is not merely as the pigmy incarnations of the depraved modesty, the surface morality, the filthy and libidinous decency of the age, but it is as the persecutors of thought that they stand before us. It is no excuse for them to say, that such treatment of Walt Whitman is justifiable, because his book appears to them bad. Waiving every other consideration, I have to inform them that on this subject they should not permit themselves the immodesty of a judgment. It is not for such as they to attempt to prison in the poor cell of their opinion the vast journey and illumination of the human mind. No matter what the book seems to them, they should remember that an author deserves to be tried by his peers, and that a book may easily seem to some persons quite another thing from what it really is to others.

Here is Rabelais, a writer who wears all the crowns; but even Mr. Harlan would consider Walt Whitman white as purity beside him. "Filth," "zany-ism," "grossness," "profligacy," "licentiousness," "sensuality," "beastli-ness"—these are samples of the epithets which have fallen, like a rain of ex-crement, on Rabelais for three hundred years. And yet it is of him that the holy-hearted Coleridge—an authority of the first order on all purely literary or ethical questions—it is of him that Coleridge says, and says justly: " I " could write a treatise in praise of the *moral elevation* of Rabelais' work " which would make the Church stare, and the Conventicle groan, and yet " would be the truth, and nothing but the truth." The moral elevation of Rabelais! A great criticism, a needed word. It is just. No matter for seeming—Rabelais is good to the very core. Rabelais' book, viewed with reference to ensemble, viewed in relation, viewed in its own proper quality by other than cockney standards, is righteous to the uttermost extreme. So is the work of Walt Whitman, far other in character, and far less obnoxious to criticism than that of Rabelais, but which demands at least as liberal a judgment, and which it is not for any deputy, however high in office, to assign to shame.

I know not what further vicissitude of insult and outrage is in store for this great man. It may be that the devotees of a castrated literature, the earth-worms that call themselves authors, the confectioners that pass for poets, the flies that are recognized as critics, the bigots, the dilettanti, the prudes and the fools, are more potent than I dream to mar the fortunes of his earthly hours; but above and beyond them uprises a more majestic civilization in the immense and sane serenities of futurity; and the man who has achieved that sublime thing, a genuine book; who has written to make his land greater, her citizens better, his race nobler; who has striven to serve men by communicating to them that which they least know, their own nature, their own experience; who has thrown into living verse a philosophy designed to exalt life to a higher level of sincerity, reality, religion; who has torn away disguises and illusions, and restored to commonest things, and the simplest and roughest people, their divine significance and natural, antique dignity, and who has wrapped his country and all created things as with splendors of sunrise, in the beams of a powerful and gorgeous poetry—that man, whatever be the clouds that close around his fame, is assured illustrious; and when every face lowers, when every hand is raised against him, turning his back upon his day and generation, he may write upon his book, with all the pride and grief of the calumniated Æschylus, the haughty dedication that poet graved upon his hundred dramas: To Time!

And Time will remember him. He holds upon the future this supreme claim of all high poets—behind the book, a life loyal to humanity. Never, if I can help it, shall be forgotten those immense and divine labors in the hospitals of Washington, among the wounded of the war, to which he voluntarily devoted himself, as the best service he could render to his struggling country, and which illustrate that boundless love which is at once the dominant element of his character, and the central source of his genius. How can I tell the nature and extent of that sublime ministration? During those years, Washington was a city in whose unbuilt places and around whose borders were thickly planted dense white clusters of barracks. These were the hospitals—neat, orderly, rectangular, strange towns, whose every citizen lay drained with sickness or wrung with pain. There, in those long wards, in rows of cots on either side, were stretched, in all attitudes and aspects of mutilation, of pale repose, of contorted anguish, of death, the martyrs of the war; and among them, with a soul that tenderly remembered the little children in many a dwelling mournful for those fathers, the worn and anxious wives, haggard with thinking of those husbands, the girls weeping their spirits from their eyes for those lovers, the mothers who from afar yearned to the bedsides of those sons, walked Walt Whitman, in the spirit of Christ, soothing, healing, consoling, restoring, night and day, for years; never failing, never tiring, constant, vigilant, faithful; performing, without fee or reward, his self-imposed duty; giving to the task all his time and means, and doing every-thing that it is possible for one unaided human being to do. Others fail, others flag; good souls that came often and did their best, yield and drop away; he remains. Winter and summer, night and day, every day in the week, every week in the year, all the time, till the winter of '65, when for a few hours daily, during six months, his duties to the Government detain him; after that, all the time he can spare, he visits the hospitals. What does he do? See. At the red aceldama of Fredericksburg, in '62–'3, he is in a hospital on the banks of the Rappahannock; it is a large, brick house, full of wounded and dying; in front, at the foot of a tree, is a cart-load of amputated legs, arms, hands, feet, fingers; dead bodies shrouded in army blankets are near; there are fresh graves in the yard; he is at work in the house among the officers and men, lying, unclean and bloody, in their old clothes; he is upstairs and down; he is poor, he has nothing to give this time, but he writes letters for the wounded; he cheers up the desponding; he gives love. Some of the men, war-sad, passionately cling to him; they weep; he will sit for hours with them if it gives them comfort. Here he is in Washington, after Chancellorsville, at night, on the wharf; two boat-loads of wounded (and oh, such wounded!) have been landed; they lie scattered about on the landing, in the rain, drenched, livid, lying on the ground, on old quilts, on blankets; their heads, their limbs bound in bloody rags; a few torches light the scene; the ambulances, the callous drivers are here; groans, sometimes a scream, resound through the flickering light and the darkness. He is there, moving around; he soothes, he comforts, he consoles, he assists to lift the wounded into the ambulances; he helps to place the worst cases on the stretchers; his kiss is warm upon the pallid lips of some who are mere children; his tears drop upon the faces of the dying. Here he is in the hospitals of Washington—the Campbell, the Patent Office, the Eighth Street, the Judiciary, the Carver, the Douglas, the Armory Square. He writes letters; he writes to fathers, mothers, brothers, wives, sweethearts; some of the soldiers are poor penmen; some cannot get paper and envelopes; some fear to write lest they should worry the folks at home; he writes for them all; he uses that genius which shall endure to the latest generation, to say the felicitous, the consoling, the cheering, the prudent, the best word. He goes through the wards, he talks cheerfully, he distributes amusing reading matter; at night or by day, when the horrible monotony of the hospital weighs like lead on every soul, he reads to the men; he is careful to sit away from the cot of any poor fellow so sick or wounded as to be easily disturbed, but he gathers into a large group as many as he can, and amuses them with some story or enlivening game, like that of "Twenty Questions," or recites some little poem or speech, or starts some discussion, or with some device dispels the gloom. For his daily occupation, he goes from ward to ward, doing all he can to hearten and revive the spirits of the sufferers, and keep the balance in favor of their recovery. Usually, his plan is to pass, with haversack strapped across his shoulder, from cot to cot, distributing small gifts; his theory is that these men, far from home, lonely, sick at heart, need more than anything some practical token that they are not forsaken, that some one feels a fatherly or brotherly interest in them; hence, he gives them what he can; to particular cases, entirely penniless, he distributes small sums of money, fifteen cents, twenty cents, thirty cents, fifty cents, not much to each, for there are many, but under the circumstances these little sums are and mean a great deal. He also distributes and directs envelopes, gives letter paper, postage stamps, tobacco, apples, figs, sweet biscuit, preserves, blackberries; gets delicate food for special cases; sometimes a dish of oysters or a dainty piece of meat, or some savory morsel for some poor creature who loathes the hospital fare, but whose appetite may be tempted. In the hot weather he buys boxes of oranges and distributes them, grateful to lips baked with fever; he buys boxes of lemons, he buys sugar, to make lemonade for those parched throats of sick soldiers; he buys canned peaches, strawberries, pears; he buys ice cream and treats the whole hospital; he buys whatever luxuries his limited resources will allow, and he makes them go as far as he can. Where does he get the means for this expenditure? For Walt Whitman is poor; he is poor, and has a right to be proud of his poverty, for it is the sacred, the ancient, the immemorial poverty of goodness and genius. He gets the means by writing for newspapers; he expends all he gets upon his boys, his darlings, the sick and maimed soldiers—the young heroes of the land who saved their country, the laborers of America who fought for the hopes of the world. He adds to his own earnings the contributions of noble souls, often strangers, who, in Boston, in New York, in Providence, in Brooklyn, in Salem, in Washington and elsewhere, have heard that such a man walks the hospitals, and who volunteer to send him this assistance; when at last he gets a place under Government, and till Mr. Harlan turns him out, he has a salary which he spends in the same way; sometimes his wrung heart gets the better of his prudence, and he spends till he himself is in difficulties. He gives all his money, he gives all his time, he gives all his love. To every inmate of the hospital something, if only a vital word, a cheering touch, a caress, a trifling gift; but always in his rounds he selects the special cases, the sorely wounded, the deeply despondent, the homesick, the dying; to these he devotes himself; he buoys them up with fond words, with caresses, with personal affection; he bends over them, strong, clean, cheerful, perfumed, loving, and his magnetic touch and love sustain them. He does not shrink from the smell of their sickening gangrene; he does not flinch from their bloody and rotten mutilations; he draws nigher for all that; he sticks closer; he dresses those wounds; he fans those burning temples; he moistens those parched lips; he washes those wasted bodies; he watches often and often in the dim ward by the sufferer's cot all night long; he reads from the New Testament, the words sweeter than music to the sinking soul; he soothes with prayer the bedside of the dying; he sits, mournful and loving, by the wasted dead. How can I tell the story of his labors? How can I describe the scenes among which he moved with such endurance and devotion, watched by me, for years?

Few know the spectacle presented by those grim wards. It was hideous. I have been there at night when it seemed that I should die with sympathy if I stayed;—when the horrible attitudes of anguish, the horizontal shapes of cadaver on the white cots, the quiet sleepers, the excruciated emaciations of men, the bloody bandages, the smell of plastered sores, the dim lamplight, the long white ward, the groans of some patient half hidden behind a screen, naked, shorn of both arms, held by the assistant upon a stool, made up a scene whose well-compounded horror is unspeakable. Now realize a man without worldly inducement, without reward, from love and compassion only, giving up his life to scenes like these; foregoing pleasure and rest for vigils, as in chambers of torture, among the despairing, the mangled, the dying, the forms upon which shell and rifle and sabre had wrought every bizarre atrocity of mutilation; immuring himself in the air of their sighs, their moans, the mutter and scream of their delirium; breathing the stench of their putrid wounds; taking up his part and lot with them, living a life of privation and denial, and boarding his scanty means for the relief and mitigation of their anguish. That man is Walt Whitman! I said his labors have been immense. The word is well chosen. I speak within bounds when I say that, during those years, he has been in contact with, and, in one form or another, either in hospital or on the field, personally ministered to upward of one hundred thousand sick and wounded men. You mothers of America, these were your sons! Faithfully, and with a mother's love, he tended them for you! Many and many a life has he saved—many a time has he felt his heart grow great with that delicious triumph—many a home owes its best beloved to him. Sick and wounded, officers and privates, the black soldiers as well as the white, the teamsters, the poor creatures in the contraband camps, the rebel the same as the loyal—he did his best for them all; they were all sufferers, they were all men.—Let him pass. I note Thoreau's saying, that he suggests something more than human. It is true. I see it in his book and in his life. To that something more than human which is also in all men—to the hour of judgment, to the hour of sanity, let me resign him. Not for such as I to vindicate such as he. Not for him, perhaps, the recognition of his day and generation. But a life and deeds like his, lightly esteemed by men, sink deep into the memory of Man. Great is the stormy fight of Zutphen; it is the young lion of English Protestantism springing in haughty fury for the defence of the Netherlands from the bloody ravin of Spain; but Philip Sidney passing the flask of water from his own lips to the dying soldier looms gigantic, and makes all the foreground of its noble purpose and martial rage; and whatever be the verdict of the present, sure am I that hereafter and to the latest ages, when Bull Run and Shiloh and Port Hudson, when Vicksburg and Stone River and Fort Donelson, when Pea Ridge and Chancellorsville and Gettysburg and the Wilderness, and the great march from Atlanta to Savannah, and Richmond rolled in flame, and all the battles for the life of the Republic against her last internal foe are gathered up in accumulated terraces of struggle upon the mountain of history, well-relieved against those bright and bloody tumultuous giant tableaux, and all the dust and thunder of a noble war, the men and women of America will love to gaze upon the stalwart form of the good gray poet, bending to heal the hurts of their wounded and soothe the souls of their dying, and the deep and simple words of the last great martyr will be theirs,— "Well, *he* looks like A MAN."

So let me leave him. And if there be any who think this tribute in bad taste, even to a poet so great, a person so unusual, a man so heroic and loving, I answer, that when, on grounds of taste, foes withhold detraction, friends may withhold eulogy; and that at any rate I recognize no reason for keeping back just words of love and reverence when, as in this case, they must glow upon the sullen foil of the printed hatreds of years. To that long record of hostility, I am only proud to be able to oppose this record of affection. And with respect to the crowning enmity of the Secretary of the Interior, let no person misjudge the motives upon which I denounce it. Personally, apart from this act, I have nothing against Mr. Harlan. He is of my own party; and my politics have been from my youth essentially the same as his own. I do not know him; I have never even seen him; I criticise no attitude nor action of his life but this; and I criticise this with as little personality as I can give to an action so personal. I withhold, too, as far as I can, every expression of resentment; and no one who knew all I know of this matter could fail to credit me with singular and great moderation. For, behind what I have related, there is another history, every incident of which I have recovered from the obscurity to which it was confided; and, as I think of it, it is with difficulty that I restrain my just indignation. Instead of my comparatively cold and sober treatment, this transaction deserves rather the pitiless exposure, the measureless, stern anger, the red-hot steel scourge of Juvenal. But I leave untold its darkest details, and, waiving every other consideration, I rest solely and squarely on the general indignity and injury this action offers to intellectual liberty. I claim that to expel an author from a public office and subject him to public contumely, solely because he has published a book which no one can declare immoral without declaring all the grand books immoral, is to affix a penalty to thought, and to obstruct the freedom of letters. I declare this act the audacious captain of a series of acts, and a style of opinions whose tendency and effect throughout Christendom is to dwarf and degrade literature, and to make great books impossible, except under pains of martyrdom. As such, I arraign it before every liberal and thoughtful mind. I denounce it as a sinister precedent; as a ban upon the free action of genius; as a logical insult to all-commanding literature; and as in every way a most serious and heinous wrong. Difference of opinion there may and must be upon the topics which in these pages I have grouped around it, but upon the act itself there can be none. As I drag it up here into the sight of the world, I call upon every scholar, every man of letters, every editor, every good fellow everywhere who wields the pen, to make common cause with me in rousing upon it the full tempest of reprobation it deserves. I remember Tennyson, a spirit of vengeance over the desecrated grave of Moore; I think of Scott rolling back the tide of obloquy from Byron; I see Addison gilding the blackening fame of Swift; I mark Southampton befriending Shakespeare; I recall Du Bellay enshielding Rabelais; I behold Hutten fortressing Luther; here is Boccaccio lifting the darkness from Dante, and scattering flame on his foes in Florence; this is Bembo protecting Pomponatius; that is Grostête enfolding Roger Bacon from the monkish fury; there, covered with light, is Aristophanes defending Æschylus; and if there lives aught of that old chivalry of letters, which in all ages has sprung to the succor and defence of genius, I summon it to act the part of honor and duty upon a wrong which, done to a single member of the great confraternity of literature, is done to all, and which flings insult and menace upon every immortal page that dares transcend the wicked heart or the constricted brain. God grant that not in vain upon this outrage do I invoke the judgment of the mighty spirit of literature, and the fires of every honest heart!

WILLIAM DOUGLAS O'CONNOR.

TWO SUBSEQUENT LETTERS.

A NOTEWORTHY incident following the publication of Mr. O'Connor's pamphlet is embodied in the subjoined correspondence. The defence of the poet appears to have been received by the literary journals of the United States with a complete unanimity of abuse and ridicule. Among these reviews was one in the New York "Round Table" of January 20th, 1866, penned by a minor poet, of considerable distinction in New York literary circles, Mr. Richard Henry Stoddard. His article, written in a vein of flippant insolence and containing a number of insulting references to Mr. O'Connor's previous literary work, was nevertheless relieved by the admission, however carelessly made, that Mr. Harlan "deserved and deserves to be pilloried in the contempt of thinking men for this wanton insult to literature in the person of Mr. Whitman." This remark, imbedded in a column of rude persiflage, like a filament of gold in an acre of sage and alkali, was the only observation adverse to Mr. Harlan's act which appeared in any American literary journal, and appears to have suggested the necessity for the following curiously clumsy and lying parry, made a week later (January 27th) in the "Round Table" by Mr. Charles Lanman, a gentleman of considerable literary pretensions, the author of the "Biographical Dictionary of Congress," formerly, it is said, secretary to Daniel Webster, and at this time one of the officers of the Interior Department under Mr. Harlan. The line of defence chosen for the Secretary by one of his officers and friends is so extraordinary as to add a new feature of outrage to an already sufficiently scandalous transaction. Mr. Lanman's communication was as follows:

WASHINGTON, January 19th, 1866.

To THE EDITOR OF THE "ROUND TABLE."

SIR: Your notice of "The Good Gray Poet" contains one important error that I desire, as a friend of Secretary Harlan, to correct. You intimate, or, rather, reiterate the charge of Mr. Walt Whitman's defender—that the author of *Leaves of Grass* was removed from a clerkship because of his *religious* opinions. To this statement I give the most positive denial; and to substantiate it I have only to mention the fact that there are employed in the Interior Department gentlemen of every possible shade of religious opinion. Although the Hon. Secretary is a high-minded and Christian gentleman, he has never, in a single instance, questioned an employé in regard to his religious belief, and for the very good reason that with those beliefs he has nothing to do. Nor is he in the habit of removing subordinates from office for their political opinions. Drunkards and incompetent men he does not consider fit to be intrusted with the business of the nation, and when such men are reported to him, they are very likely to be discharged. For removing Mr. Whitman from a clerkship there were two satisfactory reasons: he was wholly unfit to perform the duties which were assigned to his desk; and a volume which he published and caused to be circulated through the public offices was so coarse, indecent, and corrupting in its thought and language, as to jeopardize the reputation of the Department.

· Respectfully yours,

CHARLES LANMAN.

To this indescribable document Mr. O'Connor replied in the "Round Table" of a week later (February 3d) as follows

WASHINGTON, January 26th, 1866.

To THE EDITOR OF THE "ROUND TABLE."

SIR: Allow me a few words of reply to Mr. Charles Lanman's extraordinary letter in your last issue respecting the accusation brought against Mr. Harlan by my pamphlet, "The Good Gray Poet."

As the statements of that letter are unfounded in every particular, they are probably as unauthorized as they are gratuitous. Nobody ever charged that Mr. Whitman was removed by the Secretary of the Interior "because of his religious opinions." I certainly made no such charge, nor did your reviewer.

Mr. Lanman's other assertions are equally hardy. It is not true that Mr. Whitman was removed because "he was wholly unfit to perform the duties which were assigned to his desk." On the contrary, Mr. Harlan himself said at the time of the dismissal that he had no fault to find with Mr. Whitman in regard to the performance of his official duties, but that he was discharged solely and only for being the author of *Leaves of Grass*. Nor is it true that Mr. Whitman was removed because he published and circulated in the Department any volume whatever. *Leaves of Grass* was published years ago, and has been for some time out of print. "Drum-Taps," Mr. Whitman's recent book, consists mainly of poems of the war, and does not contain one word that even Mr. Harlan could accuse.

This disposes of Mr. Lanman's statements. But I note the color he gives his letter by the insinuated word "drunkards," and whenever he has the courage to put that as a charge which he has only ventured to put as an innuendo, I may deal with it and him.

The facts are precisely as I have stated them in my pamphlet, and whatever rejoinder any volunteer may choose to hazard, *those facts Mr. Harlan himself will never deny.*

You will, perhaps, permit me this opportunity to express my obligations to your reviewer. In his notice of my pamphlet he says that the Secretary of the Interior " deserved and deserves to be pilloried in the contempt of thinking men for this wanton insult to literature in the person of Mr. Whitman." I thank him for those words. Coupled with such a condemnation of the outrage I denounce, no affront, no ridicule heaped on me or my writings can excite in my mind any feeling unmixed with gratitude. Shaftesbury, in England, is, if report says truly, a bigot peer, and Walter Savage Landor wrote poems which almost rivalled the license of the Roman ; but if ever the lord, as the head of a Department, had dismissed the poet from an official station for his verses, the British press, whatever it thought of the poetry, would have stirred from John o' Groat's to Land's End with a tumult of denunciation whose impulse would have swept over the continent. I want a similar spirit here ; and it matters very little what is said of my compositions, if the press and people of this country, by their resentment at an attempt to impose checks and penalties on intellectual liberty and the freedom of letters, and by their rebuke of a gross violation of the proprieties of the administration of a great Department, show that they are not below the decent level of Europe.

Very respectfully,

W. D. O'Connor.

PART II.

WHEN the true poet comes, how shall we know him—
　　By what clear token,—manners, language, dress?
Or shall a voice from Heaven speak and show him:
　　Him the swift healer of the Earth's distress!
Tell us that when the long-expected comes
　　At last, with mirth and melody and singing,
We him may greet with banners, beat of drums,
　　Welcome of men and maids, and joy-bells ringing;
　　　　And, for this poet of ours,
　　　　Laurels and flowers.

Thus shall ye know him—this shall be his token:
　　Manners like other men, an unstrange gear;
His speech not musical, but harsh and broken
　　Shall sound at first, each line a driven spear;
For he shall sing as in the centuries olden,
　　Before mankind its earliest fire forgot;
Yet whoso listens long hears music golden.
　　How shall ye know him?　Ye shall know him not
　　　　Till ended hate and scorn,
　　　　To the grave he's borne.
　　　　　　　　RICHARD WATSON GILDER.

CHAPTER I.

HISTORY OF LEAVES OF GRASS.

WALT WHITMAN began to write for the periodical press at the age of fourteen years—was engaged as editor at maturity and afterwards—and continues as contributor to newspapers and magazines to this day. If all he has ever written were collected, it would probably make many good-sized volumes. I have no knowledge of any of the pieces in *Leaves of Grass* before the publication of the first edition in 1855. Walt Whitman tells us in one of the prose prefaces preserved in *Specimen Days*, that he had more or less consciously the plan of the poems in his mind for eight years before, and that during those eight years they took many shapes; that in the course of those years he wrote and destroyed a great deal; that, at the last, the work assumed a form very different from any at first expected; but that from first to last (from the first definite conception of the work in say 1853–'54, until its completion in 1881) his underlying purpose was *religious*. It seems that so much was clear in his mind from the beginning, but how the plan was to be formulated seemed not at all clear, and had to be toilsomely worked out. A great deal else, of course, had to be present in his mind besides the intention. In the "Song of the Answerer," enumerating other elements necessary for such an enterprise, he says,

Divine instinct, breadth of vision, the law of reason, health, rudeness of body,
    withdrawnness,
Gayety, sun-tan, air-sweetness—such are some of the words of poems.

These he had, and beneath all, and above all, and including all, lying below consciousness, he had in unparalleled perfection that rarest master faculty which we call moral elevation. Along with these, his race-stock, immediate ancestry, mode of upbringing, outer life, surroundings, and American equipment, have to

(135)

be taken into account. It is upon these that he himself always lays the most weight. He once said to the present writer, " The "fifteen years from 1840 to 1855 were the gestation or formative "periods of *Leaves of Grass*, not only in Brooklyn and New York, "but from several extensive jaunts through the States—including "the Western and Southern regions and cities, Baltimore, Cin- "cinnati, Chicago, St. Louis, New Orleans, Texas, the Mississippi "and Missouri Rivers, the great lakes and Niagara, and through "New York from Buffalo to Albany. Large parts of the poems, "and several of them wholly, were incarnated on those jaunts or "amid these scenes. Out of such experiences came the physi- "ology of *Leaves of Grass*, in my opinion the main part. The "psychology of the book is a deeper problem; it is doubtful "whether the latter element can be traced. It is, perhaps, only "to be studied out in the poems themselves, and is a hard study "there."

At another time, speaking with more than usual deliberation to a group of medical men, friends of his, in answer to their in- quiries, on an occasion where I was present, he said, " One main "object I had from the first was to sing, and sing to the full, the "ecstasy of simple physiological Being. This, when full develop- "ment and balance combine in it, seemed, and yet seems, far "beyond all outside pleasures; and when the moral element and "an affinity with Nature in her myriad exhibitions of day and "night are found with it, makes *the happy Personality*, the true "and intended result (if they ever have any) of my poems." This last sentence contains a key to the central secret of *Leaves of Grass*—that this book, namely, represents a man whose ordi- nary every-day relationship with Nature is such that to him mere existence is happiness.

The problem then before him was to express not what he heard, or saw, or fancied, or had read, but one far deeper and more diffi- cult to express, namely, Himself. To put the man Walt Whitman in his book, not especially dressed, polished, prepared, not for con- ventional society, but for Nature, for God, for America—given as a man gives himself to his wife, or as a woman gives herself to her husband—whole, complete, natural—with perfect love, joy, and trust.   This is something that, as I believe, was never before dared or done in literature.   This is the task that he set for himself, and that he has accomplished.   If the man were merely an ordinary person, such a purpose, such a book, written with absolute sincerity, would possess the most extraordinary interest ; but *Leaves of Grass* has an interest far greater, derived from the exceptional personality which is embodied in it.   Such was, in outline or brief suggestion, the intention with which it was written, and the reason for writing it.   Then I think a profound part of the forecasting of the work was the way in which many things were left open for future adjustment.

By the spring of 1855, Walt Whitman had found or made a style in which he could express himself, and in that style he had (after, as he has told me, elaborately building up the structure, and then utterly demolishing it, five different times) written twelve poems, and a long prose preface which was simply another poem. Of these he printed a thousand copies.   It was a thin quarto, the preface filling xii., and the body of the book 95 pages, on rather poor paper, and in the type printers call "English."   The large title-page has the words "LEAVES OF GRASS, Brooklyn, New York, 1855," only.   Facing the title is the miniature of a man who looks about thirty-five to forty years old.   He wears a broad-brimmed, wide-awake hat, has a large forehead and strongly-marked features.   The face (to my mind) expresses sadness and good nature.   No part of the face is shaved.   The beard is clipped rather short and is turning gray.   The figure is shown down to the knees.   This is Walt Whitman from life in his thirty-sixth year.   The picture was engraved on steel by McRae, of New York, from a daguerreotype taken one hot day in July, 1854, by Gabriel Harrison, of Brooklyn.   (The same picture is used in the current 1882 edition.)   The twelve poems constituting the body of the book are unnamed, except for the words *Leaves of Grass*, which are used as a page heading throughout, and besides as a heading to some, but not all, of the individual pieces.   Giving those twelve 1855 poems the names that they bear in the ultimate 1882 edition, the first eleven are :

1. Song of Myself.
2. A Song for Occupations.
3. To Think of Time.
4. The Sleepers.
5. I Sing the Body Electric.
6. Faces.
7. Song of the Answerer.
8. Europe the 72d and 73d Years of These States.
9. A Boston Ballad (1854).
10. There was a Child went forth.
11. Who Learns my Lesson complete.

The twelfth, though retained in every edition until the present, 1882, is omitted from that. Its name in the 1876 edition is "Great are the Myths."

The book now being manufactured, copies of it were left for sale at various bookstores in New York and Brooklyn. Other copies were sent to magazines and newspapers, and others to prominent literary men. Of those that were placed in the stores none were sold. Those that were sent to the press were, in quite every instance, either not noticed at all, laughed at, or reviewed with the bitterest and most scurrilous language in the vocabulary of the reviewer's contempt. Those sent to eminent writers were in several instances returned, in some cases accompanied by insulting notes.

The first reception of *Leaves of Grass* by the world was in fact about as disheartening as it could be. Of the thousand copies of this 1855 edition, some were given away, most of them were lost, abandoned, or destroyed. It is certain that the book quite universally, wherever it was read, excited ridicule, disgust, horror, and anger. It was considered meaningless, badly written, filthy, atheistical, and utterly reprehensible. And yet there were a few, a very few indeed, who suspected from the first that under that rough exterior might be something of extraordinary beauty, vitality, and value. Among these was Ralph Waldo Emerson, then at the height of his splendid fame. He wrote to Walt Whitman the following letter:

CONCORD, MASS., *July 21st, 1855.*

DEAR SIR,—I am not blind to the worth of the wonderful gift of *Leaves of Grass*. I find it the most extraordinary piece of wit and wisdom that America has yet contributed. I am very happy in reading it, as great power makes us happy. It meets the demand I am always making of what seems the sterile and stingy Nature, as if too much handiwork or too much lymph in the temperament were making our Western wits fat and mean.   I give you joy of your free and brave thought.   I have great joy in it.   I find incomparable things, said incomparably well, as they must be.   I find the courage of treatment which so delights us, and which large perception only can inspire.

I greet you at the beginning of a great career, which yet must have had a long foreground somewhere, for such a start.   I rubbed my eyes a little, to see if this sunbeam were no illusion; but the solid sense of the book is a sober certainty.   It has the best merits, namely, of fortifying and encouraging.

I did not know, until I last night saw the book advertised in a newspaper, that I could trust the name as real and available for a post-office.

I wish to see my benefactor, and have felt much like striking my tasks, and visiting New York to pay you my respects.

R. W. EMERSON.

This letter was eventually published (at first refused by Walt Whitman, but on second and pressing application he consented), at the request of Chas. A. Dana, then managing editor of the " New York Tribune."   Though it could not arrest, it did service in partially offsetting the tide of adverse feeling and opinion which overwhelmingly set in against the poet and his book. Walt Whitman has since been censured for printing a so-called private communication of opinion, not intended for the public. In answer to this, besides no proof that the letter was meant to be private, the editor of the " Tribune," who was a personal friend of both Walt Whitman and Mr. Emerson, would probably have been a judge in such matters, and he sought it for the columns of his paper, as legitimate and proper to both parties. It may be mentioned here that vastly as the two men, R. W. Emerson and Walt Whitman, differ in the outward show of their expression, there are competent scholars who accept both equally, and use them to complement each other.*

The next year, 1856, the second edition of *Leaves of Grass* was published by Fowler & Wells, 308 Broadway, N. Y., but the

---

* Emerson is the "knight-errant of the moral sentiment;" Whitman accepts the whole "relentless kosmos," and theoretically, at least, seems to blur the distinction between right and wrong.   Emerson's pages are like beds of roses and violets; Whitman's like masses of sun-flowers and silken-tasselled maize.   Emerson soars upward in Plato's chariot over the "flickering Dæmon film" into the pure realm "where all form in one only form dissolves," and when he returns his face and his raiment are glistening with light caught from that pure

firm did not put its name on the title-page. The volume is a small 16mo. of 384 pages. The same miniature of the author is used. The words *Leaves of Grass* are the page-heading throughout that part of the volume containing the poems, and besides this general title, each poem has a name, but in no instance exactly the same as it bears in later issues. The total number of poems in this edition is thirty-two. The twenty new poems are—(giving them as before the names they bear in the 1882–'83 edition):

1. Unfolded out of the Folds.
2. Salut au Monde.
3. Song of the Broadaxe.
4. By Blue Ontario's Shore.
5. This Compost.
6. To You.
7. Crossing Brooklyn Ferry.
8. Song of the Open Road.
9. A Woman Waits for Me.
10. A poem a large part of which is left out of the later editions, but which is partly preserved in "On the Beach at Night Alone."
11. Excelsior.
12. Song of Prudence.
13. A poem which now makes part of the "Song of the Answerer."
14. Assurances.
15. To a Foil'd European Revolutionaire.
16. A short poem part of which is afterwards incorporated in "As I sat Alone by Blue Ontario's Shore," and the rest of it omitted from subsequent editions.
17. Miracles.
18. Spontaneous Me.
19. A poem called "Poem of The Propositions of Nakedness," afterward called "Respondez," and printed in every edition subsequent to the 2d down to that of 1882–'3—but omitted from that.
20. A Song of the Rolling Earth.

The prose preface of the first edition did not appear as such in this second edition, but part of it was embodied in a few of the

world of perfect types. But Whitman is like the ash-tree Ygdrasil, whose triple fountain-nourished root symbolizes what was done, what is done, and what will be done, and the roaring storm-tossed boughs of it reach through the universe and bear all things in their arms. Emerson is the sweet and shining Balder; Whitman, Thor with hammer and belt of strength. Toss into the sunlight a handful of purest mountain lake water; the thousand droplets that descend, flash and burn with whitest light, and on the silvery surface of each a miniature world lies softly pictured in richest iridescence. Like these droplets are Emerson's sentences. But the writings of Whitman are the golden mirror of the moon lifted up out of immensity by some giant hand, that it may throw the refulgence of the sun down among the dark forests of earth, over its fair cities, sweet, flowery fields, and dark blue seas, concealing nothing, lighting earth's passion and its pain, its murders, its hatred and its hideousness, as well as its music, its poetry and its flowers.—*Lecture* of W. SLOANE KENNEDY.

new pieces, especially in " By Blue Ontario's Shore," " Song of the Answerer," " To a Foil'd European Revolutionaire," and " Song of Prudence." The poems extend to page 342. The rest of the volume, called " Leaves Droppings," is made up, first, of Emerson's letter to Walt Whitman, preceding—second, a long letter to Emerson in reply—and third, of twenty-six pages of criticisms of the first edition, taken from various quarters, a few favorable, the rest intensely bitter. (Extracts from some of these criticisms are given in the Appendix to Part II. of this vol.) Not only was this edition also savagely criticised, but so extreme was the feeling excited by it, that some good people in New York seriously contemplated having the author indicted and tried for publishing an obscene book. From this step they were only deterred by the consideration that, whatever might be the estimation which his book deserved, the man Walt Whitman was so popular in New York and Brooklyn, that it would be impossible to get a jury to find him guilty.

If any of the poems of *Leaves of Grass* can be put before the rest, we may say that upon the publication of the second edition the fundamental and important parts of the author's work were done, the foundations squarely and solidly laid, and the lines of the edifice drawn with a sure hand. The work, although far from completed, was already of supreme beauty and of infinite value. What then did men say of it? They received it with such a unanimous howl of execration and refusal, that after the sale of a small number of copies, Fowler & Wells, the publishers, thinking it might seriously injure their business, then very flourishing, peremptorily threw it up, and the publication of *Leaves of Grass* ceased. For the next four years the history of the work is a blank.

I am not sure but the attitude and course of Walt Whitman, these following years, form the most heroic part of all. He went on his way with the same enjoyment of life, the same ruddy countenance, the same free, elastic stride, through the tumult of sneers and hisses, as if he were surrounded by nothing but applause; not in the slightest degree abashed or roused to resent.

ment by the taunts and opposition. The poems written directly after the collapse of this second edition (compare, for instance, "Starting from Paumanok," and "Whoever you are, holding me now in hand,") are, if possible, more sympathetic, exultant, arrogant, and make larger claims than any. So far, the book had reached no circulation worth mentioning; probably not a hundred copies had been sold of both first and second editions. It is likely that at the time when the publishers of the second edition withdrew it from the market not a thousand people had read it, and not one in fifty of these would have the least idea what it was about.

Toward the end of the year 1856 Thoreau called upon Walt Whitman (Emerson had twice already visited him), and shortly afterwards T. wrote a letter to a friend, extremely curious as showing the impression made by the poet at that time upon so fine a genius and so sensible a man as the Walden hermit. The uncertain tone of the letter, and the contradictions in it, are remarkably suggestive:

CONCORD, December 7th, 1856.

MR. B .... That Walt Whitman of whom I wrote to you is the most interesting fact to me at present. I have just read his second edition (which he gave me) and it has done me more good than any reading for a long time. Perhaps I remember best the "Poem of Walt Whitman, an American" [now called "Song of Myself"] and the "Sun-down Poem" [now called "Crossing Brooklyn Ferry"]. There are two or three pieces in the book which are disagreeable, to say the least; simply sensual. He does not celebrate love at all. It is as if the beasts spoke. I think that men have not been ashamed of themselves without reason. No doubt there have always been dens where such deeds were unblushingly recited, and it is no merit to compete with their inhabitants. But even on this side he has spoken more truth than any American or modern that I know. I have found his poem exhilarating, encouraging. As for its sensuality—and it may turn out to be less sensual than it appears— I do not so much wish that those parts were not written, as that men and women were so pure that they could read them without harm, that is, without understanding them. One woman told me that no woman could read it—as if a man could read what a woman could not. Of course, Walt Whitman can communicate to us no new experience, and if we are shocked, whose experience is it we are reminded of?

On the whole, it sounds to me very brave and American, after whatever deductions. I do not believe that all the sermons, so called, that have been preached in this land, put together, are equal to it for preaching. We ought to rejoice greatly in him. He occasionally suggests something a little more than human. You can't confound him with the other inhabitants of Brooklyn or New York. How they must shudder when they read him! He is awfully good. To be sure, I sometime feel a little imposed on. By his heartiness and broad generalities he puts me into a liberal frame of mind, prepared to see wonders—and, as it were, sets me upon a hill, or in the midst of a plain,—stirs me up well, and then throws in—a thousand of brick! Though rude and sometimes ineffectual, it is a great primitive poem, an alarum or trumpet-note ringing through the American camp. Wonderfully like the Orientals, too, considering that, when I asked him if he had read them, he answered, " No; tell me about them."

I did not get far in conversation with him, two more being present—and among the few things that I chanced to say, I remember that one was, in answer to him as representing America, that I did not think much of America, or of politics, and so on—which may have been somewhat of a damper to him.

Since I have seen him, I find that I am not disturbed by any brag or egotism in his book. He may turn out the least of a braggart of all, having a better right to be confident.

He is a great fellow.   H. D. T.

During 1857-'8-'9 *Leaves of Grass* was out of print. In 1860 a third edition appeared, very much larger and handsomer than either of the preceding, published by Thayer & Eldridge, of Boston, beautifully printed on heavy white paper, and strongly bound in cloth—a volume of 456 pages, containing the 32 poems of the second edition, and 122 new ones. Many of the pieces have individual names, but most of them are named by groups. The words *Leaves of Grass* constitute the headline on the left-hand page throughout the volume; the right-hand page bears the name of the poem or group of poems. The likeness of the author, which accompanies the two earlier editions (and which appears again in the sixth as well as the late complete one), is replaced in the third by another, only used in this edition; an engraving on steel, from an oil painting by Charles Hine, (a valued artist-friend of Walt Whitman)—one of the most striking and interesting likenesses of the poet that has ever been made. The chief thing to note about this third edition is that not one word of the poems which had given such terrible offence in the earlier issues is omitted. The author has not swerved a hair's breadth from the line upon which he set out. The volume breathes the same all-generous spirit as the earlier issues; the same faith in God, the same love of man, perfect patience, and the largest and most absolute tolerance. In this edition those poems treating especially of sexual passions and acts are, for the first time, grouped together under one name, "Children of Adam" (written here "Enfans d'Adam"). Walt Whitman was advised, urged, even implored by his friends to omit or at least modify these pieces. An old and intimate personal friend, urging him one day to leave them out, said to him, "What in the world do you want to put in that stuff for, that nobody can read?" He answered with a smile, "Well, John, if you need to ask that question, it is evident at any rate that the book was not written for you."

In the course of the summer of 1860, while Walt Whitman was in Boston, putting that third edition through the press, Emerson came to see him, and presently said, "When people want to talk in Boston, they go to the Common; let us go there." So they went to the Common, and Emerson talked for something like two hours on the subject of "Children of Adam." He set forth the impolicy, the utter inadvisability of those poems. Walt Whitman listened to all he had to say; he did not argue the point, but when Emerson made an end, he said quietly, "My mind is not changed; I feel, if possible more strongly than ever, that those pieces should be retained" "Very well," said Emerson, "then let us go to dinner." *

---

* In "The Critic" for December 3d, 1881, Walt Whitman gives the following account of the interview: "Up and down this breadth by Beacon Street, between these same old elms, I walked for two hours, of a bright, sharp February midday twenty-one years ago, with Emerson, then in his prime, keen, physically and morally magnetic, armed at every point, and when he chose, wielding the emotional just as well as the intellectual. During those two hours he was the talker, and I the listener. It was an argument—statement—reconnoitring, review, attack, and pressing home (like an army corps in order, artillery, cavalry, infantry), of all that could be said against that part (and a main part) in the construction of my poems, 'Children of Adam.' More precious than gold to me that dissertation (I only wish I had it now verbatim). It afforded me, ever after, this strange and paradoxical lesson; each point of E.'s statement was unanswerable, no judge's charge ever more complete or convincing—I could never hear the points better put—and then I felt down in my soul the clear and unmistakable conviction to disobey all, and pursue my own way. 'What

This third edition, which came out early in the summer of 1860, was the first that had any sale at all. There was less out-cry about it than about the first and second. A class of men had begun to appear—a very few—who, having more or less absorbed *Leaves of Grass*, were in a position to hold in check the army of detractors. Although it could not be said that public opinion was becoming even partially favorable, still a hearing was beginning to be established, and here and there both in America and England, individuals were rising up to defend the book and strike a blow in its advocacy. Just at this time when the enterprise looked encouraging, the Secession War ruined (among much else) the book-publishing trade. Thayer, Eld-ridge failed, and *Leaves of Grass* was again out of print. Soon after (in 1862) Walt Whitman went to the seat of war (see *Specimen Days*), and poetry was forgotten, or at least laid aside, in the vast, vehement, all-devouring interests and duties of the time, and the succeeding years.

Late in 1865 was published "Drum Taps"—poems com-posed on battle-fields, in hospitals, or on the march, among the sights and surroundings of the war, saturated with the spirit and mournful tragedies of that time, including in a supplement, "When Lilacs Last in the Door-yard Bloom'd," commemora-ting the death of President Lincoln. Then in 1867, the war being well over, and the ordinary avocations of peace resumed, the poet (he had at the time a clerkship in the office of the Attorney-General, at Washington) brought out the fourth edi-tion, including all the poems written down to that period. This volume in size and shape is very similar to the current edition. It contains 470 pages and 235 poems. All the old ones are re tained, and about 80 new ones added. The title-page bears the words "LEAVES OF GRASS, New York, 1867." This fourth edi-tion contains no portrait. It is fairly printed (from the type) on good paper, but is not nearly as handsome a volume as the third edition.

have you to say, then, to such things?' said E., pausing in conclusion. 'Only that while I can't answer them at all, I feel more settled than ever to adhere to my own theory, and exemplify it,' was my candid response. Whereupon we went and had a good dinner at the American House."

The fifth edition was issued in 1871. It consisted of one good-sized, good-looking volume (384 pages), and a brochure, same paper and type, called "Passage to India" (120 pages). The total number of poems in this issue is 263—all the old, and a few new ones, especially the aforesaid "Passage to India." This edition was printed from new plates, on thick white paper, and is the handsomest edition published up to that time. In it all the old poems are carefully revised. This is known as the Washington edition. The title-page bears the words "LEAVES OF GRASS, Washington, D. C., 1871." This, like the fourth, contains no portrait. It supplied such moderate demand (mostly in England) as existed during five years.

Early in 1872 Walt Whitman was invited by the students of Dartmouth College, Hanover, New Hampshire, to deliver what is called "the Commencement Poem." He accepted, went on there, had a good time, and the piece given was published in book-form in New York soon after under the name of "As a Strong Bird on Pinions Free." It had no sale at all. (In the present, 1882 edition, it is called "Thou Mother with thy Equal Brood.")

In 1876 the author printed the sixth edition. This—for several reasons, the most interesting and valuable of all—is in two volumes, one called *Leaves of Grass* (printed from the same plates as the corresponding volume in the fifth edition), and the other, "Two Rivulets." The last named is made up of "Democratic Vistas," "Passage to India" (printed from the plates used in the fifth edition), and, along with these, four collections of prose and verse, called respectively, "Two Rivulets," "Centennial Songs, 1876," "As a Strong Bird on Pinions Free," and, in prose, "Memoranda During the War." The total number of pages is 734, and the total number of poems 288. Each volume contains the author's autograph, and the two books include three portraits. It will not be many years before copies of this Centennial edition will bring almost anything that holders of them like to ask. The poems contained in it are all included (with many alterations, some omissions, additions, etc.) in the 1882 issue; and most of the prose is included in *Specimen Days*.

The next (seventh) edition of *Leaves of Grass* is that of James R. Osgood & Co., Boston, 1881–'82. The text is packed as closely together as possible in one volume of 382 pages, long primer type, containing 293 distinct poems. A few of the old ones are omitted (generally for the reason that what they contained was expressed elsewhere), in some instances two are run into one, and quite a number of new pieces added. The text throughout has been thoroughly revised, hundreds of slight alterations have been made, in many places words and lines omitted, and as frequently, in other places, words and lines added. The arrangement and the punctuation have been materially altered for the better, and the poems are so joined and blended by slight alterations in the text and by juxtaposition, that *Leaves of Grass* now becomes a unit in a sense it had never been before. The original design of the author, formed twenty-six years before, has taken shape, and stands in this volume completed.

It is usual to speak, as I have done, of the different " editions" of *Leaves of Grass,* but this term, in one sense, is scarcely correct, for an essential point about the work is not only its identical but its cumulative character. Those seven different issues are simply successive expansions or growths, strictly carrying out the one idea.

A peculiarity of Walt Whitman has been his careful attention to the minutest details of typography (he is a printer himself, be it remembered) in all the issues of *Leaves of Grass,* and especially in the final one. Instead of sending on his copy and receiving back proofs by mail, he goes personally to Boston, takes a little room in the printing office, settles on the size of page, kind of type, how the pieces shall run on, etc. After which, for six or seven weeks, every line is vigilantly scanned ; every day for two or three hours he is at Rand & Avery's (the printing office and foundry) reading proofs, sometimes to the third and fourth revision. On the completion of the plates, he remarked that if there was anything amiss in the material body of the work, it should be charged to him equally with its spiritual sins, for he had had his own way about it all.

The subsequent withdrawal of the firm of J. R. Osgood & Co. from publishing that seventh edition of *Leaves of Grass* makes it necessary to relate somewhat in detail both how they came to be, and how, in a short five or six months, they ceased to be, such publishers. In May, 1881, J. R. Osgood wrote to Walt Whitman, asking if he had in hand and was disposed to bring out a new and complete edition of his poetic works. Walt Whitman wrote back that such an enterprise was contemplated by him, but before entering upon any negotiation, it needed to be distinctly understood that not a piece or line of the old text was intended by him to be left out ; this was an absolute pre-requisite. Osgood & Co. then wrote asking if they could see the copy. Walt Whitman sent it immediately. Osgood & Co. wrote back formally offering to publish, and mentioning terms, which were fixed at a royalty of twenty-five cents on every two-dollar copy sold. The contract being made, the poet went on to Boston, and was there two months (September and October, 1881) engaged in seeing the poems properly set up. This seventh and completed *Leaves of Grass* was published latter part of November, 1881. The sale commenced fairly. Several hundred copies went to London, and Walt Whitman's royalty from the winter and early spring issues amounted to nearly five hundred dollars.

March 1st, 1882, Oliver Stevens, Boston District Attorney (under instructions from Mr. Marston, State Attorney-General, see further on), sends an official letter* to Osgood & Co. that he intends to institute suit against *Leaves of Grass* and for its suppression, under the statutes regarding obscene literature. A list of pieces and passages is soon after officially specified, and it is

---

* Here is this curious document:

Commonwealth of MASSACHUSETTS,
District Attorney's Office,
BOSTON, 24 Court House, *March 1st, 1882.*

MESSRS. J. R. OSGOOD & Co.

Gentlemen,—Our attention has been officially directed to a certain book, entitled *Leaves of Grass*, Walt Whitman, published by you. We are of the opinion that this book is such a book as brings it within the provisions of the public statutes respecting obscene literature, and suggest the propriety of withdrawing the same from circulation, and suppressing the edition thereof; otherwise the complaints which are proposed to be made will have to be entertained. I am, yours truly,

(Signed)   OLIVER STEVENS, *District Attorney,*

intimated that upon these being erased and left out, the publication may continue. March 21st, Osgood & Co. write Walt Whitman, forwarding this list,* and asking if the words, lines, and pieces specified could be left out. March 23d, Walt Whitman writes Osgood & Co., " The list, whole and several, is rejected " by me, and will not be thought of under any circumstances." A week afterwards, Osgood & Co. write Walt Whitman, " The official mind has declared it will be satisfied if the pieces ' To a Common Prostitute ' and ' A Woman Waits for Me ' are left out," and that those two so left out, the book can then go on unmolested. (Osgood & Co. add that they have suspended the publication and sales, and that orders are waiting.) Walt Whitman peremptorily rejects the proposal to leave out the two pieces. Osgood & Co. (April 13th, 1882) courteously but decidedly write that they cannot afford to be drawn into any suit of the kind threatened by the Boston officials, but must give up *Leaves of Grass*, and that they are ready to turn over the plates to Walt Whitman's purchase, (these plates were so consigned to him, and no cash royalty ever paid), adding, " We feel it right to say, that it is not we who have fixed inflexible conditions under which this matter could be decided—those conditions have been fixed by yourself." (There is an interior history of the persons and their animus behind the scenes, in Boston, who egged on Messrs. Marston and Stevens, which has not yet come to the light, but may, some day.)

---

* The following is the list referred to—(same paging as in the 1882 edition):

PAGE	LINES	PAGE	LINES
31,	15th and 16th.	88, 89,	" A Woman Waits for Me."
32,	19th to 22d (inclusive).	90, 91,	Whole of 90 and 91, to line 11 (inclu-
37,	14th and 15th.		sive).
48,	20th to 29th (inclusive).	94,	First six lines and half of 7th to words
49,	11th to 20th (inclusive).		" indecent calls " (inclusive).
52,	The remainder of paragraph twenty-	216,	" The Dalliance of the Eagles."
	eight, beginning at the 12th line.	266,	21st and 22d.
59,	11th and 12th.	299, 300,	" To a Common Prostitute."
66,	15th and 16th.	303,	2d and 3d.
79,	21st and 22d.	325,	The remainder of the 4th line from
80,	Entire passage from 14th line, ending		bottom, beginning with words " he
	with words " And you, stalwart		with his palm."
	loins," on page 81.	331,	9th and 10th.
84,	1st to 7th (inclusive).	355,	13th to 17th (inclusive).
87,	13th to 28th (inclusive).		

After such plain narration of the facts, perhaps the keenest and most deserved comment upon this whole transaction (it was fitting that the one who attended to Hon. Mr. Harlan in 1865–6 should also sum up the Marston-Stevens-Osgood affair in 1882) is a letter by William D. O'Connor, printed in the "New York Tribune" of May 25th, 1882, from which the following are extracts:

If it were not for unduly trenching upon your space, I would like to show you the passages which the State District-Attorney pronounced obscene, and demanded expurgated. The list furnished by this holy and intelligent man is before me, and has twenty-two specifications. Four of the passages specified relate to the poet's democratic theory of the intrinsic sacredness and nobility of the entire human physiology—identical with the famous declaration of Novalis that the body is the temple of the Holy Ghost; and involve, specially in one or two instances, a rapt celebration of the acts and organs of chaste love. Another passage describes the identification through sympathy of one's self with lawless or low-down persons. A sixth passage under ban is devoted to the majestic annunciation of woman as the matrix of the generations—the doctrine that her greatness is the mould and condition of all the greatness of man. Another proscribed passage consists of ten pictorial lines, worthy of Æschylus, in which the poet describes the grand and terrible dalliance of two eagles, high aloft in the bright air, above a river road. A seventh passage specially required to be expunged is the poem nobly entitled "To a Common Prostitute"—I say nobly, because even the large sense of the composition is enlarged by its title. The piece is simply indicative of the attitude of ideal humanity in this age toward even the lowest or most degraded, and is conceived throughout in the sublime spirit of our times, whose theory abandons no one nor anything to loss or ruin, recognizing amelioration as the law of laws, and good as the final destiny of all. It is incredible that a poem whose whole staple, on the face of it, is to assure the unfortunate Magdalen that not until Nature excludes her shall she be excluded from consideration and sympathy, and to promise her the redemption of the superior life—whose entire thesis is plainly and undeniably supreme charity and faith in the human ascension—should appear to any mind as an expression of obscenity. However, as Swedenborg reminds us, to the devils perfumes are stinks. The eighth quarry of the State District-Attorney is the piece entitled, "A Woman Waits for Me." If the defence of this poem is to carry with it dishonor, I court that dishonor. Nothing that the poet has ever written, either in signification or in splendid oratoric music, has more the character of a sanctus; nothing in modern literature is loftier and holier. Beginning with an inspired declaration of the absolute conditioning power of sex—a declaration as simply true as sublime—the poet, using sexual imagery, as Isaiah and Ezekiel, as all the prophets, all the great Oriental poets, have used it before him, continues his dithyramb in exalted affirmation of the vital procreative effects of his book upon the women, that is to say upon the future of America. And this glorious conviction of a lofty mission—the consciousness, in one form or another, of every philosopher, every apostle, every poet who has worked his thought for the human advancement—the faith and the consolation of every sower of the light who has looked beyond the hounding hatreds of the present to the next ages—the eminently pure, the eminently enlightened, the supereminently judicial Boston District-Attorney considers obscene! The remaining fourteen passages marked by his condemnation I need not discuss, as they are all included in the first edition of the work indorsed by Emerson.

As for the part taken by Messrs. Osgood & Company in this shameful transaction, what is said should have the conciseness of a brand. It was no new book they had undertaken to publish—it had been the talk of two worlds for over a quarter of a century. They knew its noble repute in the highest quarters, and they also knew what shadows might be cast upon it by booby bigotry, by foul sour prudery mincing as purity, or by rotten carnality in its hypocrite mask of virtue. Knowing all this, facing possible consequences in their agreement to publish without expurgation, and having voluntarily sought the publication of the volume, I say it was their duty as gentlemen to stand by the bargain they had solicited, and it was no less their interest as men of business to advertise the State-Attorney's ridiculous menace in the boldest type their printers could furnish, and bid him come on with his prosecution! Time enough to give in when Sidney Bartlett had failed to make a Massachusetts jury see that in literature we must allow free expressions if we are going to have free expression;—time enough to own defeat when Sidney Bartlett or Charles O'Conor failed to make plain, as either would not have failed to make plain to even Mr. Oliver Stevens's comprehension, the difference between Biblical courage of language and intrinsic intellectual impurity. But Messrs. Osgood & Company leave their Pavia unfought, and lose everything, including honor. They might have braced themselves with the remembrance of Woodfall, standing prosecution heaped on prosecution, in his dark fidelity to Junius. They might have gathered grit by trying to imagine John Murray flinching from the publication of Byron. On the contrary, shaking in abject cowardice at the empty threat of this legal bully, they meanly break their contract with the author, abandon the book they had volunteered to issue, and drop from the ranks of great publishers into the category of hucksters whose business cannot afford a conscience.

It only remains to point the moral and adorn the tale with the name of the Boston District-Attorney. I have called the transaction in which he appears as the prime mover shameful, but the word is limp and colorless in its application to such an outrage upon the liberty of thought as he has committed.

The sense of it makes every fibre of one's being seem interknitted with lightning. On such a subject no thinking man or woman in such a country as ours will reflect with cold composure. The action of this lawyer constitutes a reef which threatens with shipwreck every great book of every great author, from Aristophanes to Molière, from Æschylus to Victor Hugo; and the drop of blood that is calm in view of such an outrage proclaims us bastard to the lineage of the learned and the brave! To-day Oliver Stevens has become the peril of Shakespeare. He knows well, no one knows it better, that under his construction of the statutes neither Shakespeare nor the Bible could be circulated, and no one better knows than he that neither of those books is obscene. He knows well, Emerson and a host of scholars and men of letters in both continents bearing witness, that Walt Whitman's book is no more within the meaning of the statutes than Shakespeare or the Bible, but he also knows that the charge he has brought against the one lies with at least equal force against the others, and if he does not continue his raid upon the great literature, it is only because his courage is not equal to his logic. Even his bolder and brassier ally in this holy war, Mr. Anthony Comstock,—even he tempers valor with discretion for the nonce, and says he " will not prosecute the publishers of the classics, unless they specially advertise them"! There are contingencies, it seems, in which the great works of the human mind will be brought under the operation of "the statutes against obscene literature." Who knows, since fortune favors the brave and enterprising, but that we may yet, step by step, succeed in bringing the Fourteenth century into the Nineteenth, and reërect Montfaucon—that hideous edifice of scaffolds reared by Philippe le Bel, where the blackened corpse of Glanus swung beside the carcass of the regicide for having translated Plato, and where Peter Albin dangled gibbeted beside the robber for having published Virgil? If this fond prospect is still somewhat distant, it is only, it seems, because Mr. Anthony Comstock lets his I dare not wait upon I would, and delays the initial step until the classics are "specially" advertised. Meanwhile Mr. Oliver Stevens also waits for fresh relays of courage, and as yet only ventures to attempt to crush Walt Whitman. For that act of daring he shall reap the full harvest of reward. We will see whether in this country and in this century he can suppress by law the work of a man of genius, and fail of his proper recompense. He has arrested in Massachusetts the superb book which is the chief literary glory of our country in the capitals of Europe—the book of the good gray nurse who nourished the wounded and tended many a dying soldier through our years of war—and for that valiant action I promise Mr. Stevens his meed of immortal remembrance. He has the solemn comfort of having been unknown yesterday; I can offer him the glorious assurance that he will not be forgotten to-morrow.

The Marston-Stevens-Osgood assault, however, instead of

bringing about the result intended (a suppression of *Leaves of Grass*), immediately produced quite the contrary effect. The book was taken up by a Philadelphia house, Rees Welsh & Co., to whose miscellaneous business David McKay succeeded, and the latter is now publisher both of the completed poems, and of the late prose work, *Specimen Days.* Of *Leaves of Grass* the first Philadelphia edition (without the omission of a line or word) was ready in the latter part of September, 1882, and all sold in one day. And there has been quite a general and steady sale since.

It is this issue, comprehending all, that I allude to throughout the present volume as the completed 1882 (or 1882-'83) edition. It includes several touches and additions, minor but significant, not in any previous issue.

CHAPTER II.

ANALYSIS OF THE POEMS, ETC.

ALTHOUGH, as already stated, Walt Whitman has written much
else, yet the two now published volumes, 1882–'83, the one of
verse, *Leaves of Grass*, and the other of prose, *Specimen Days
and Collect*, may be considered (at any rate so far) as containing
all that he cares to preserve. For the purpose of comment, the
prose writings may be divided into, First, the early tales and
sketches in the Appendix. Secondly, the section of *Collect* which
includes several pieces of the highest excellence, entitling the
author to take equal rank with the greatest masters of prose composition. These essays—especially "Democratic Vistas," "Ori-
gins of Attempted Secession," "Preface to 1855 Issue of *Leaves
of Grass*," "Poetry To-day in America"—are not only of the
greatest value inherently in themselves, but as presenting the
prose, intellectual, discriminating, common-sense side of American Democracy, of which *Leaves of Grass* exhibits the poetical
aspect. They thus counterpart one another, and the prose essays
show (what if we read the poetry only we might be inclined to
doubt) that the man who saw the future glories of American civilization which are set forth in the poetic work, saw also, and fully
saw, the mean and threatening facts which are visible to ordinary
men in the present, and which they (many of them) think is all
there is to see. Thirdly, the first half, or third, of *Specimen
Days* (formerly called "Memoranda during the War") is, as far
as I know, by far the best work yet written from which to get an
idea of the Secession struggle of 1860–'65—who were engaged
in it, what they actually did, and how they felt and suffered. Its
want of literary form makes it the more valuable. Had the author
from his notes distilled a finished work, he must inevitably have
included coloring and shading from his own after-feelings and

reflections; but as actually jotted down on the battle-fields and in the hospitals, surrounded by the events, scenes, persons depicted, it is clearly the reproduction of living incidents under the direct observation of the writer, absolutely truthful and una-dorned. Fourthly, the last one hundred and twenty pages of *Specimen Days* stands in a category by itself; its correct name taken alone would be "The Diary of an Invalid," and it is as such that it has its extraordinary and unique value. As *Leaves of Grass* is, from one point of view, a picture of perfect ideal health, so may this section of *Specimen Days* be received as the ideal (though entirely real) picture of sickness. It will remain forever a record of how a heroic soul faced and without dejection quietly and bravely passed through continued grief, poverty, the imminency of death, and great suffering both of mind and body, lasting for years. Never before from amid such circumstances came such a voice. *Leaves of Grass* teaches us to strive, to aspire, and to dare; *Specimen Days* an equally good lesson, that of forti tude, cheerfulness, and even joyousness in defiance (though not in a spirit of defiance) of all and any ills.

Lastly comes *Leaves of Grass*, the real work of the author's life—or from another (and more correct) point of view the image of his real work, which was his life itself. After the long period of its own and its author's growth, we have it at last in the 1882 –'83 edition, completed as conceived twenty-six years ago. Dur-ing that time every line has been pondered again and again with the greatest care. Though the result of spontaneity and spiritual impulse, and invariably started thence, the file has in no wise been forgotten. Every word and expression found not to come up to the standard has been cut out. The new material as pre pared has been fitted into its place; the old, from time to time, torn down and re-arranged. Now it appears before us, perfected like some grand cathedral that through many years or intervals has grown and grown until the original conception and full de sign of the architect stand forth.

In examining this book, the first thing that presents itself for remark is its name, by no means the least significant part. It

would indeed be impossible to select for the volume a more perfect title. Properly understood, the words express what the book
contains and is. Like the grass, while old as creation, it is
modern, fresh, universal, spontaneous, not following forms, taking
its own form, perfectly free and unconstrained, common as the
commonest things, yet its meaning inexhaustible by the greatest
intellect, full of life itself, and capable of entering into and
nourishing other lives, growing in the sunshine (*i. e.*, in the full,
broad light of science), perfectly open and simple, yet having
meanings underneath; always young, pure, delicate and beautiful to those who have hearts and eyes to feel and see, but coarse,
insignificant and worthless to those who live more in the artificial,
(parlors, pictures, traditions, books, dress, jewels, laces, music,
decorations, money, gentility), than in the natural, (the naked and
rude earth, the fresh air, the calm or stormy sea, men, women,
children, birds, animals, woods, fields, and the like).

I might say here a preparatory word or two about the absence
of ordinary rhyme or tune in Walt Whitman's work. The question cannot be treated without a long statement, and many premises. Readers used to the exquisite verbal melody of Tennyson
and Longfellow may well wince at first entering on *Leaves of
Grass.* So does the invalid or even well person used to artificial warmth and softness indoors, wince at the sea, and gale, and
mountain steeps. But the rich, broad, rugged rhythm and inimi-
table interior music of *Leaves of Grass* need not be argued for
or defended to any real tone-artist. It has already been told
how, during the gestation of the poems, the author was saturated
for years with the rendering by the best vocalists and performers
of the best operas and oratorios. Here is further testimony on
this point, from a lady, a musician and art-writer, Mrs. Fanny
Raymond Ritter, wife of Music-Professor Ritter of Vassar College

Those readers who possess a musical mind cannot fail to have been struck
by a peculiar characteristic of some of Whitman's grandest poems. It is apparently, but only superficially, a contradiction. A fault that critics have most
insisted upon in his poetry is its independence of, or contempt for, the canons
of musico-poetical art, in its intermittent, irregular structure and flow. Yet the

characteristic alluded to which always impressed me as inherent in these—especially in some of the Pindaric " Drum-Taps "—was a sense of strong rhythmical, pulsing, *musical* power. I had always accounted to myself for this contradiction, because I, of course, supposed the poet's nature to be a large one, including many opposite qualities; and that as it is impossible to conceive the Universe devoid of those divinely musical forces, Time, Movement, Order, a great poet's mind could not be thought of as an imperfect, one-sided one, devoid of any comprehension of or feeling for musical art. I knew, too, that Whitman was a sincere lover of art, though not practically formative in any other art than poetry. Therefore, on a certain memorable Olympian day at the Ritter-house, when Whitman and Burroughs visited us together, I told Whitman of my belief in the presence of an overwhelming musical pulse, behind an apparent absence of musical form in his poems. He answered with as much sincerity as geniality, that it would indeed be strange if there were no music at the heart of his poems, for more of these were actually inspired by music than he himself could remember. Moods awakened by music in the streets, the theatre, and in private, had originated poems apparently far removed in feeling from the scenes and feelings of the moment. But above all, he said, while he was yet brooding over poems still to come, he was touched and inspired by the glorious, golden, soul-smiting voice of the greatest of Italian contralto singers, Marietta Alboni. Her mellow, powerful, delicate tones, so heartfelt in their expression, so spontaneous in their utterance, had deeply penetrated his spirit, and never, as when subsequently writing of the mocking-bird or any other bird-song, on a fragrant, moonlit summer night, had he been able to free himself from the recollection of the deep emotion that had inspired and affected him while he listened to the singing of Marietta Alboni.

The volume (final edition 1882–'83) opens with ten pages of short poems called "Inscriptions," some of which were written after the body of the work, and are reflections upon its intention and meaning. They cannot be understood until the book itself has been studied, and its scope and power more or less realized. Here, for instance, is one of them :

Shut not your doors to me, proud libraries,
For that which was lacking on all your well-fill'd shelves, yet needed most, I
    bring,
Forth from the war emerging, a book I have made,
The words of my book nothing, the drift of it everything,
A book separate, not link'd with the rest, nor felt by the intellect,
But you, ye untold latencies, will thrill to every page.

And here another:

Lo, the unbounded sea,
On its breast a ship starting, spreading all sails, carrying even her moonsails;
The pennant is flying aloft as she speeds, she speeds so stately—below emulous
    waves press forward,
They surround the ship with shining curving motions and foam.

The first of these, I suppose, could not be in any degree explained to a person who knew nothing of *Leaves of Grass.* The second admits of a certain degree of explanation which, however, would have to be taken on trust by such a person. The ship is the book, the ocean is the human mind. The large ship, with all sails set, starts on her voyage; as she presses through the water, the waves (the resistances the book meets) roll from her bows and down her sides. The angry, hostile criticisms and clamors are the bubbles of foam in the wake.

The first poem of any length, "Starting from Paumanok," appeared first in the third (1860) edition, though it was written in 1856, immediately after the second (1856) edition was published. It is an introduction or overture. In it the author sets forth what he is going to do. He says he intends to celebrate man's soul and his body—to drop in the soil of the general human character the germs of a greater religion than has hitherto appeared upon the earth. He says he will sing the song of companionship, and write the evangel-poem of comrades and of love. Referring to "Children of Adam," he says:

And sexual organs and acts! do you concentrate in me—for I am determin'd
    to tell you with courageous clear voice to prove you illustrious.

And toward the end of the poem, as a final admonition, he says to the reader:

For your life adhere to me;
(I may have to be persuaded many times before I consent to give myself
    really to you—but what of that?
Must not Nature be persuaded many times?)

No dainty dolce affettuoso I;
Bearded, sun-burnt, gray-neck'd, forbidding, I have arrived,
To be wrestled with as I pass for the solid prizes of the universe,
For such I afford whoever can persevere to win them.

The stress of the book opens with the poem (hitherto named "Walt Whitman," now) "Song of Myself," the largest and most important that the author has produced, and perhaps the most important poem that has so far been written at any time, in any language. Its magnitude, its depth and fulness of meaning, make it difficult, indeed impossible, to comment satisfactorily upon. In the first place, it is a celebration or glorification of Walt Whitman, of his body, and of his mind and soul, with all their functions and attributes—and then, by a subtle but inevitable implication, it becomes equally a song of exultation, as sung by any and every individual, man or woman, upon the beauty and perfection of his or her body and spirit, the material part being treated as equally divine with the immaterial part, and the immaterial part as equally real and godlike with the material. Beyond this it has a third sense, in which it is the chant of cosmical man (the *être supreme* of Comte)—of the whole race considered as one immense and immortal being. From a fourth point of view it is a most sublime hymn of glorification of external Nature. The way these different senses lie in some passages one behind the other, and are in others inextricably blended together, defies comment. But beyond all, the chief difficulty in criticising this, as all other poems in *Leaves of Grass*, is that the ideas expressed are of scarcely any value or importance compared with the passion, the never-flagging emotion, which is in every line, almost in every word, and which cannot be set forth or even touched by commentary. If, again, the reviewer tries to impress the deeper meaning upon his reader by quoting passages, he finds that this expedient is equally futile, because no extract will make upon the reader an impression at all corresponding to that produced by the same lines upon a person to whom the whole poem is familiar. The "Song of Myself" is not only a celebration of man (any man), his soul and body, but it is a celebration of everything else as well (necessarily so, since, as Walt Whitman expresses it, "Objects gross and the unseen soul are one")—of the earth and all there is upon it—of the universe, and of the Divine Spirit that animates it—that *is* it. The reader is not merely told that these things are good, and persuaded or argued into believing it (that has been done a thousand times, and is a small matter), but he is brought into contact with, and absolutely fused in the living mind of Walt Whitman, to whom these things are so, not as a matter of speculation and belief, but as a matter of vital existence and identity: and as he reads the poem (it may be for the fifth or the fiftieth time), the state of mind of the author inevitably (in some measure) passes over to the reader, and he practically becomes the author—becomes the person who thinks so, knows so, feels so. But, until this point is reached (and with many readers, so far, it is never reached), the poem is necessarily more or less meaningless, and besides is displeasing from what critics call its "egotism," a quality well known to the author, who (in the first as well as subsequent editions) says:

> I know perfectly well my own egotism,
> Know my omnivorous lines, and must not write any less,
> And would fetch you whoever you are flush with myself.

When the reader is brought "flush" with or up to the spiritual level of the book (if this ever happens), he finds, as Walt Whitman tells him, that it is himself talking just as much as the man who wrote the book—that in fact the "ego" is the reader fully as much as the writer. The poet speaks for himself in the first place of course, but he speaks also just as much for others, as he says :

> It is you talking just as much as myself, I act as the tongue of you,
> Tied in your mouth, in mine it begins to be loosen'd.

Then the range is outdoors almost perpetually. No critic of the poems can fail to notice the entire absence of any bookshelf or easy-chair character in them. Many readers will consider it a fault; at any rate the pieces, from first to last, give out nothing of the atmosphere of a permanent indoor home.*

---

* "Poets' Homes" for 1879 (Mrs. Mary Wager-Fisher) says: As to Walt Whitman's home, it must be confessed that he has none, and for many years has had none in the special sense of "home;" neither has he the usual library or "den" for composition and work. He composes everywhere—years ago, while writing *Leaves of Grass*, sometimes on the New York and Brooklyn ferries, sometimes on the top of omnibuses in the roar of Broadway, or

One peculiarity is the indirectness of the language in which it is written. This is at first a serious obstacle to the comprehension of the poems, but after the key has been found, it adds materially to the force and vividness of expression. In places where a thought or fact is expressed in the usual direct manner, there is frequently a second and even a third meaning underlying the first. The following examples, which are taken from the "Song of Myself," will serve to give an idea of the feature in question, which belongs more or less to the whole volume:

Houses and rooms are full of perfumes, the shelves are crowded with perfumes,
I breathe the fragrance myself and know it and like it,
The distillation would intoxicate me also, but I shall not let it.

The atmosphere is not a perfume, it has no taste of the distillation, it is odorless,
It is for my mouth forever, I am in love with it,
I will go to the bank by the wood and become undisguised and naked,
I am mad for it to be in contact with me.

In this passage "Houses and rooms" are the schools, religions, philosophies, literature; "perfumes" are their modes of thought and feeling; the "atmosphere" is the thought and feeling excited in a healthy and free individual by direct contact with Nature; to be "naked" is to strip off the swathing, suffocating folds and mental wrappings derived from civilization.

Stop this day and night with me, and you shall possess the origin of all poems,

means, Live with me (with my book) until my mode of thought and feeling becomes your mode of thought and feeling.

I have heard what the talkers were talking, the talk of the beginning and the end,

---

amid the most crowded haunts of the city, or the shipping by day—and then at night, often in the democratic amphitheatre of the Fourteenth Street Opera House. The pieces in his "Drum Taps" were all prepared in camp, in the midst of war scenes, on picket or the march, in the army. He now spends the summers mostly at a solitary farm "down in Jersey," where he likes best to be by a secluded, picturesque pond on Timber Creek. It is in such places, and in the country at large, in the West, on the Prairies, by the Pacific—in cities too, New York, Washington, New Orleans, along Long Island shore where he well loves to linger, that Walt Whitman has really had his place of composition.

means, I have studied what has been taught in the philosophies and religious systems as to the Creation or the final destinies and purposes of men and things.

I am satisfied—I see, dance, laugh, sing;
As the hugging and loving bed-fellow sleeps at my side through the night, and withdraws at the peep of the day with stealthy tread,
Leaving me baskets cover'd with white towels swelling the house with their plenty,
Shall I postpone my acceptation and realization and scream at my eyes
That they turn from gazing after and down the road,
And forthwith cipher and show me to a cent,
Exactly the value of one and exactly the value of two, and which is ahead?

means, I am contented and happy as I am; refreshed with sleep, I have all I need; that being the case, shall I put off the enjoyment of life, and blame myself that I do not take part with the world in studies, money-making, ambition and the like, or spend my time calculating what is best to do, say, etc.?

Long enough have you dream'd contemptible dreams;
Now I wash the gum from your eyes,
You must habit yourself to the dazzle of the light and of every moment of your life;

Long have you timidly waded holding a plank by the shore;
Now I will you to be a bold swimmer,
To jump off in the midst of the sea, rise again, nod to me, shout, and laughingly dash with your hair;

means, You have long enough been degraded by ancient superstitions, followed the systems, the schools, the religions handed down from old times, all taken for granted, wanting courage to look for yourselves; now I propose to have you face all things and your fortunes with confidence and faith, and live a free and joyful life.

I swear I will never again mention love or death inside a house,

means, I will never more think, or have you think, of love or death in the conventional ways, with the old limitations (the walls of the house) or with the feeling of dread (in the case of death).

And filter and fibre your blood,

means, and purify and strengthen your spiritual nature.

These examples might be multiplied to almost any extent, for a large part of this poem, as of all *Leaves of Grass*, is made up of language which I have characterized as indirect, but which, when understood, is seen to be more direct than any other. This "Song of Myself" is, in the highest sense of the word, a religious poem. From beginning to end it is an expression of Faith, the most lofty and absolute that man has so far attained. There are passages in it expressive of love or sympathy, but taken as a whole, the groundwork and vivifying spirit of the poem is Faith.

Following the "Song of Myself," comes the group called "Chil dren of Adam." ("He that will deepest serve men," says De Foe, "must not promise himself that he shall not anger them.") These poems having been misunderstood, as was indeed inevitable at first, have given rise to condemnatory criticism not only against the pieces themselves (which really form a small proportion of the whole work), but against the rest of the book, and its author. Perhaps these poems can only be justified as they justify themselves, by altering the mental attitude of society and literature towards the whole subject treated in them ; and this of course will take time, no doubt several generations. For, though to a few thoughtful people, women as well as men, these parts either require no justification, or are already justified by the process indicated, yet probably the vast majority of persons now living in the most civilized countries could never be got to believe, and could never if they tried make themselves see, that the mental attitude represented by Walt Whitman is higher and better (as it certainly is, and time will prove it) than has before existed towards all things relating to sex. The following on the subject is from a criticism by Joseph B. Marvin in the Boston quarterly "Radical" for August, 1877 :

There are two phases of Whitman's poetry we have barely alluded to : his treatment of sex, and his form of expression ; his celebration of amativeness, and his art. It is these, chiefly, that have given offence. As to the first—as to sexuality—there is an instinct of silence, which, it is said, Whitman, in his group of poems entitled "Children of Adam" rudely ignores and overrides. But so does the physiologist and the true physician ignore this instinct and break the silence: and properly so. And this poet of Democracy is a physician of both soul and body. He comes to diagnosticate the disease in the intellect, in the art, in the heart, of America to-day. And what does his discriminating eye discern? He sees that there is a false sense of shame attaching, in the modern mind, to the sexual relation. There is tacit admission among men and women everywhere, in our time, that there is inherent vileness in this relation, in sex itself, and in the body. We come honestly enough by this belief. The tradition is very old. It began with Judaism, and Christianity has maintained it. The Church chants it in her litanies; and Puritanism has emphasized it, and formulated it into an iron creed. The body's vileness is traced back in our traditions even to the beginning of the human race. Nor is there any concession of the possibility of purification on the earth. Was it not time that one came who should break the long silence about sexuality? who should show that what men have been dumb about, and ashamed of, through all these years, is not foul, but holy—holy as love; holy as birth, and fatherhood, and motherhood, to which it all pertains? And who, better than the poet, was entitled and qualified to perform this service? For, to him, the real is visible always in its ideal relations. And did not the achievement of this high task and service devolve naturally and especially upon the poet of Democracy; upon him who is distinctively the attestor and celebrator of the greatness and the divineness in men and women; who is the interpreting, rapt Lucretius of *human* nature? Before Whitman came, there had been plenty of half-praise of human nature, and no end of the demagogue's vulgar flattery. But at last comes one who reveres mankind; by whom all, *all* of man is honored; and in whose eyes sexuality, the body, the soul, are equally pure and sacred. Again, was it not fitting that he who has celebrated death as has no other poet, should likewise celebrate birth: and not only birth, but the prelude of birth,—procreation and begetting?

And now at length, the task achieved, this service to humanity performed, let the instinct of silence, if you will, again prevail. The purpose for which the spell was broken is accomplished. The flesh is freed from its false repute. The "fall" is finished. Henceforth humanity ascends. Democracy now for the first time interpreted and understood, man may begin to achieve his destiny intelligently, and in fulness of self-respect.

But even if this spiritual necessity and emergency had not existed, it may easily be shown that Whitman is justified, from a literary and artistic point of view, in all that he has written of the amative passion. In his large celebration of humanity, one of the incidental undertakings, subservient to his larger purpose, was the cataloguing of mankind's myriad belongings and relations. He would write the inventory of man's illimitable possessions. He would assure him of his own riches; and, by these means, impressing him with some approximate sense of his own importance, he might hope to arouse within him the self-assurance and the lofty pride which are the basis of individuality and true Democracy. And, read in the rapt spirit of joy and adoration in which they were written, these mere lists and schedules become sublimest poems. But what kind of an inventory of the attributes and endowments of mankind would that be which omitted sexuality; the amative act; procreation? Not thus did antique genius record the natural history of man. The men of the Bible, and of the "Iliad," and of Shakespeare's dramas, were lusty, and loved, and wived, and begot children. Has all this changed in our time? Is ours the age of the neuter gender? It would seem so from our popular literature.

A critic of our popular literary school avers that there is not an impure word in Shakespeare, but that Whitman is obscene. Such a declaration as this is the result of a literary glamour which renders moral discrimination simply impossible. Every line of Shakespeare is justified by the standard of supreme art; but whether the critic means to say that the great dramatist's writings are free from textual impurities, or from moral licentiousness, his assertion is equally untrue and absurd. There is not a play of Shakespeare in which the text is not altered upon the stage to suit the prudery of our time; and this critic himself could hardly be persuaded, notwithstanding his assertion, to read "Venus and Adonis" to a miscellaneous company. But Walt Whitman, though he is gross and rude, is always pure. His grossness is the grossness of Nature, of rude health. Shakespeare's treatment of the amorous passion is often that of the gallant and the voluptuary. Whitman's never; for, though he celebrates the sensuous, he never writes in the interest of sensuality, but of fatherhood and maternity. He avows and rejoices in the deliciousness of sex; but, like Plato in the "Republic," he demands sanity and health in it all, and as the result of it all. He is the one poet, in all time, who has celebrated sex in the interest of human progress; in the service of health,—physical and moral,—of equality, Democracy, religion. They who think they find him obscene, in truth find Nature obscene,—find themselves obscene.

Leaves of Grass is really the largest single step ever taken in this special line of progress towards sexual purity. Sexual shame as an *inherent* rule or concept in the normal mind, being abolished (as it must eventually be), it does not follow that sexual organs, acts and feelings should be paraded or unveiled. There is no corresponding feeling of shame connected with our feelings towards our own genesis, our fathers and mothers, our children, our most intimate friends, or with our religious feelings, or our deepest feelings towards Nature. ·What is wanted (and must be done) is to abolish the feeling of inherent shame, to make recognized in the hearts of all, the purity, holiness and perfect sanity of the sexual relation in itself, in its normality, and then leave this feeling to take its place with all the other deep and strong emotions.

Next after " Children of Adam," comes the group of poems called " Calamus." As the " Song of Myself " sets before us an exalted moral attitude toward the universe at large, and leads us to realize and acquire (each for him or her self) this higher and happier mode of thought and feeling—as "Children of Adam" does the same service for us towards all things relating to sex, so " Calamus " presents to us an equally advanced moral state in another direction—an exalted friendship, a love into which sex does not enter as an element. The following, on this subject, is from an article entitled " Walt Whitman the Poet of Joy," by Standish O'Grady, in the " Gentleman's Magazine," London, December, 1875 :

Of the new ideas which Whitman has cast as seed into the American brain, the importance which he attaches to friendship is the most remarkable. This appears to have been a subject over which he has brooded long and deeply. It is not possible that Whitman could have written as he has upon this and kindred subjects if he were merely a cultivated brain and nothing more. A thin-blooded, weak-spirited man may, doubtless, like Swedenborg, strike profound truths through sheer force of intellect, or may use violent and swelling language with little dilatation in his spirit; but there is a genuineness and eloquence in Whitman's language concerning friendship which preclude the possibility of the suspicion that he uses strong words for weak feelings. It must not be forgotten that, though now latent, there is in human nature a capacity for friendship of a most absorbing and passionate character. The Greeks were well acquainted with that passion, a passion which in later days ran riot and assumed abnormal forms; for the fruit grows ripe first, then overripe, and then rots. In the days of Homer friendship was an heroic passion. The friendship of Achilles and Patroclus was for many centuries the ideal after which the young Greeks fashioned their character. Nowadays friendship means generally mere consentaneity of opinions and tastes. With the Greeks it was a powerful physical feeling, having physical conditions. Beauty was one of those conditions, as it is now between the sexes. In the dialogues of Plato we see the extraordinary nature of the friendships formed by the young men of his time, the passionate absorbing nature of the relation, the craving for beauty in connection with it, and the approaching degeneracy and threatened degradation of the Athenian character thereby—which Plato vainly sought to stem, both by his own exhortations and by holding up the powerful example of Socrates. There cannot be a doubt but that with highly developed races friendship is a passion, and like all passions more physical than intellectual in its sources and modes of expression.

I will sing the song of companionship ;
I will show what alone must finally compact These ;
I believe These are to found their own ideal of manly love, indicating it in me ;
I will therefore let flame from me the burning fires that were threatening to consume me ;
I will lift what has too long kept down those smouldering fires ;
I will give them complete abandonment ;
I will write the evangel-poem of comrades, and of love ;
For who but I should understand love, with all its sorrow and joy?
And who but I should be the poet of comrades ?

This is strong language, and doubtless genuine. Pride and love, I have said, Whitman considers the two hemispheres of the brain of humanity, and by love he means not alone benevolence and wide sympathy and the passion that embraces sexual relation, but that other passion which has existed before, and whose latent strength the American poet here indicates as a burning and repressed flame. Elsewhere he speaks of the sick, sick dread of unreturned friendship, of the comrade's kiss, the arm round the neck—but he speaks to sticks and stones; the emotion does not exist in us, and the language of his evangel-poems appears simply disgusting.

Yes, "disgusting" to fops and artificial scholars and prim gentlemen of the clubs—but sane, heroic, full-blooded, natural men will find in it the deepest God-implanted voices of their hearts.

The next poem is called "Salut au Monde," and is, as its name implies, a salutation to the whole of the rest of the world, sent in America's name. It begins in a low key, broad and calm, but becomes more and more impassioned as it proceeds, until towards its close the intensity of the feeling expressed becomes almost painful.

The "Song of the Open Road," which follows next in order, is one of the supremely great poems of *Leaves of Grass*. It is a mystic and indirect chant of aspiration toward a noble life, a vehement demand to reach the very highest point that the human soul is capable of attaining—to join the "great companions," "the swift and majestic men, the greatest women," who have from age to age shown what human life might be. This is a religious poem in the truest and best sense of the term. Not the imitative sense in which "Paradise Regained," "The Course of Time," or "Yesterday, To-day and Forever," are religious poems; they go back to other poems, other books, and depend on them for their meaning. But this and the other chants of *Leaves of Grass* go back to Nature and the soul of man, and derive thence their meaning.

But it is unnecessary and would take too much space to review the whole book in detail, and to show, as might be shown, how the whole poem (for *Leaves of Grass* is really *one* poem) has for its purpose simply to carry exalted morality into all the affairs and relations of life—to exhibit it, for instance, in "Salut au Monde" and "Faces," as toward the lower races and classes of mankind; in "Memories of President Lincoln," "To Think of Time," and many other poems, as toward death; in "So Long" and "Years of the Modern," as toward the future generally; in "To You," and numerous other pieces, as toward average humanity; in "Our Old Feuillage," as toward the United States of to-day, and in the "Song of the Broadaxe," as toward the special future of America. In the third (1860) edition, the last-named poem contained the following lines, which have been left out of later issues, I suppose as being too fully and frankly personal, but for that very reason they shall have a place here. They form a life-picture that might be readily recognized in New York City or Brooklyn, on the East River there, or Broadway, by those who can carry their reminiscences back twenty-five or thirty years:

His shape arises,
Arrogant, masculine, naïve, rowdyish,
Laugher, weeper, worker, idler, citizen, countryman,
Saunterer of woods, stander upon hills, summer swimmer in rivers or by the
    sea,
Of pure American breed, of reckless health, his body perfect, free from taint
    from top to toe, free forever from headache and dyspepsia, clean-
    breathed,

Ample-limbed, a good feeder, weight a hundred and eighty pounds, full
  blooded, six feet high, forty inches round the breast and back,
Countenance sunburnt, bearded, calm, unrefined,
Reminder of animals, meeter of savage and gentleman on equal terms,
Attitudes lithe and erect, costume free, neck gray and open, of slow move-
  ment on foot,
Passer of his right arm round the shoulders of his friends, companion of the
  street,
Persuader always of people to give him their sweetest touches, and never their
  meanest,
A Manhattanese bred, fond of Brooklyn, fond of Broadway, fond of the life
  of the wharves and the great ferries,
Enterer everywhere, welcomed everywhere, easily understood after all,
Never offering others, always offering himself, corroborating his phrenology,
Voluptuous, inhabitive, combative, conscientious, alimentive, intuitive, of
  copious friendship, sublimity, firmness, self-esteem, comparison, indi-
  viduality, form, locality, eventuality,
Avowing by life, manners, works, to contribute illustrations of results of The
  States,
Teacher of the unquenchable creed, namely, egotism,
Inviter of others continually henceforth to try their strength against his.

The poem entitled "The Answerer" is a description of the full
poet (Walt Whitman or any other). The term is given a higher
meaning here than it usually bears. The class of men usually
called poets are here called "singers," and the word *Poet* is used
for another, a smaller and far higher order of man. Of that
higher order "The Answerer" says:

Him all wait for, him all yield up to, his word is decisive and final,
Him they accept, in him lave, in him perceive themselves as amid light,
Him they immerse, and he immerses them.

The singers do not beget, only the Poet begets,
The singers are welcom'd, understood, appear often enough—but rare has the
  day been, likewise the spot, of the birth of the maker of poems, the
  Answerer,
(Not every century nor every five centuries has contain'd such a day, for all
  its names.)

Before "The Answerer" can be appreciated, it is essential that
Leaves of Grass as a whole should be pretty thoroughly absorbed,
and the true rank of its author realized.

Passing now over a large number of poems, many of them as great as any in the volume, we come to a group which has a special celebrity, namely, "Drum-Taps." These, with the exception of a few, are short pieces, and to my mind not by any means equal to those which, in date of composition, preceded them. The fire that burned in "Song of Myself," "Children of Adam," "Calamus," "The Song of the Open Road," "Salut au Monde," "Faces," "Songs before Parting," and some other pieces, with such almost unbearable heat and radiance, was beginning to die out. They are, it is true, the most beautiful poems Walt Whitman has written. They to-day, and probably for many years (perhaps always), will have more readers and admirers than any other portion of his works, but they would never (not a thousand such poems) alter materially for the better a human life. They help the others, and are important, perhaps essential, as taking their place with the rest. They are warmed by the divine fire,* but not capable alone of kindling that fire in another human soul. Many clever critics (like Th. Bentzon, the reviewer of *Leaves of Grass* in the "Revue des deux Mondes") admire "Drum-Taps" immensely, while they find the "Song of Myself" "nonsense." According to such reviewers Walt Whitman was, when he wrote these pieces, at the end of his apprenticeship, and beginning to write good verses! He was certainly progressing, but in what sense? A few more steps of the same length in the same direction, towards beauty of execution with loss of strength —towards fulness of expression with loss of suggestion—towards greater polish and facility of pleasing with loss of power of arousing and vivifying—and Walt Whitman would be upon the plane of the "great poets" of the Nineteenth century. But, thank God, he can never take those steps. He is safe from this fate. The day will come when he will be popular, but it will be when men grow up to him, not when he comes down to them. In "Drum-Taps" Walt Whitman's genius has "not yet lost all its original brightness, nor appears less than Archangel ruined."

---

* The London "Nineteenth Century" (December, 1882) says of "Drum-Taps," "It contains some of the most magnificent and spirit-stirring trumpet-blasts, as well as some of the most deeply moving aspects of suffering and death, ever expressed by poet."

It is still divine, still immeasurably above (not by degree merely, but by kind) that of every other poet of the present time, but it is not the genius that poured out the fiery torrent of the earlier poems. Had we never known those, we might think that words could not convey greater passion than they are made to bear in some of " Drum-Taps ; " but now we know better. And it is not only in amount but also in kind of passion that " Drum-Taps " fall short. The splendid faith of the earlier poems is not extinct, indeed, in these, but it is greatly dimmed. On the other hand, love and sympathy are as strongly expressed here as anywhere else in *Leaves of Grass.* I have been told by a person who knew the poet well, and who was living in Washington when " Drum-Taps " were being composed, that he has seen Walt Whitman at this time turn aside into a doorway or other out-of-the-way place on the street, and take out his note-book to write some lines of these poems, and while he was so doing he has seen the tears run down his cheeks. I can well believe this, for there are poems in " Drum-Taps " that can scarcely be read aloud after their full meaning has once been felt. But the tears shed by Walt Whitman in writing these poems, while they indicate to us clearly the passionate sympathy which dictated them, show also a loss of personal force (*i. e.* faith) in the man who some years before wrote " Children of Adam " and " Calamus " without flinching.

From " Drum-Taps " to the end of the volume (1882 edition) there are one hundred and twenty pages of poetry, most of it belonging to the first order of excellence, a good deal of it written in what may be called the " Song of Myself " period. " By Blue Ontario's Shore," for instance, was nearly all published in the 1855 edition, but at that time in the shape of a prose preface. The " Sleepers " was also published in that edition, and ranks among the very great poems. It is a representation of the mind during sleep—of connected, half-connected, and disconnected thoughts and feelings as they occur in dreams, some commonplace, some weird, some voluptuous, and all given with the true and strange emotional accompaniments that belong to them. Sometimes (and these are the most astonishing parts of the poem) the vague emotions, without thought, that occasionally arise in sleep, are given as they actually occur, apart from any idea—the words having in the intellectual sense no meaning, but arousing, as music does, the state of feeling intended. It is a poem that with most people requires a great deal of study to make anything of it, but to certain minds it would, no doubt, be plain at once.

The next group, called " Whispers of Heavenly Death,'' contains some exquisite poems on that subject, of which the following is perhaps a fair sample:

I need no assurances, I am a man who is preoccupied of his own soul;
I do not doubt that from under the feet and beside the hands and face I am
    cognizant of, are now looking faces I am not cognizant of—calm and
    actual faces,
I do not doubt but the majesty and beauty of the world are latent in any iota
    of the world,
I do not doubt I am limitless, and that the universes are limitless—in vain I
    try to think how limitless,
I do not doubt that the orbs and the systems of orbs play their swift sports
    through the air on purpose, and that I shall one day be eligible to do
    as much as they, and more than they,
I do not doubt that temporary affairs keep on and on millions of years,
I do not doubt interiors have their interiors, and exteriors have their exteriors,
    and that the eyesight has another eyesight, and the hearing another
    hearing, and the voice another voice,
I do not doubt that the passionately-wept deaths of young men are provided
    for, and that the deaths of young women and the deaths of little chil-
    dren are provided for,
(Did you think Life was so well provided for, and Death, the purport of all
    Life, is not well provided for?)
I do not doubt that wrecks at sea, no matter what the horrors of them, no
    matter whose wife, child, husband, father, lover, has gone down, are
    provided for, to the minutest points,
I do not doubt that whatever can possibly happen anywhere at any time, is
    provided for in the inherences of things,
I do not think Life provides for all, and for Time and Space, but I believe
    Heavenly Death provides for all.

How a man who spent his whole life writing just such poems as that (and what is better, *living* them) can be considered by a vast majority of the community an irreligious person is one of those terrible mysteries which may be explained a hundred times, but remains incomprehensible at last. Or consider the " Prayer of Columbus " (really, under a thin disguise, the prayer of Walt Whitman)—the deep below deep of meaning and feeling in those passionate, most religious lines:

> O, I am sure they really came from Thee,
> The urge, the ardor, the unconquerable will,
> The potent, felt, interior command, stronger than words,
> A message from the heavens whispering to me, even in sleep;
> These sped me on.
>
> One effort more, my altar this bleak sand:
> That Thou, O God, my life hast lighted
> With ray of light, steady, ineffable, vouchsafed of Thee,
> Light rare, untellable, lighting the very light,
> Beyond all signs, descriptions, languages;
> For that, O God, be it my latest word, here on my knees,
> Old, poor and paralyzed, I thank Thee.
>
> My terminus near,
> The clouds already closing in upon me,
> The voyage balked, the course disputed, lost,
> I yield my ships to Thee.
>
> My hands, my limbs grow nerveless,
> My brain feels rack'd, bewilder'd;
> Let the old timbers part, I will not part,
> I will cling fast to Thee, O God, though the waves buffet me,
> Thee, Thee at least I know.

How is it possible for any one to look into the heart here thrown open, and not recognize what kind of man it belongs to ?

The volume concludes with " So Long," a sublime farewell, of which the following is the last part:

> My songs cease, I abandon them,
> From behind the screen where I hid I advance personally solely to you.
>
> Camerado, this is no book,
> Who touches this touches a man,
> (Is it night? are we here together alone?)
> It is I you hold and who holds you,
> I spring from the pages into your arms—decease calls me forth.

O how your fingers drowse me,
Your breath falls around me like dew, your pulse lulls the tympans of my ears,
I feel immerged from head to foot,
Delicious, enough.

Enough O deed impromptu and secret,
Enough O gliding present—enough O summ'd-up past.

Dear friend whoever you are take this kiss,
I give it especially to you, do not forget me,
I feel like one who has done work for the day to retire awhile,
I receive now again of my many translations, from my avataras ascend-
    ing, while others doubtless await me,
An unknown sphere more real than I dream'd, more direct, darts awak-
    ening rays about me, *So long!*
Remember my words, I may again return,
I love you, I depart from materials,
I am as one disembodied, triumphant, dead.

CHAPTER III.

ANALYSIS OF POEMS, CONTINUED.

I HAVE now reviewed briefly from my point of view the book in which Walt Whitman has, as far as such a thing is possible, embodied himself. It remains to state as well as I can the inner and more specific significance of the poems. After their unquestionable birthmarks, so different from European models or from any copied or foreign type whatever,* the first thing to be noticed about *Leaves of Grass* (this is what strikes nearly every one immediately upon trying to read it) is the difficulty to the ordinary, even intelligent reader, of understanding it. On this point my own experience has been as follows. About eighteen years ago, I began to read it. For many months I could see absolutely nothing in the book, and at times I was strongly inclined to believe that there was nothing in it to see. But I could not let it alone; although one day I would throw it down in a sort of rage at its want of meaning, the next day or the day after I would take it up again with just as lively an interest as ever, persuaded

---

* The London " Times " (June, 1878), in an article on the death of William Cullen Bryant, takes for its main theme this excessive imitativeness of American poets, and their entire want of special nativity, adding, " Unless Walt Whitman is to be reckoned among the poets, American verse, from its earliest to its latest stages, seems an exotic, with an exuberance of gorgeous blossom, but no principle of reproduction."

The same English journal (March 25, 1882), in an editorial on the death of Longfellow, continues in a similar strain, "We are not forgetting his ' Hiawatha' when we say that he might have written his best poems with as much local fitness in our own Cambridge as in its namesake across the Atlantic;" and sulkily adds : " We are told that in Walt Whitman's rough, barbaric, untuned lines, full of questionable morality, and unfettered by rhyme, is the nucleus of the literature of the future. That may be so, and the *Leaves of Grass* may prove, as is predicted, the foundation of a real American literature, which will mirror the peculiarities of the life of that continent, and which will attempt to present no false ideal. Yet we shall be surprised if the new school, with its dead set towards ugliness and its morbid turn for the bad sides of nature, will draw people wholly away from the stainless pages, rich in garnered wealth, fancy and allusions, and the sunny pictures, which are to be found in the books of the poet who has just died."

that there was something there, and determined to find out what that might be. At first as I read, it seemed to me the writer was always on the point of saying something which he never actually said. Page after page seemed equally barren of any definite statement. Then after a time I found that a few lines here and there were full of suggestion and beauty. Gradually these bright spots, as I may call them, grew larger, more numerous and more brilliant, until at last the whole surface was lit up with an almost unearthly splendor.

And still I am well aware that I do not yet fully understand this book. Neither do I expect ever to understand it entirely, though I learn something more about it almost every day, and shall probably go on reading it as long as I live. I doubt whether I fully understand any part of it. For the more it is studied the more profound it is seen to be, stretching out vista beyond vista apparently interminably. Now it may seem strange that any person should go on reading a book he could not understand, and, consequently, could in the ordinary way take no interest. The explanation is that there is the same peculiar magnetism about *Leaves of Grass* as about Walt Whitman himself, so that people who once really begin to read it and get into the range of its attraction, must go on reading it whether they comprehend it or not, or until they do comprehend it. As Walt Whitman says:

> I teach straying from me, yet who can stray from me?
> I follow you whoever you are from the present hour,
> My words itch at your ears till you understand them.

But after all, granting that this is true, is it worth while to read any book for years on the mere chance of understanding it at last? Certainly it would not be worth while with many books, but I will answer for it that no one who reads *Leaves of Grass* so as to understand it at all will ever repent the time and pains. For this is not a book that merely amuses or instructs. It does neither of these in the ordinary sense, but it does far more than amuse or instruct. It is capable of making whoever wishes to be so, wiser, happier, better; and it does these not by acting on the intellect, by telling us what is best for us, what we ought to do and avoid doing, and the like, but by acting directly on the moral nature itself, and elevating and purifying that. Why is this book so hard to understand? In the first place it is worth while to notice that the author of *Leaves of Grass* was himself well aware of this difficulty, as he says in the two following and in many other places

But these leaves conning you con at peril,
For these leaves and me you will not understand,
They will elude you at first, and still more afterward, I will certainly elude you,
Even while you should think you had unquestionably caught me, behold !
Already you see I have escaped from you.

Then in the lines " To a Certain Civilian :'

Did you ask dulcet rhymes from me?
Did you seek the civilian's peaceful and languishing rhymes?
Did you find what I sang erewhile so hard to follow?
Why I was not singing erewhile for you to follow, to understand—nor am I now;
(I have been born of the same as the war was born,
The drum-corps' rattle is ever to me sweet music—I love well the martial dirge,
With slow wail and convulsive throb leading the officer's funeral;)
What to such as you anyhow such a poet as I? therefore leave my works,
And go lull yourself with what you can understand, and with piano-tunes,
For I lull nobody, and you will never understand me.

Are we to conclude that Walt Whitman wished and intended his writings to be difficult of comprehension? I do not think so at all. I think he would gladly have every one comprehend him at once if possible. Must we suppose then that he had not the ability to so write as to make himself easily intelligible? that in fact he is deficient in the faculty of clear expression? On the contrary I should say that Walt Whitman is a supreme master of the art of expression. In a case like this there is some one else besides the poet who may be to blame, and perhaps the fault may lie with—the reader. Must we say then that ordinary men, or even able men (for many of these have tried to read *Leaves*

of Grass and failed), have not sufficient intelligence to comprehend the book ?   No, I neither say nor believe this.

The fact is, in the ordinary sense, there is nothing to understand about *Leaves of Grass* which any person of average intelligence could not comprehend with the greatest ease.   The secret
of the difficulty is, that the work, different from every popular
book of poetry known, appeals almost entirely to the moral
nature, and hardly at all to the intellect—that to understand it
means putting oneself in emotional, and not simply mental relation with its author—means to thoroughly realize Walt Whitman
—to be in sympathy with the heart and mind of perhaps the
most advanced nature the world has yet produced.   This, of
course, is neither simple nor easy.   *Leaves of Grass* is a picture
of the world as seen from the standpoint of the highest moral
elevation yet reached.   It is at the same time an exposition of
this highest moral nature itself.   The real difficulty is for an
ordinary person to rise to this spiritual altitude.   Whoever can
do so, even momentarily, or in imagination, will never cease to
thank the man by whose aid this was accomplished.   It is such
assistance which Walt Whitman is destined to give to large
sections of the human race, and doubtless it is this which he
refers to in the following passages :

I am he bringing help for the sick as they pant on their backs,
And for strong upright men I bring yet more needed help.

Behold, I do not give lectures or a little charity,
When I give I give myself.

I bring what you much need yet always have,
Not money, amours, dress, eating, erudition, but as good,
I send no agent or medium, offer no representative of value, but offer the value
   itself.

For I myself am not one who bestows nothing upon man and woman,
For I bestow upon any man or woman the entrance to all the gifts of the universe.

Now, in the mouth of any man known to history, with very few
exceptions, these claims would be ludicrous.   They would not,
however, have been ludicrous if we suppose them made by such

men as Siddhartha Guatama, Confucius, Zoroaster, or Moham-
med, for these men did as far as it was possible in their times and
lands what Walt Whitman in these verses promises to do now,—
that is, they bestowed their own higher natures upon all who
came under their influence, gave them the help they most needed,
and opened to them (the best gift of all) the way to a higher
spiritual life. They made such claims, and fulfilled them. Walt
Whitman too makes them. Can he fulfil them? I say he has
done so, and that he will do so throughout the future.

But let us examine this question and these claims a little more
in detail, and see what they really mean. Whoever will consider
them will see that they all amount essentially to the same thing,
which is a promise on Walt Whitman's part to bestow upon any
person who asks it, and who will put his or her mind in full relation with the poems, moral elevation. In other words, he will
give to such person a greater amount of faith, a greater power
of affection, and will consequently reduce in that person the lia-
bility to, and the capacity of, fear and hate. Now, love and faith
are the elements of which happiness is composed, and hate and
fear (their opposites) are the elements of which unhappiness is
composed. If, therefore, Walt Whitman can produce in us moral
elevation, he will increase our true happiness, and this, to my
mind, is the most valuable of all the "gifts of the universe," so
far, at all events, as we know at present. Again: modern
science has made it capable of proof that this universe is so
constructed as to justify on our part love and faith, and not
hate and fear. For this reason, the man who has in his composition the most love and faith, and the least hate and fear,
will stand (other things being equal) in the closest relation to
universal truth,—that is, he will be the wisest man. If, then,
Walt Whitman gives us moral elevation, he will also give wisdom,
which, it seems to me, is clearly another of the chief "gifts of
the universe." Yet once more: conduct flows from moral nature.
The man with a low moral nature who is full of hate and fear,
and the compounds of these, such as envy and jealousy, cannot
possibly live a beneficent and happy life. On the other hand,

it is inconceivable that the man who is full of love and faith should, on the whole, live a bad life. So that moral elevation, besides giving us happiness and wisdom, gives us also the power and inclination to lead good lives; and this, I should say, is another "gift of the universe" really worth having, in contradistinction to mere wealth, education, social position, or fame, which the current standards make the main objects of existence.

Let us not forget that of all mental qualities, exceptional moral elevation is the hardest to see. So true is this, that in the whole history of our race, as far back as it is known, every man, without one exception, who has stood prominently in advance of and above his age by this quality, has not only not been considered exceptionally good, but has been in every instance looked upon by the majority of his contemporaries as a bad man, and has been consequently traduced, banished, burned, poisoned, or crucified.

In philosophy, science, art, religion, men's views, their ways of looking at things, are constantly altering. And it is equally plain that on the whole they are altering for the better—are constantly acquiring a more just and worthy mental attitude towards their surroundings, towards each other, and towards Nature. This progress necessitates the constant abandonment of old ideas, and the constant taking up of new intellectual and moral positions. These successive readjustments are always the cause of more or less social, political, and literary disturbance. The antagonism is naturally deeper and stronger in the case of religious and social changes than new departures in science, philosophy, or art, since in religious tenets the feelings are more deeply involved. The men who initiate such readjustments of the soul of man to its environment are the master minds of the race. These are the men Walt Whitman calls Poets. He says: "The true Poet is not the follower of beauty, but the august master of beauty." That is to say, he does not take merely the matter recognized as beautiful already and make it the theme of his verse, or amuse himself and his readers by dressing it up and admiring and praising it. This, in the language of *Leaves of Grass*, is the office of a "singer," not of a "Poet;" to do this is to be a follower of beauty. But the Poet is the master of beauty, and his mastery consists in commanding and causing things which were not before considered beautiful to become so. How does he do this? Before this question can be answered we must understand why one thing is beautiful to us and another not—why persons, combinations, etc., that are beautiful to one are often not so to another—and why one man sees so much beauty in the world, another so little. The explanation is, that beauty and love are correlatives; they are the objective and subjective aspects of the same thing. Beauty has no existence apart from love, and love has no existence apart from beauty. Beauty is the shadow of love thrown upon the outer world. We do not love a person or thing because the person or thing is beautiful, but whatever we love, that is beautiful to us, and whatever we do not love, is not beautiful. And the function of the true Poet is to love and appreciate all things, nationalities, laws, combinations, individuals. He alone illustrates the sublime reality and ideality of that verse of Genesis, how God after His entire creation looked forth, "and pronounced it *all* good." A parallel statement would be true of Faith. As that which is seen from without inwards is love, and seen from within outwards is beauty, so that which seen from without inwards is faith, is goodness when seen from within outwards.

The human race began by fearing or distrusting nearly everything, and trusting almost nothing; and this is yet the condition of savages. But from time to time, men arose who distrusted and feared less and less. These men have always been considered impious by those about them; but for all that, they have been the saviors and progressists of the race, and have been recognized as such when their views and feelings penetrated the generations succeeding them. Such evolution has always been going on, and will continue. So far, fear has been a part of every accepted religion, and it is still taught that to destroy fear is to destroy religion. But if faith is to increase, fear, its opposite, must continually decrease and at last disappear. Fear is the basis of superstition. Faith, its opposite, along with love, is the basis of religion.   I know it is still said by some to-day in the name of religion, that men should hate this and that—sin for instance, and the devil, and that they should fear certain things, such as God and the Judgment.   But this really is irreligion, not religion.

An important feature of *Leaves of Grass* is what I would call its continuity or endlessness.   It does not teach something, and rest there.   It does not make, in morals and religion, an important step in advance, and stop satisfied with that.   It has unlimited vista.   It clears the way ahead, with allowance and provision for new advances far, far beyond anything contained in itself.   It brings no one to "a terminus," nor teaches any one to be "content and full."   It is a ceaseless goad, a never-resting spur.   To those to whom it speaks, it cries continually, forward ! forward ! and admits of no pause in the race.   A second trait is its universality.   There is nothing of which humanity has experience that it does not touch upon more or less directly.   There must have been a deliberate intention on the part of the author to give the book this all-embracing character, and no doubt that was one reason for the catalogues of objects in a few of the poems which have so irritated the critics.   I have often tried to think of something objective or subjective, material or immaterial, that was not taken cognizance of by *Leaves of Grass,* but always failed. A third feature is the manner in which the author avoids (either of set purpose, or more likely by a sure instinct) dealing specifically with any topics of mere class or ephemeral interest (though he really treats these too through the bases upon which they rest), and concerns himself solely with the elementary subjects of human life, which must necessarily have perennial interest.

Leaves of Grass is curiously a different book to each reader. To some, its merit consists in the keen thought which pierces to the kernel of things—or a perpetual and sunny cheeriness, in which respect it is the synonyme of pure air and health; to others it is chiefly valuable as being full of pictorial suggestions; to a third class of men it is a new Gospel containing fresh revelations of divine truth; to a fourth it is charged with ideas and suggestions in practical life and manners; to some its large, sweet, clear, animal physiology is its especial charm; to some, the strange abysses of its fervid emotions.* Upon still others (on whom it produces its full effect), it exerts an irresistible and divine power, strengthening and elevating their lives unspeakably, driving them from all meanness and toward all good, giving them no rest, but compelling them to watch every act, word, thought, feeling—to guard their days and nights from weakness, baseness, littleness, or impurity—at the same time giving them extraordinary power to accomplish these ends.

There is still another class (altogether the most numerous so far), who see in the book nothing of all these fine things or good uses. To them it suggests contempt for laws and social forms, appears coarse, prosaic, senseless, full of impure ideas, and as seeking the destruction of religion, and all that is decent in human life. If men were really, as theologians tell us, inclined by Nature to evil, I could imagine *Leaves of Grass* might on the whole do some serious harm. But since, as I think is certainly the case, (for who would not rather be healthy than sick? loved than hated? happy than wretched?) humanity on the whole is far more disposed to good than evil, there is no question that whatever stimulates and encourages the native growth and independent vigor of the mind, as it does, must in the final result be beneficial.

Leaves of Grass belongs to a religious era not yet reached, of which it is the revealer and herald. Toward that higher social and moral level the race was inevitably tending—and thither, even without such an avant-courier, it would still eventually have reached. This book, however, will be of incalculable assistance in the ascent. As John Burroughs has suggested, it may have to wait to be authoritatively assigned to literature's

---

* The London "Nineteenth Century" (December, 1882), in the course of an article on Walt Whitman, says, " He has a power of passionate expression, of strong and simple utterance of the deepest tones of grief, which is almost or altogether without its counterpart in the world."

highest rank, first by the lawgivers of the Old World, before America really acknowledges her own offspring in Walt Whitman's work.* With the incoming moral state to which it belongs, certain cherished social and religious forms and usages are incompatible; hence the deep instinctive aversion and dread with which it is regarded by the ultra-conventional and conservative. Just so, in their far-back times, was Zoroastrianism, Buddhism, Mohammedanism, Christianity, and every new birth received. Our whole theory of property, of individual ownership (for example) is by implication condemned by the spirit of the book, and when its level is reached, our present ideas and practice in this department will seem as backward and outré as the ownership and transfer of one man by another seems to us now. So also our church-going, bible-reading, creeds, and prayers, will appear from its vantage-ground mere make-believes of religion, hollow shells whose kernels have long since imperceptibly mouldered into dust. So does one birth of Time succeed another. So is it still as ever true that the gods are devoured by their own children—that what the deepest and holiest heart-throbs of the race have brought into being, is again successively overwhelmed and destroyed by the legitimate offspring of those same spiritual impulses.

Every marked rise in the moral nature, when it has become diffused over broad sections of the race, necessitates and inspires as its accompaniment, new manners, new social forms, new politics, new philosophies, new literatures, and above all, new religious forms. For moral elevation is the mainspring of all these, and of the world's progress—the rising tide upon which float all the fleets and argosies, as well as all the driftwood and foam,

---

* The London "Nineteenth Century" of December, 1882, already alluded to, says : "The mass of his countrymen were not and are not strong enough to accept him. They have perhaps too little confidence in their own literary originality to appreciate duly one from among themselves who breaks through all the conventional usages of literature; they have too much squeamish delicacy to admit to their society one who is so brutally outspoken and unrefined. It is necessary perhaps that this writer, for we need not be zealous to claim for him the title of poet, should be first accepted in the Old World before he can be recognized by the New, which at present can see nothing in literature but by reflected light. Strange irony of fate, if such should be the destiny of one who cast off the conventional forms, in order to free himself and his country from Old-World influences!"

the ascending sap which vitalizes all the fruit of human life. *Leaves of Grass* is the initiative of such a rise, the preface and creator of a new era. This old world has seen many such new departures, and is to see many more before it is done. They have always been begun by one man, embodying what suspends in nebulous forms through the humanity of the time, and from him have spread more or less over the earth's surface. And for their basis these movements have had invariably, since the invention of writing, and in some instances before that time, *a book*, to embody themselves and radiate from. *Leaves of Grass* is such a book. What the Vedas were to Brahmanism, the Law and the Prophets to Judaism, the Avesta and Zend to Zoroastrianism, the Kings to Confucianism and Taoism, the Pitakas to Buddhism, the Gospels and Pauline writings to Christianity, the Quràn to Mohammedanism, will *Leaves of Grass* be to the future of American civilization. Those were all Gospels; they all brought good news to man, fitting his case at the period, each in its way and degree. They were all " hard sayings " and the rankest heresy at first, just as *Leaves of Grass* is now. By and by it too will be received, and in the course of a few hundred years, more or less, do its work and become commonplace like the rest. Then new Gospels will be written upon a still higher plane.

In the mean time, *Leaves of Grass* is the bible of Democracy, containing the highest exemplar of life yet furnished, and suited to the present age and to America. Within it is folded (as the oak in the acorn, or the man in the new-born babe) a new spiritual life for myriads of men and women.

Very few people have any conception what such books are to those who first receive them—what enthusiasm and devotion they inspire—what reckless abandonment to the new feeling of spiritual exaltation they kindle—how they absorb all life, and make the old worldly interests poor and contemptible—how they light up new joys, and end by placing existence on a higher plane. As few to-day realize this, though they have heard and read of it all their lives, so no one, except those who have felt it, can realize what *Leaves of Grass* is to the first men and women who experience its power.

16

Then from a merely literary, technical, pictorial point of view,
where else are so depicted in living words the complex storms of
action in the midst of which we of the Nineteenth century live
—the trains on the railways, the steam and sail ships and their
cargoes, the myriads of factories, the interminable stretches of
cultivated land, the towns and villages, with thousands of throb-
bing lives—curious flashes of the life of wildest Nature (as in
"The Man-of-war Bird "*)—the geography of the globe, the
diverse races, circumstances, employments—fraternal love and
fratricidal strife—the arming for the war, 1861-65, the fields of
battle, victory, defeat, the heaped burial trenches, the hospitals
filled with mangled and maimed, the final disbandment of the
soldiers—the scenery of a Continent, its rivers, lakes, bays, prairies, mountains, forests, the crags and ravines of Colorado and
California, the vast fertile spread of the Prairie States, the snows
and wildernesses of the North, the warm bayous and lagoons of
the South, the great cities to the East—all the shows of the sea,
of the sky, of the seasons—sexual passions, religious mystery, the
records of the past, the facts of the present, the hopes of the
future—the splendors of life, the equal splendors of death—all
the speculations and imaginations of man, all the thoughts of his
composite mind, all the visions of his dreaming soul, all the beats
of his great heart, all the works of his giant hands—the seething
crowds, the passionate longings of men and women everywhere,
their fervor and their ceaseless striving, their intense egoism and
equally intense sympathy, the attractions and repulsions that sway
them from moment to moment, the contradictory forces that
dwell in every soul, the passion and energy of the globe.   For
all these—not in polished literary descriptions, but with their
own life and heat and action—make up *Leaves of Grass.*   Its
themes and treatment, so august, so complex (yet uniform), so
tremendous, how curious it is to see the book sneered at for
"want of form."   Criticism of it from such point of view were

---

* There is a bit of literary history about this piece. It was sent to the American magazines—first to " Scribner's," by whom it was returned with a contemptuous note from the
principal editor. Then to, and rejected by, one after another of nearly all the principal
monthlies. Then to London to the " Athenæum," promptly accepted, paid for, and published.

a senseless waste of time. Its form will be unprecedently beautiful to all who know its spirit, and to those who do not, it is a matter of no consequence. The function of first-class works is not to follow forms already instituted, but to institute new forms. "He who would achieve the greatest production of art," said Voltaire, "must be the pupil of his own genius." The language in which a book is written will never finally save or condemn it ; only the soul of the book counts, nothing else is of any lasting consequence. The three first Gospels were chiefly written by quite illiterate people, and they have no pretensions at all to "style." St. Paul's epistles were written in very bad Greek, and had perhaps still less pretension to mere literary excellence. But in those books lived and through them shone the Soul of a Divine Man. How many hundred tons of classically correct poems, essays, speeches, letters, and dramas have they outlived ! and how many will they still outlive ! Walt Whitman will endure, not as having reached or conformed to any existing standard, but as having set one up.

Other first-class poets possess a mental scope and grandeur that dwarf ordinary humanity, and intimate existences higher than those of earth. They excite in us admiration and wonder, give us glimpses of celestial beauty and joy, but leave us intrinsically as we were—or perhaps fill us with pain at our own inherent littleness. While no reader of *Leaves of Grass* (once entering their meaning and influence) fails to absorb every piece, every page, every line, as intensely *his*—how strangely different, in their effect, the hitherto accepted poems ! We revel amid the beauty, fulness, majesty and art, of the plots and personages of the "Iliad," "Odyssey," or "Æneid," or in Shakespeare's immortal plays, or Spenser or Milton, or "La Légendes des Siècles," or Goethe's masterpieces, or Tennyson's "Idyls." With them the reader passes his time as in sumptuous dreams or feasts, far from this miserable every-day world, man's actual and vulgar experience, one's own sphere. He enjoys those incomparable works like some sweet, and deep, and beautiful intoxication. But a mortifying and meagre consciousness invariably follows. Not for *him* the stage where Achilles and

Coriolanus and Lancelot so grandly tread. He himself dwindles to a mere nothing in comparison with such exceptional types of humanity. However splendid the pageant and the shows of the march, a latent humiliation brings up the rear. Was it not time one should arise to show that a few selected warriors and heroes of the past, even the gods, have not monopolized and devoured (nay, have hardly entered into) the grandeur of the universe, or of life and action, or of poems? arise to "shake out," for common readers, farmers, mechanics, laborers, "carols stronger and haughtier than have ever yet been heard upon the earth"? Well did Thoreau, after reading and visiting Walt Whitman, hit the centre of the matter by exclaiming "*He is Democracy.*" For what possible service in that department so great as to practically demonstrate to each of the countless mass of common lives that its scope and sphere are as divine, as heroic, as illuminated, as "eligible," as any? As pure air, wholesome food, clear water, sunshine, pass into and become the life of the body, so do these *Leaves* interpenetrate and nourish the soul that is fitted to receive them. The others stand outside our identity; this poet comes within, and interfuses and incorporates his life with each of us. We share his health, strength, savage freedom, fierce self-assertion, fearlessness, tamelessness. We take part in his large, rugged humanity, his tender love and steadfast faith. The others are for hours of clearness and calm. He suits equally well (perhaps better) with worry, hard work, illness, and affliction. Every-day lives, common employments, become illustrious. For you, "whoever you are," the past has been, the present exists, and the future will exist.

A word, (I ought to have given it farther back) as to the curious *catalogue character,* so hesitatingly dwelt on by not a few—even by Emerson. The latter wrote to Carlyle, sending him an early *Leaves of Grass*, in 1856: "If, on reading, you think its pages the catalogue of an auctioneer, you can light your pipe with them." The book is doubtless open to a charge of the kind. Only it is as if the primary Creator were the "auctioneer," and the spirit in which the lists are made out is the *motif* of all vitality, all form. Or, a new Adam, in a modern and more complex Paradise, here gives names to everything—to mechanics' trades, tools—to our own days, and their commonest objects.

In still hours, reading the biblic poems of the ages, and entirely possessed with them, flits through the brain the phantom thought that in the impalpable atmosphere of those poems' expression and endeavor, man's ultimata are involved; and all the rest, however multitudinous, is only preparation and accessory.

I have been so occupied with the features portrayed through the preceding pages that I have said nothing on a point, or series, partly personal, by no means least in giving character to Walt Whitman and his works. His position in the history of his country is a peculiar one. Receiving the traditions of Washington from men who had seen and talked with that great chieftain —of the old Revolutionary War from those who had been part of it—as a little boy, held in the arms of Lafayette, and his childish lips warmly pressed with a kiss from the French warrior —his youth passed amid the scenes and reminiscences of the gloomy Battle of Brooklyn—the direct memories of that whole contest, of the adoption of the American Constitution, of the close of the last century, and of Jefferson, Adams, Paine, and Hamilton, saturating, as it were, his early years—he brings on and connects that receding time with the Civil War of 1861-'65 —with the persons and events of our own age—with Lincoln, Grant, Sherman, Lee, the Emancipation Proclamation, the fights around Richmond, and the surrender at Appomattox. Then, the Secession War over, he merges it, or at least the spirit of it, in oblivion. The brotherhood of the States re-united, now indissolubly, he chants a tender and equal sorrow for the Southern as for the Northern dead—in one of his last utterances passionately invoking the Muse, through himself, in their behalf:

Give me exhaustless, make me a fountain,
That I exhale love from me wherever I go, like a moist perennial dew,
For the ashes of all dead soldiers South or North.

Until a long period elapses few will know what the pages of *Leaves of Grass* bestow on America. Granting all its unprecedented thrift and material power, the question arises to serious inquiry, Is the New World Republic actually a success on any but lower grounds? Is there not, to its heart-action and blood-circulation to-day, a profound danger, a pervading lack of something to be supplied, without which its richest and amplest fruits will continually turn to ashes? It is in response to such inquiry, and supply to such deficiency (or rather to suggest the means of every man supplying it within himself, and as part of himself) I consider Walt Whitman's life and poems unspeakably important.

APPENDIX

TO PART II.

CONTEMPORANEOUS NOTICES

1855 TO 1883.

SELECTIONS FROM CONTEMPORANEOUS CRITICISMS, LETTERS, NEWSPAPER NOTICES, ETC., AMERICAN AND FOREIGN.

To recover what was distinctively said of any important past event or person, at the time of his or its advent—what the wise ones had to predict —would it not indeed afford lessons of the deepest, sometimes of an unquestionably comic, significance? Judgments formed of men by their contemporaries have also a certain interest apart from their individual truth or falsity; for it was true at least that such things were thought of the man. Considered in this way, the opinions about Walt Whitman have a value, and, as I think, a great value, in the estimation of his character. At any rate, there is the refracted light—and future ages may estimate no more powerful one—which a majority of the criticisms of the Nineteenth century on *Leaves of Grass* pour over the criticisers themselves, and the society and times whose impressions they utter.

One thing to be remarked, on the least attempt at massing the collection, is the extent and number of European notices of the poems and their author, often at great length and much detail, contrasted by comparative silence in leading American quarters, the monthlies and quarterlies. About all the attention to the book during the last two years, from these latter authorities (though the newspaper press has been copious), consists, for example, in this precious judgment of three lines, at the close of its critical budget in "Harper's Monthly," January, 1882, describing the final edition of the poems as "a congeries of bizarre rhapsodies that are neither sane verse nor intelligible prose, by Walt Whitman, entitled *Leaves of Grass.*" In the British Islands and cities, London, Edinburgh, and Dublin, the poet has a far more settled status, if not more appreciative readers, than in his own country. The "London Times," in its mention of him, while it does not indorse or eulogize his works, always speaks of him with entire respect, admitting that he is the only *American* poet, native and democratic. Though not yet popularly read on the European continent, he is often noticed, welcomed, sometimes translated, in German, Hungarian, Danish, and Italian periodicals. The Russian "Zagranitschuy Viestnik" (Foreign Messenger), St. Petersburg monthly, in one of its 1882 numbers, has a long article on American literature, nearly a quarter being devoted to high and appreciative comments on *Leaves of Grass*

17 (193)

and its author. For the guidance of those who may desire to further pursue this branch of inquiry, I give a list of some of these past and late statements and sources:

Leaves of Grass Imprints. Thayer & Eldridge. Boston, 1860. 64 pages, 16mo.

Notes on Walt Whitman as Poet and Person. By John Burroughs. Second edition. 126 pages, 12mo. J. S. Redfield. New York, 1871.

Walt Whitman. "Revue des Deux Mondes." Paris, June 1, 1872. By Th. Bentzon.

Walt Whitman, the Poet of Joy. By Arthur Clive. "Gentleman's Magazine." London, December, 1875.

The Poetry of Democracy: Walt Whitman. "Studies in Literature." By Prof. Edward Dowden. London, 1878.

The Flight of the Eagle. "Birds and Poets." By John Burroughs. Boston: Houghton & Mifflin, 1878.

Walt Whitman. "Scribner's Monthly." New York, November, 1880. By Edmund Clarence Stedman.

Walt Whitman. "Buster og Masker." By Rudolf Schmidt. Copenhagen, 1882.

Walt Whitman. "Nineteenth Century." London, December, 1882. By G. C. Macaulay.

Walt Whitman. "Sonntagsblatt der New-Yorker Staats-Zeitung." December, 1882. Three numbers. By Dr. Karl Knortz.

Regarding the excerpts that follow, it will be seen at the first glance that their verdicts, both *pro* and *con*, are of the very strongest. How can such extremely contradictory opinions and feelings be explained? Perhaps it is best to let each find a solution for himself, or simply leave the whole matter to be settled by time. One thing may, however, be said, that if Walt Whitman is really the sort of man and poet his opponents say, it would be impossible to account for the feeling entertained and the view taken by his disciples. On the other hand, if his friends are right in their estimation of him, there is no difficulty at all in accounting both for the intense antipathy felt toward the man and the falsehoods circulated about him, and for the extreme hostility with which *Leaves of Grass* has been received. Then a fact of no small significance: It is plain to those who have watched the currents and utterances excited by the poet and his works, that the opposition to them (though still strong and active, as it is no doubt best it should be) is steadily declining, while appreciation of both is broadening and deepening every day.

The excerpts are collected at random; they are made more for the future than the present. To have been exact, the objurgatory notices ought to have occupied three-fourths of the collection. I give enough, however, to show the animus of all; then devote the rest to further illustration of the idea and purpose out of which my book has arisen.

From the Brooklyn "Daily Times," September 29, 1855.

WALT WHITMAN, A BROOKLYN BOY. *Leaves of Grass:* (a volume of Poems, just published.)—To give judgment on real poems, one needs an account of the poet himself. Very devilish to some, and very divine to some, will appear these new poems, the *Leaves of Grass;* an attempt, as they are, of a live, naïve, masculine, tenderly affectionate, rowdyish, contemplative, sensual, moral, susceptible and imperious person, to cast into literature not only his own grit and arrogance, but his own flesh and form, undraped, regardless of foreign models, regardless of modesty or law, and ignorant or silently scornful, as at first appears, of all except his own presence and experience, and all outside of the fiercely loved land of his birth, and the birth of his parents and their parents for several generations before him. Politeness this man has none, and regulation he has none. The effects he produces are no effects of artists or the arts, but effects of the original eye or arm, or the actual atmosphere or grass or brute or bird. You may feel the unconscious teaching of the presence of some fine animal, but will never feel the teaching of the fine writer or speaker.

Other poets celebrate great events, personages, romances, wars, loves, passions, the victories and power of their country, or some real or imagined incident—and polish their work, and come to conclusions, and satisfy the reader. This poet celebrates himself, and that is the way he celebrates all. He comes to no conclusions, and does not satisfy the reader. He certainly leaves him what the serpent left the woman and the man, the taste of the tree of the knowledge of good and evil, never to be erased again.

What good is it to argue about egotism? There can be no two thoughts on Walt Whitman's egotism. That is what he steps out of the crowd and turns and faces them for. Mark, critics! for otherwise is not used for you the key that leads to the use of the other keys to this well-enveloped yet terribly in earnest man. His whole work, his life, manners, friendships, writing, all have among their leading purposes an evident purpose, as strong and avowed as any of the rest, to stamp a new type of character, namely his own, and indelibly fix it and publish it, not for a model but an illustration, for the present and future of American letters and American young men, for the South the same as the North, and for the Pacific and Mississippi country, and Wisconsin and Texas and Canada and Havana, just as much as New York and Boston. Whatever is needed toward this achievement he puts his hand to, and lets imputations take their time to die.

First be yourself what you would show in your poem—such seems to be this man's example and inferred rebuke to the schools of poets. He makes no allusions to books or writers; their spirits do not seem to have touched him; he has not a word to say for or against them, or their theories or ways. He never offers others; what he continually offers is the man whom our Brooklynites know so well. Of American breed, of reckless health, his body perfect, free from taint from top to toe, free forever from headache and dyspepsia, full-blooded, six feet high, a good feeder, never once using medicine, drinking water only—a swimmer in the river or bay or by the seashore—of straight attitude and slow movement of foot—an indescribable style evincing indifference and disdain—ample limbed, weight a hundred and eighty-five pounds, age thirty-six years [1855]—never dressed in black, always dressed freely and clean in strong clothes, neck open, shirt-collar flat and broad, countenance of swarthy transparent red, beard short and well mottled with white, hair like hay after it has been mowed in the field and lies tossed and streaked—face not refined or intellectual, but calm and wholesome—a face of an unaffected animal—a face that absorbs the sunshine and meets savage or gentleman on equal terms—a face of one who eats and drinks and is a brawny lover and embracer—a face of undying friendship and indulgence toward men and women, and of one who finds the same returned many fold —a face with two gray eyes where passion and hauteur sleep, and melancholy stands behind them—a spirit that mixes cheerfully with the world—a person singularly beloved and welcomed, especially by young men and mechanics— one who has firm attachments there, and associates there—one who does not associate with literary and elegant people—one of the two men sauntering along the street with their arms over each other's shoulders, his companion some boatman or ship-joiner, or from the hunting-tent or lumber-raft—one who has that quality of attracting the best out of people that they present to him none of their meaner and stingier traits, but always their sweetest and most generous traits—a man never called upon to make speeches at public dinners, never on platforms amid the crowds of clergymen, or professors, or aldermen, or Congressmen—rather down in the bay with pilots in their pilot boats—or off on a cruise with fishers in a fishing smack—or with a band of laughers and roughs in the streets of the city or the open grounds of the country—fond of New York and Brooklyn—fond of the life of the wharves and the great ferries, or along Broadway, observing the endless wonders of that thoroughfare of the world—one whom, if you would meet, you need not expect to meet an extraordinary person—one in whom you will see the singularity which consists in no singularity—whose contact is no dazzling fascination, nor requires any deference, but has the easy fascination of what is homely and accustomed—of something you knew before, and was waiting for —of natural pleasures, and well-known places, and welcome familiar faces— perhaps of a remembrance of your brother or mother, or friend away or dead —there you have Walt Whitman, the begetter of a new offspring out of literature, taking with easy nonchalance the chances of its present reception, and, through all misunderstandings and distrusts, the chances of its future reception.

From " The Critic," London, England, 1855.

We should have passed over this book, *Leaves of Grass*, with indignant contempt, had not some few Transatlantic critics attempted to "fix" this Walt Whitman as the poet who shall give a new and independent literature to America—who shall form a race of poets as Banquo's issue formed a line of kings. Is it possible that the most prudish nation in the world will adopt a poet whose indecencies stink in the nostrils? We hope not; and yet there is a probability, and we will show why, that this Walt Whitman will not meet with the stern rebuke which he so richly deserves. America has felt, oftener perhaps than we have declared, that she has no national poet—that each one of her children of song has relied too much on European inspirations, and clung too fervently to the old conventionalities. It is therefore not unlikely that she may believe in the dawn of a thoroughly original literature, now there has arisen a man who scorns the Hellenic deities, who has no belief in, perhaps because he has no knowledge of, Homer and Shakespeare; who relies on his own rugged nature, and trusts to his own rugged language, being himself what he shows in his poems. Once transfix him as the genesis of a new era, and the manner of the man may be forgiven or forgotten. But what claim has this Walt Whitman to be thus considered, or to be considered a poet at all? We grant freely enough that he has a strong relish for Nature and freedom, just as an animal has; nay, further, that his crude mind is capable of appreciating some of Nature's beauties; but it by no means follows that, because

Nature is excellent, therefore art is contemptible. Walt Whitman is as unacquainted with art, as a hog is with mathematics. His poems—we must call them so for convenience—twelve in number, are innocent of rhythm, and resemble nothing so much as the war-cry of the Red Indians. Indeed, Walt Whitman has had near and ample opportunities of studying the vociferations of a few amiable savages. Or rather, perhaps, this Walt Whitman reminds us of Caliban flinging down his logs, and setting himself to write a poem. In fact, Caliban, and not Walt Whitman, might have written this :

> I too am not a bit tamed—I too am untranslatable,
> I sound my *barbaric yawp* over the roofs of the world.

Is this man with the "barbaric yawp" to push Longfellow into the shade, and he meanwhile to stand and "make mouths" at the sun? The chance of this might be formidable were it not ridiculous. That object or that act which most develops the ridiculous element carries in its bosom the seeds of decay, and is wholly powerless to trample out of God's universe one spark of the beautiful. We do not, then, fear this Walt Whitman, who gives us slang in the place of melody, and rowdyism in the place of regularity. The depth of his indecencies will be the grave of his fame, or ought to be, if all proper feeling is not extinct. The very nature of this man's compositions excludes us from proving by extracts the truth of our remarks; but we, who are not prudish, emphatically declare that the man who wrote page 79 of the *Leaves of Grass* deserves nothing so richly as the public executioner's whip. Walt Whitman libels the highest type of humanity, and calls his free speech the true utterance of *a man :* we, who may have been misdirected by civilization, call it the expression of *a beast.*

From the New York "*Criterion,*" November 10, 1855.

Thus, then, we leave this gathering of muck to the laws which, certainly, if they fulfil their intent, must have power to suppress such obscenity. As it is entirely destitute of wit, there is no probability that any would, after this exposure, read it in the hope of finding that; and we trust no one will require further evidence, for, indeed, we do not believe there is a newspaper so vile that would print confirmatory extracts.

In our allusions to this book, we have found it impossible to convey any, even the most faint idea of its style and contents, and of our disgust and detestation of them, without employing language that cannot be pleasing to ears polite ; but it does seem that some one should, under circumstances like these, undertake a most disagreeable yet stern duty. The records of crime show that many monsters have gone on in impunity, because the exposure of their vileness was attended with too great indelicacy.

Emerson to Carlyle, 1856.

One book, last summer, came out in New York, a nondescript monster, which yet had terrible eyes and buffalo strength, and was indisputably American—which I thought to send you ; but the book throve so badly with the few to whom I showed it, and wanted good morals so much, that I never did. Yet I believe now again, I shall. It is called *Leaves of Grass*—was written and printed by a journeyman printer in Brooklyn, New York, named Walter Whitman ; and after you have looked into it, if you think, as you may, that it is only an auctioneer's inventory of a warehouse, you can light your pipe with it.—*Letters published 1883.*

From the Boston " Intelligencer," May 3, 1856.

We were attracted by the very singular title of the work to seek the work itself, and what we thought ridiculous in the title is eclipsed in the pages of this heterogeneous mass of bombast, egotism, vulgarity, and nonsense. The beastliness of the author is set forth in his own description of himself, and we can conceive no better reward than the lash for such a violation of decency as we have before us. Speaking of "this mass of stupid filth," the "Criterion" says: "It is impossible to imagine how any man's fancy could have conceived it, unless he were possessed of the soul of a sentimental donkey that had died of disappointed love." This book should find no place where humanity urges any claim to respect, and the author should be kicked from all decent society as below the level of the brute. There is neither wit nor method in his disjointed babbling, and 't seems to us he must be some escaped lunatic raving in pitiable delirium.

From " Fourteen Thousand Miles Afoot," 1859.

Nothing can more clearly demonstrate the innate vulgarity of our American people, their radical immodesty, their internal licentiousness, their unchastity of heart, their foulness of feelings, than the tabooing of Walt Whitman's *Leaves of Grass.* It is quite impossible to find a publisher for the new edition which has long since been ready for the press, so measureless is the depravity of public taste. There is not an indecent word, an immodest expression, in the entire volume; not a suggestion which is not purity itself; and yet it is rejected on account of its indecency! So much do I think of this work by the healthiest and most original poet America has produced, so valuable a means is it of rightly estimating character, that I have been accustomed to try with it of what quality was the virtue my friends possessed. How few stood the test I shall not say. Some did, and praised it beyond measure. These I set down without hesitation as radically pure, as "born again," and fitted for the society of heaven and the angels. And this test I would recommend to every one. Would you, reader, male or female, ascertain if you be actually modest, innocent, pure-minded? read the *Leaves of Grass.* If you find nothing improper there, you are one of the virtuous and pure. If, on the contrary, you find your sense of decency shocked, then is that sense of decency an exceedingly foul one, and you, man or woman, a very vulgar, dirty person.

The atmosphere of the *Leaves of Grass* is as sweet as that of a hay-field. Its pages exhale the fragrance of Nature. It takes you back to man's pristine state of innocence in Paradise, and lifts you Godwards. It is the healthiest book, morally, this century has produced ; and if it were reprinted in the form of a cheap tract, and scattered broadcast over the land, put into the hands of youth, and into the hands of men and women everywhere, it would do more towards elevating our nature, towards eradicating this foul, vulgar, licentious, sham modesty which so degrades our people now, than any other means within my knowledge. What we want is not outward, but inward modesty; not external, but internal virtue; not silk and broadcloth decency, but a decency infused into every organ of the body and faculty of the soul. Is modesty a virtue? Is it then worn in clothes? Does it hang over the shoulders, or does it live and breathe in the heart? Our modesty is a Jewish phylactery, sewed up in the padding of a coat, and stitched into a woman's stays.

From the Brooklyn "City News," October 10th, 1860.

LEAVES OF GRASS IMPRINTS. Boston: Thayer & Eldridge, Publishers. In this little supplement (a sort of wake after the ship) appear to be gathered a portion of those notices, reviews, etc. (especially the condemnatory ones), that have followed the successive issues of Walt Whitman's *Leaves of Grass.* The history of that composition, so far, is curious. It has already had three births, or successive issues. The first poems consisted of a thin quarto volume of 96 pages, in Brooklyn, in 1855. It comprised eleven pieces, and was received with derision by the literary lawgivers. The only exception was a note from Ralph Waldo Emerson. In 1857 a second issue, a very neat 16mo volume of 384 pages, was published in New York, containing thirty-two poems. The third issue, containing, large and small, one hundred and fifty-four poems, superbly printed (it is indeed universally pronounced, here and in England, a perfect specimen of choice typography), came forth in Boston the current year, 1860.

Such is the book to which this curious collection of criticisms refers. The poem itself (for *Leaves of Grass* all have a compact unity) may be described, in short terms, as the Song of the sovereignty of One's self—and the Song of entire faith in all that Nature is, universal and particular—and in all that belongs to a man, body and soul. The egotistical outset, " I celebrate myself," and which runs in spirit through so much of the volume, speaks for him or her reading it precisely the same as for the author, and is invariably to be so applied. Thus the book is a gospel of self-assertion and self-reliance for every American reader—which is the same as saying it is the gospel of Democracy. •

A man "in perfect health" here comes forward, devoting his life to the experiment of singing the New World in a New Song—not only new in spirit, but new in letter, in form. To him America means not at all a second edition, an adaptation of Europe—not content with a new theory and practice of politics only—but above its politics, and more important than they, inaugurating new and infinitely more generous and comprehensive theories of Sociology, Literature, Religion, and Comradeship.

We therefore do not wonder at the general *howl* with which these poems have been received both in America and in Europe. The truth about the book and its author is, that they both of them confound and contradict several of the most cherished of the old and hitherto accepted canons upon the right manner and matter of men and books—and cannot be judged thereby;—but aim to establish new canons, and can only be judged by them. Just the same as America itself does, and can only be judged.

Neither can the song of *Leaves of Grass* ever be judged by the intellect— nor suffice to be read merely once or so, for amusement. This strange song (often offensive to the intellect) is to be felt, absorbed by the soul. It is to be dwelt upon—returned to, again and again. It wants a broad space to turn in, like a big ship. Many readers will be perplexed and baffled by it at first; but in frequent cases those who liked the book least at first will take it closest to their hearts upon a second or third perusal. A peculiar native idiomatic flavor is in it, to many disagreeable. There is no denying, indeed, that an essential quality it takes from its author, is (as has been charged) the quality of the celebrated New York "rough," full of muscular and excessively virile energy, full of animal blood, masterful, striding to the front rank, allowing none to walk before him, full of rudeness and recklessness, talking and acting his own way, utterly regardless of other people's ways.

The cry of indecency against *Leaves of Grass* amounts, when plainly stated, about to this: Other writers assume that the sexual relations are shameful in themselves, and not to be put in poems. But our new bard assumes that those very relations are the most beautiful and pure and divine of any— and in that way he "celebrates" them. No wonder he confounds the ortho- dox. Yet his indecency is the ever-recurring indecency of the inspired Bib- lical writers—and is that of innocent youth, and of the natural and untainted man in all ages. In other words, the only explanation the reader needs to bear in mind to clear up the whole matter is this: The subjects about which such a storm has been raised, are treated by Walt Whitman with unprece- dented boldness and candor, but always in the very highest religious and es- thetic spirit. Filthy to others, *to him* they are *not* filthy, but "illustrious." While his "critics" (carefully minding never to state the foregoing fact, though it is stamped all over the book) consider those subjects in *Leaves of Grass* from the point of view of persons standing on the lowest animal and infidelistic platform. Which, then, is really the "beast"?

Those who really know Walt Whitman will be amused beyond measure at the personal statements put forth about him in some of these criticisms. We believe it was Dr. Dictionary Johnson who said that persons of any celebrity may calculate how much truth there is in histories and written lives, by weigh- ing the amount of that article in the stuff that is printed or gossiped about themselves.

From "*The Cosmopolite*," *Boston, August 4th, 1860.*

In no other modern poems do we find such a lavish outpouring of wealth. It is as if, in the midst of a crowd of literati bringing handfuls of jewels, a few of pure metal elaborately wrought, but the rest merely pretty specimens of pinchbeck, suddenly a herculean fellow should come along with an entire gold mine. Right and left he scatters the glittering dust,—and it is but dust in the eyes of those who look only for pleasing trinkets. Out of his deep Californian sacks, mingled with native quartz and sand, he empties the yellow ore,—sufficient to set up fifty small practical jewellers dealing in galvanized ware, if they were not too much alarmed at the miner's rough garb to ap- proach and help themselves. Down from his capacious pockets tumble astonishing nuggets,—but we, who are accustomed to see the stuff never in its rude state, but only in fashionable shapes of breastpins or caneheads, start back with affright, and scream for our toes.

It is much to be regretted that treasures of such rare value are lost to the age through the strange form and manner in which they are presented. But it is time lost blaming the miner. Perhaps he could have done differently, perhaps not; at all events, we must take him as he is, and, if we are wise, make the best of him.

The first and greatest objection brought against Walt Whitman and his *Leaves of Grass* is their indecency. Nature is treated here without fig-leaves; things are called by their names, without any apparent sense of modesty or shame. Of this peculiarity—so shocking in an artificial era—the dainty reader should be especially warned. But it is a mistake to infer that the book is on this account necessarily immoral. It is the poet's design, not to entice to the perversion of Nature, which is vice, but to lead us back to Nature, which in his theory is the only virtue. His theory may be wrong, and the manner in which he carries it out repulsive, but no one who reads and understands him will question the sincerity of his motives, however much may be doubted the wisdom of attempting in this way to restore mankind to the days of un- draped innocence.

In respect of plain speaking, and in most respects, the *Leaves* more resemble the Hebrew Scriptures than do any other modern writings. The style is wonderfully idiomatic and graphic. The commonest daily objects and the most exalted truths of the soul, this bard of Nature touches with the ease and freedom of a great master. He wonders at all things, he sympathizes with all things and with all men. The nameless something which makes the power and spirit of music, of poetry, of all art, throbs and whirls under and through his verse, affecting us we know not how, agitating and ravishing the soul. And this springs so genuinely from the inmost nature of the man, that it always appears singularly in keeping even with that extravagant egotism, and with those surprisingly quaint or common expressions, at which readers are at first inclined only to laugh. In his frenzy, in the fire of his inspiration, are fused and poured out together elements hitherto considered antagonistic in poetry,—passion, arrogance, animality, philosophy, brag, humility, rowdyism, spirituality, laughter, tears, together with the most ardent and tender love, the most comprehensive human sympathy which ever radiated its divine glow through the pages of poems.

From the "Boston Post," 1860.

We have alluded just now to our incapability of comprehending the writings of Swedenborg, but still more, in some parts, do we acknowledge ourselves nonplussed and puzzled by these *Leaves of Grass*. It would be more correct, however, to say how utterly at a loss we are to understand by what motive or impulse so eminent a lecturer and writer, and, as we have always understood, with all his crotchety ideas and pantheistic prattlings, so pure-minded a man as R. Waldo Emerson could have written that eulogy of the *Leaves*, which certainly acted as our chief inducement for inspecting their structure.

Grass is the gift of God for the healthy sustenance of his creatures, and its name ought not to be desecrated by being so improperly bestowed upon these foul and rank leaves of the poison-plants of egotism, irreverence, and of lust run rampant and holding high revel in its shame!

We see that the volume arrogantly assumes to itself the claim of founding an original and independent American Literature. Woe and shame for the Land of Liberty if its literature's stream is thus to flow from the filthy fountain of licentious corruption! Little fear, however, should we have of such an issue from the *Leaves* themselves. The pure and elevated moral sense of America would leave them to decay and perish amid their own putridity. But there *is* danger of their corrupting influences being diffused and extended to the great injury of society, when leaders of our literature, like Emerson, are so infatuated in judgment, and so untrue to the most solemn responsibilities of their position, as to indorse such a prurient and polluted work;—to address its author in such terms as these, "I give you joy of your free and brave thought—I have great joy in it—I wish to see my benefactor."

The most charitable conclusion at which we can arrive is, that both Whitman's *Leaves* and Emerson's laudation had a common origin in temporary insanity!

It in no degree shakes our judgment to find more than one eminent Review coinciding more or less in the praise of this work, to which we ourselves by no means deny the possession of much originality of thought and vigor of expression. No amount, however, of such merits can, in the judgment of sound and honest criticism,—whose bounden duty it is to endeavor to guide the mind of the nation in a healthy, moral course—atone for the exulting audacity of Priapus-worshiping obscenity, which marks a large portion of the volume. Its vaunted manliness and independence, tested by the standard of a truthful judgment, is nothing but the deification of Self, and defiance of the Deity;—its liberty is the wildest license; its love the essence of the lowest lust!

From the Cincinnati "Commercial," 1860.

Perhaps our readers are blissfully ignorant of the history and achievements of Mr. Walt Whitman. Be it known, then, that he is a native and resident of Brooklyn, Long Island, born and bred in an obscurity from which it were well he never had emerged. A person of coarse nature, and strong, rude passions, he has passed his life in cultivating, not the amenities, but the rudenesses of character; and instead of tempering his native ferocity with the delicate influences of art and refined literature, he has studied to exaggerate its deformities, and to thrust into his composition all the brute force he could muster from a capacity not naturally sterile in the elements of strength. He has undertaken to be an artist, without learning the first principles of art, and has presumed to put forth "poems," without possessing a spark of the poetic faculty. He affects swagger and independence, and blurts out his vulgar impertinence under a full assurance of "originality."

From the London "Literary Gazette," July 7th, 1860.

Of all the writers we have ever perused Walt Whitman is the most silly, the most blasphemous, and the most disgusting. If we can think of any stronger epithets we will print them in a second edition.

From the "Allgemeine Zeitung" (Augsburg.) May 10, 1868.

Walt Whitman.
Von Ferdinand Freiligrath.

Walt Whitman! Wer ist Walt Whitman?

Die Antwort lautet: ein Dichter! Ein neuer amerikanischer Dichter! Seine Bewunderer sagen: der erste, der einzige Dichter welchen Amerika bisher hervorgebracht. Der einzige specifisch amerikanische Dichter. Kein Wandler in den ausgetretenen Spuren der europäischen Muse, nein, frisch von der Prairie und den Ansiedlungen, frisch von der Küste und den großen Flüssen, frisch aus dem Menschengewühl der Häfen und der Städte, frisch von den Schlachtfeldern des Südens, den Erdgeruch des Bodens, der ihn gezeugt, in Haar und Bart und Kleidern; ein noch nicht Dagewesener, ein fest und bewußt auf den eigenen amerikanischen Füßen Stehender, ein große Dinge groß, wenn auch oft seltsam, Verkündender. Und weiter noch gehen die Bewunderer: Walt Whitman ist ihnen der einzige Dichter überhaupt in welchem die Zeit, die kreißende, ringende, suchende Zeit, ihren Ausdruck gefunden hat; der Dichter par excellence; der Dichter— "the poet."

So, auf der einen Seite die Bewunderer, in deren Reihen, uns sogar ein Emerson begegnet; auf der andern dann freilich die Tadler, die Herabwürdiger. Neben dem ungemessenen Lobe, der begeisterten Anerkennung der bittere, der beißende Spott, die kränkende Schmähung.

Das freilich kümmert den Dichter nicht. Das Lob nimmt er hin als ein ihm gebührendes; der Verachtung setzt er die Verachtung entgegen. Er glaubt an sich, sein Selbstgefühl ist unbegränzt. „Er ist" (sagt sein englischer Herausgeber, W. M. Rossetti) „vor allen selbst der eine Mann, welcher die ernste Ueberzeugen hegt und bekennt daß er, jetzt und in Zukunft, der Gründer einer neuen poetischen Literatur ist — einer großen Literatur — einer Literatur wie sie zu der materiellen Größe und den unberechenbaren Geschicken Amerika's im Verhältniß steht." Er glaubt daß der Columbus des Erdtheils oder der Washington der Staaten nicht wahrhaftiger ein Gründer und Auferbauer dieses Amerika's gewesen ist als er felbst in Zukunft einer fehn wird. Gewiß eine erhabene Ueberzeugung, und vom Dichter mehr als einmal in prächtigen Worten ausgesprochen — keine prächtiger als das Gedicht welches mit der Zeile beginnt:

„Kommt, unauflöslich will ich dieses Festland machen."

Das klingt stolz. Ist der Mann in seinem Rechte so zu reden? Treten wir ihm näher! Hören wir von seinem Leben und seinem Schaffen! Schlagen wir zuerst sein Buch auf!

Sind das Verse? Die Zeilen sind wie Verse abgesetzt, allerdings, aber Verse sind es nicht. Kein Metrum, kein Reim, keine Strophen. Rhythmische Prosa, Streckverse. Auf den ersten Anblick rauh, ungefüg, formlos; aber dennoch, für ein feineres Ohr, des Wohllauts nicht ermangelnd. Die Sprache schlicht, derb, gradezu, alles Ding beim rechten Namen nennend, vor nichts zurückschreckend, manchmal dunkel. Der Ton rhapsodisch, prophetenhaft, oft ungleich, das Erhabene mit dem Gewöhnlichen, bis zur Geschmacklosigkeit sogar, vermischend. Er erinnert uns zuweilen, bei aller sonstigen Verschiedenheit, an unsern Hamann, oder an Carlyle's Orakelweisheit, oder an die Paroles d'un Croyant. Aus allem heraus klingt die Bibel — ihre Sprache, nicht ihr Glaube.

Und was trägt uns der Dichter in dieser Form vor? Zunächst sich selbst, sein Ich, Walt Whitman. Dieses Ich aber ist ein Theil von Amerika, ein Theil der Erde, ein Theil der Menschheit, ein Theil des Alls. Als solchen fühlt er sich, und rollt, das Größte ans Kleinste knüpfend, immer von Amerika ausgehend und immer wieder auf Amerika zurückkommend (nur einem freien Volke gehört die Zukunft!), ein großartiges Weltpanorama vor uns auf. Durch dieses Individuum Walt Whitman und seinen Amerikanismus geht, wir möchten sagen, ein kosmischer Zug, wie er sinnenden Geistern eignen mag, die, der Unendlichkeit gegenüber, einsame Tage am Gestade des Meers, einsame Nächte unter dem gestirnten Himmel der Prairie verbracht haben. Er findet sich in allem und alles in sich. Er, der eine Mensch Walt Whitman, ist die Menschheit und die Welt. Und die Welt und die Menschheit sind ihm e i n großes Gedicht. Was er sieht und hört, was er berührt, was immer an ihn herantritt, auch das Niedrigste, das Geringste, das Alltäglichste — alles ist ihm Symbol eines Höheren, eines Geistigen. Oder vielmehr: die Materie und der Geist, die Wirklichkeit und das Ideal sind ihm eins und dasselbe. So, durch sich selbst geworden, steht er da; so schreitet er singend einher; so erschließt er, ein stolzer freier Mensch, und n u r ein Mensch, weltweite sociale und politische Perspectiven.

Eine wunderbare Erscheinung! Wir gestehen daß sie uns ergreift, uns beunruhigt, uns nicht los läßt. Zugleich aber merken wir an daß wir mit unserm Urtheil über sie noch nicht fertig, daß wir noch vom ersten Eindruck befangen sind. Unterdessen wollen wir, wahrscheinlich die ersten in Deutschland, wenigstens vorläufig Act nehmen vom Daseyn und wirken dieser frischen Kraft. Sie verdient daß unsere Dichter und Denker sich den seltsamen neuen Genossen näher ansehen, der unsere gesammte Ars poetica, der all unsere ästhetischen Theorien und Kanons über den Haufen zu werfen droht. In der That, wenn wir in diese ernsten Blätter hineingehorcht haben, wenn uns das tiefe volltönige Brausen dieser wie Meereswellen in ununterbrochener Folge auf uns einstürmenden rhapsodischen Gesätze vertraut geworden ist, so will unser herkömmliches Versemachen, unser Zwängen des Gedankens in irgendwelche überkommene Formen, unser Spielen mit Kling und Klang, unser Silbenzählen und Silbermessen, unser Sonettiren und Strophen= und Stanzenbauen uns fast kindisch bedünken. Sind wir wirklich auf dem Punkt angelangt wo das Leben, auch in der Poesie, neue Ausdrucksweisen gebieterisch verlangt? Hat die Zeit so viel und so bedeutendes zu sagen, daß die alten Gefäße für den neuen Inhalt nicht mehr ausreichen? Stehen wir vor einer Zukunftspoesie wie uns schon seit Jahren eine Zukunftsmusik verkündigt wird? Und ist Walt Whitman mehr als Richard Wagner?

From "*The Radical,*" *Boston, May, 1870.*

A WOMAN'S ESTIMATE OF WALT WHITMAN.—By Mrs. Gilchrist, England, in a letter to W. M. R.

(*Extracts.*)

. . . . I had not dreamed that words could cease to be words, and become electric streams like these. I do assure you that, strong as I am, I feel some-times as if I had not bodily strength to read many of these poems. In the series headed "Calamus," for instance, in some of the "Songs of Parting," the "Voice out of the Sea," * the poem beginning "Tears, Tears," etc., there is such a weight of emotion, such a tension of the heart, that mine refuses to beat under it,—stands quite still,—and I am obliged to lay the book down for a while. Or again, in the piece called "Walt Whitman,"† and one or two others of that type, I am as one hurried through stormy seas, over high moun-tains, dazed with sunlight, stunned with a crowd and tumult of faces and voices, till I am breathless, bewildered, half dead. Then come parts and whole poems in which there is such calm wisdom and strength of thought, such a cheerful breadth of sunshine, that the soul bathes in them renewed and strengthened. Living impulses flow out of these that make me exult in life, yet look long-ingly toward "the superb vistas of Death." Those who admire this poem, and don't care for that, and talk of formlessness, absence of metre, etc., are quite as far from any genuine recognition of Walt Whitman as his bitter de-tractors. Not, of course, that all the pieces are equal in power and beauty, but that all are vital; they grew—they were not made. We criticise a palace or a cathedral; but what is the good of criticising a forest? Are not the hitherto-accepted masterpieces of literature akin rather to noble architecture; built up of material rendered precious by elaboration; planned with subtile art, that makes beauty go hand-in-hand with rule and measure, and knows where the last stone will come before the first is laid; the result stately, fixed, yet such as might, in every particular, have been different from what it is (therefore inviting criticism), contrasting proudly with the careless freedom of Nature—opposing its own rigid adherence to symmetry to her wilful dallying with it? But not such is this book. Seeds brought by the winds from north, south, east, and west, lying long in the earth, not resting on it like the stately building, but hid in it and assimilating it, shooting upwards to be nour-ished by the air and the sunshine and the rain which beat idly against that,—each bough and twig and leaf growing in strength and beauty its own way, a law to itself, yet with all this freedom of spontaneous growth, the result in-evitable, unalterable (therefore setting criticism at naught)—above all things, vital—that is, a source of ever-generating vitality: such are these poems.

I see that no counting of syllables will reveal the mechanism of the music; and that this rushing spontaneity could not stay to bind itself with the fetters of metre. But I know that the music is there, and that I would not for some-thing change ears with those who cannot hear it. And I know that poetry must do one of two things,—either own this man as equal with her highest, completest manifestors, or stand aside, and admit that there is something come into the world nobler, diviner than herself, one that is free of the universe, and can tell its secrets as none before. I do not think or believe this, but see it with the same unmistakable definiteness of perception and full consciousness that I see the sun at this moment in the noonday sky, and feel his rays glowing down upon me as I write in the open air. What more can you ask of the words

---

* "Out of the Cradle Endlessly Rocking."   † "Song of Myself."

of a man's mouth than that they should "absorb into you as food and air, to appear again in your strength, gait, face,"—that they should be "fibre and filter to your blood," joy and gladness to your whole nature?

I am persuaded that one great source of this kindling, vitalizing power—I suppose *the* great source—is the grasp laid upon the present, the fearless and comprehensive dealing with reality. Hitherto the leaders of thought have (except in science) been men with their faces resolutely turned backwards; men who have made of the past a tyrant that beggars and scorns the present, hardly seeing any greatness but what is shrouded away in the twilight, underground past; naming the present only for disparaging comparisons, humiliating distrust that tends to create the very barrenness it complains of; bidding me warm myself at fires that went out to mortal eyes centuries ago; insisting, in religion above all, that I must either "look through dead men's eyes," or shut my own in helpless darkness. Poets fancying themselves so happy over the chill and faded beauty of the past, but not making me happy at all— rebellious always at being dragged down out of the free air and sunshine of to-day. But this poet, this "athlete, full of rich words, full of joy," takes you by the hand and turns you with your face straight forwards. The present is great enough for him, because he is great enough for it. It flows through him as a "vast oceanic tide" lifting up a mighty voice. Earth, "the eloquent, dumb, great mother," is not old, has lost none of her fresh charms, none of her divine meanings; still bears great sons and daughters, if only they would possess themselves and accept their birthright—a richer, not a poorer, heritage than was ever provided before—richer by all the toil and suffering of the generations that have preceded, and by the further unfolding of the eternal purposes. Here is one come at last who can show them how; whose songs are the breath of a glad, strong, beautiful life, nourished sufficiently, kindled to unsurpassed intensity and greatness by the gifts of the present.

You argued rightly that my confidence would not be betrayed by any of the poems in this book. None of them troubled me even for a moment; because I saw at a glance that it was not, as men had supposed, the heights brought down to the depths, but the depths lifted up level with the sunlit heights, that they might become clear and sunlit too. Always, for a woman, a veil woven out of her own soul—never touched upon even with a rough hand, by this poet. But, for a man, a daring, fearless pride in himself, not a mock modesty woven out of delusions—a very poor imitation of a woman's. Do they not see that this fearless pride, this complete acceptance of themselves, is needful for her pride, her justification? What! is it all so ignoble, so base, that it will not bear the honest light of speech from lips so gifted with "the divine power to use words"? Then what hateful, bitter humiliation for her, to have to give herself up to the reality! Do you think there is ever a bride who does not taste more or less this bitterness in her cup? But who put it there? It must surely be man's fault, not God's, that she has to say to herself, "Soul, look another way—you have no part in this. Motherhood is beautiful, fatherhood is beautiful; but the dawn of fatherhood and motherhood is not beautiful." Do they really think that God is ashamed of what He has made and appointed? And, if not, surely it is somewhat superfluous that they should undertake to be so for Him.

> "The full spread pride of man is calming and excellent to the soul"

of a woman above all. . It is true that instinct of silence I spoke of is a beautiful, imperishable part of Nature too. But it is not beautiful when it means an ignominious shame brooding darkly. Shame is like a very flexible veil, that follows faithfully the shape of what it covers—beautiful when it hides a beautiful thing, ugly when it hioes an ugly one. It has not covered what was beautiful here; it has covered a mean distrust of a man's self and of his Creator. It was needed that this silence, this evil spell, should for once be broken, and the daylight let in, that the dark cloud lying under might be scattered to the winds. It was needed that one who could here indicate for us " the path between reality and the soul" should speak. That is what these beautiful, despised poems, the " Children of Adam," do, read by the light that glows out of the rest of the volume : light of a clear, strong faith in God, of an unfathomably deep and tender love for humanity—light shed out of a soul that is " possessed of itself."

" Natural life of me faithfully praising things,
" Corroborating forever the triumph of things."

Now silence may brood again ; but lovingly, happily, as protecting what is beautiful, not as hiding what is unbeautiful : consciously enfolding a sweet and sacred mystery—august even as the mystery of Death, the dawn as the setting ; kindred grandeurs, which to eyes that are opened shed a hallowing beauty on all that surrounds and preludes them.

" O vast and well-veiled Death!
" O the beautiful touch of Death, soothing and benumbing a few moments, for reasons."

He who can thus look with fearlessness at the beauty of Death may well dare to teach us to look with fearless, untroubled eyes at the perfect beauty of Love in all its appointed realizations. Now none need turn away their thoughts with pain or shame : though only lovers and poets may say what they will— the lover to his own, the poet to all, because all are in a sense his own. None need fear that this will be harmful to the woman. How should there be such a flaw in the scheme of creation that, for the two with whom there is no com-plete life, save in closest sympathy, perfect union, what is natural and happy for the one should be baneful to the other ? The utmost faithful freedom of speech, such as there is in these poems, creates in her no thought or feeling that shuns the light of heaven, none that are as innocent and serenely fair as the flowers that grow ; would lead, not to harm, but to such deep and tender affection as makes harm or the thought of harm simply impossible. Far more beautiful care than man is aware of has been taken in the making of her, to fit her to be his mate. God has taken such care that he need take none ; none, that is, which consists in disguisement, insincerity, painful hush-ing-up of his true, grand, initiating nature. And, as regards the poet's utter-ances, which, it might be thought, however harmless in themselves, would prove harmful by falling into the hands of those for whom they are manifestly unsuitable ; I believe that even here fear is needless. For her innocence is folded round with such thick folds of ignorance, till the right way and time for it to accept knowledge, that what is unsuitable is also unintelligible to her, and, if no dark shadow from without be cast on the white page by miscon-struction or by foolish mystery and hiding away of it, no hurt will ensue from its passing freely through her hands. This is so, though it is little understood or realized by men. Wives and mothers will learn through this poet that there is rejoicing grandeur and beauty there wherein their hearts have so longed to find it ; where foolish men, traitors to themselves, poorly compre-hending the grandeur of their own or the beauty of a woman's nature, have taken such pains to make her believe there was none—nothing but miserable discrepancy.

From the " Revue des Deux Mondes," June 1, 1872. By Th. Bentzon.

(*Extracts.*)

Le mepris qu'il éprouvait pour le sentimentalisme élégant que les poëtes de l'école de Tennyson ont mis en honneur, et qui pour lui n'était qu'un verbiage plus ou moins musical, resultat d'une vie de mollesse et d'énervement, —la haine de ce genre de litterature dont l'origine selon lui est féodale, d'une certaine distinction convenue, de ce qu'il appelle les façons de la haute vie de bas-étage,—l'ambition enfin de créer une poesie Américaine proprement dite, en rapport avec l'immensité territoriale et la grandeur des destinées du Nouveau-Monde, lui inspirèrent cette œuvre, qui eut un succès prodigieux en même temps qu'elle suscita de formidables orages. Emerson n'a pas craint de designer *Leaves of Grass* comme le morceau le plus extraordinaire de sagesse et d'esprit qu'eût encore produit l'Amerique! Sans doute la forme en est souvent négligée ou même baroque. Si vous ètes imbu de vieux préjugés contre les poémes en prose, si vous tenez compte des lois de la versification, gardez vous de lire ce qu'ou a comparé avec trop d'indulgence à la poésie de la Bible et à la prose rhythmée de Platon. L'auteur déclare du reste rompre avec tous les précédens; *aujourd'hui*, voilà l'epreuve qui doit tenter le poète! A quoi bon remonter dans la nuit des générations lointaines? L'homme naturel, tel est son héros; les Etats-Unis sont en eux-mêmes le plus grand de tous les poèmes. Walt Whitman enterre le passé: il chante l'avenir, l'Amerique et la liberté; qu'on n'attende de lui rien de frivole vie de féminin. Il se pique avant touf d'une herculéenne virilité.

Ce qui nous parait aussi bizarre pour le moins que la philosophie et que la religion de M. Whitman, c'est sa morale. Il n'admet pas le mal, ou plutôt il juge que le mal et le bien se valent, puisque tous deux existent; il prend l'homme comme il est et soutient que rien ne peut être mieux que ce qui est, si les appétits grossiers jouentun grand rôle, ce doit être la condition nécessaire des choses, et nous devons l'accepter. Pourquoi dont ce qui se voit, ce que nous savons, ce qui est nécessaire, par consequent juste, ne serait-il pas proclamé dans ses vers? Appuyé sur de pareils sophismes, il n'y a point d'indécence qui le fasse reculer; la langue française refuserait à la traduction de certains morceaux érotiques. M. Walt Whitman n'admettant pas de difference entre l'homme et la femme, ni même entre la laideur et la beauté, ne peut employer le mot d'amour dans le sens ordinaire; ce mot il le prononce sans cesse, mais en l'appliquant indistinctement á tous les êtres; l'amour, en-dehors d'une fraternité universelle, n'est pour lui que le plaisir physique exprimé avec la crudité qui lui est propre. Aussi est il pénible de l'entendre parler de la femme considérée autrement que comme mère et citoyenne. Le seul hommage, presque respectueux et tres éloquent d'ailleurs, qu'il lui rende dans toute son œuvre, a pour cadre, le croirait-on, la morgue, et il s'agit d'une prostituée. En somme, une prostituée vaut-elle moins qu'une vierge?

L'Anglais, qu'il célèbre emphatiquement comme la langue du progrès, de la foi, de la liberté, de la justice, de l'egalité, de l'estime de soi, du sens commun, de la prudence, de la revolution, du courage, et qui, selon lui, exprime presque l'ine primable, l'anglais devient sons sa plume un jargon barbare souvent incompréhensible. Encore si ses " Chants democratiques " ne péchaient que par la forme; mais le fond est plus détestable encore.

On ne peut nier qu'il y ait là une certaine grandeur ct beaucoup de passion. Walt Whitman nous fait l'effect du sinistre oiseau de mer, au quel lui même s'est comparé, ses grandes ailes sombres ouvertes sur l'ocean qui le separe de l'ancien monde, et jetant au milieu des tempetes les cris de haine raques et stridens dont par malheur l'echo a retenti chez nous.

Walt Whitman excelle a décrire l'enthousiasme des recrues, l'embarquement des vieilles troupes qui arrivent de toute parts, convertes de poussière, fumant de sueur, les tentes blanches qui s'élèvent dans le camp, les salves d'artillerie au lever de l'aurore, les marches precipitées sur des routes inconues, les haltes rapides sous le ciel nocturne passemé d'etoiles éternelles; il excelle a mettre en opposition le calme immuable de la nature avec les fureurs humaines à nous faire respirer "le parfum de la guerre."

Un autre fois il nous conduit à l'ambulance, une ambulance improvisée dans la vieille église au fond des bois; les lampes voltigent, déchirant l'ombre noire d'une lueur rapide; une grande torche goudronnée, stationnaire, jette sa sauvage flamme rouge et des nuages de fumée sur les groupes confus, sur les formes vagues couchées par terre ou qui surchargent les bancs. Le poète ne nous fait grâce ni de l'odeur du sang confondue avec celle de l'éther, ni de la sueur des spasmes suprêmes, ni des éclairs qui jaillissent de l'instrument d'acier en train de travailler les chairs en lambeaux; il écarte le couverture de laine qui couvre le visage des morts, il recueille le demi-sourire que lui adresse le jeune volontaire, un enfant, en exhalant son dernier souffle; il pense au Christ mort pour ses frère, le sentiment religieux et la divine pitié relèvent la rudesse de certains details au point d'en faire une beauté de plus. Pour être juste, il fandrait tout citer de ces eloquens et farouches *Roulemens de Tambour:*—la *Tombe*, la pauvre tombe du soldat, ignorée, perdue dans les bois de la Virginie, et que le poète, qui l'a rencontrée une fois, retrouve sans cesse sons ses pieds, au milieu des rues bruyantes et des fêtes de la vie;—les *Reves de guerre*, qui nous transportent en plein carnage avec trop de musique imitative: sifflemens de balles, explosion d'obus;—le *Camp*, où nous goûtons un instant ce repos inquiet qui suit les marches forcées et précède la battaille;—la *Vision*, qui ramène au milieu de la fusillade le vétéran revenu au foyer, tandis qu' à l'heure de minnit il s'accoude sur l'oreiller de sa femme endormie, et que la douce respiration du *baby* s'élève, retombe dans le silence.

Nous voici loin des professions matérialistes dont fourmillent telles pièces radicales que nous ne citions tout a l'heure qu' avec repugnance. Walt Whitman se contredit singulièrement, et on ne saurait s'en plaindre; il ne se pique pas du reste d'être conséquent avec lui-même. Les fanatiques pretendent que la faute en est à la multiplicité d'aspects que présentent les choses et à la prodigieuse capacité de Whitman pour tout sentir et tout comprendre, à son *universalité* en un mot. Nous croyons plutôt qu'il a réussi à ecrire des choses élevées et fortes le jour où il s'est décidé à glaner dans le champ fécond de l'observation, au lieu de se perdre dans de vaines utopies, des paradoxes insensés et une philosophie malsaine dont il est loin d'être l'inventeur,—le jour où il s'est inspiré du spectacle inepuisable de la vie humaine avec ses nobles émotions, ses joies pures et ses suffrances, au lieu de prétendre, comme il l'avait fait d'abord, à partager les sensations des choses, à s'assimiler aux lilas, au silex, aux nuages, aux agneaux, aux volailles de la basse-cour, voire au vieil ivrogne qui se traine en trébuchant hors de la taverne!

Il est remarquable que, lorsque Whitman choisit bien ses sujets [as in "Drum Taps"] la forme est toujours plus correcte, ce qui prouve que la noblesse de l'expression est inséparable de celle de la pensée. Le poème tant vanté de "Walt Whitman" ["Song of Myself"] nous ramène en pleine brutalité, en plein égoïsme, en plein paradoxe. Nous y avous cependant recueilli une belle pensée qui nous fait espérer que le spiritualisme purifiera peut-être un jour, si l'orgueil du poète de l'avenir le permet, cette muse revolutionnaire qui l'a trop longtemps inspiré. À la suite d'une comparaison entre la nuit et la mort, il s'ecrie :

Je trouvais le jour plus beau que tout le reste, jusqu'à ce que j'eusse contemplé les beautés de ce qui n'est pas le jour.
Je croyais que notre globe terrestre etait assez, jusqu'à ce que se fussent élevées sans bruit autour de lui des myriades d'autres globes ;
Je vois maintenant que la vie ne peut tout me montrer, de même que le jour ne le peut, je vois que je dois attendre ce que me montrera la mort.

Restons sur ces vers de bon augure. Sans admettre que le prétendu Christophe Colomb de l'art Américain ait découvert des régions jusqu' ici inexplorées, on ne peut nier qu'il possède à un haut degré la passion, la verve patriotique et un salutaire mépris de la banalité ; mais que lui et ses imitateurs (puis qu'il doit être, hélas ! le père d'une longue génération de poètes) cessent de croire que la grossièreté soit de la force, la bizarrerie de l'originalité, la licence une noble hardiesse. Qu'ils ne confondent pas l'obscurité du langage avec la profondeur, le cynisme avec la franchise, le vacarme avec la musique ;—qu'ils ne fassent pas appel à la haine, à l'envie, aux plus mauvais sentimens de l'âme sous pretexte de la réveiller ;—qu'ils se degagent des inspirations factices qui feraient croire en les lisant à un mangeur de haschich ou à un de ces buveurs de whisky mêlé de poudre, comme il en existe, assure-t-on, dans quelques coins sauvages de leur patrie ;—qu'ils respectent la pudeur des femmes, puisqu'ils les placent, disent-ils, plus haut qu'elles n'ont jamais été ;—qu'ils prennent une attitude plus digne que celle de boxeur ;—qu'ils permettent au monde de les juger, au lieu de se juger euxmême avec une si altière confiance en leur mérite et leur destinées futures, avec un enivrement si comique de leur propre personnalité. Camarade ! crie Walt Whitman en terminant, après des prophéties qui prouvent qu'il croit écrire un nouvel évangile, camarade, ceci n'es pas un livre . . . . Quiconque le touche touche un homme !

From the New York "Graphic," November 25th, 1873.—By Matador.

(Extracts.)

It takes seven years to learn to appreciate Walt Whitman's poetry. At least it took me precisely that time, and I divided it as follows : For four years I ridiculed *Leaves of Grass* as the most intricate idiocy that ·. preposterous pen had ever written. During the next two years I found myself occasionally wondering if, after all, there might not be some glimmer of poetic beauty in Whitman's ragged lines. And then during the last year of my Walt Whitman novitiate the grandeur and beauty and melody of his verse, its vast and measureless expression of all human thoughts and emotions, were suddenly revealed to me. I understand it now. I have learned its purpose and caught the subtle melody of its lines.

Carelessly looked at, *Leaves of Grass* is a formless aggregation of lines without definite purpose and without the slightest pretence of prosody. Closer search shows the thread that guides one through the maze, and demonstrates its artistic plan. Whitman professes to express all the thoughts and feelings common to humanity,—whatever you or I may have felt, whether in moments of joy or sorrow ; whatever you or I may have thought, whether it was true or false, honorable or shameful, our feelings and thoughts are expressed in this cosmical poem. It is this vastness of design that forbids the easy comprehension of the poem ; that, permitting to the careless observer only a view of a rough stone here or a misshapen gargoyle there, reveals its true proportions only to the slow and careful survey that sees it from all sides, and, passing over details, grasps the final meaning of the whole.

There is much that seems trivial and ugly and meaningless and repulsive in *Leaves of Grass* when viewed only in detail. These things, however, have their place. Without them the poem would not be complete. Without them it would lack the universality hinted at in the name, *Leaves of Grass.* . . .

There is another sort of descriptive poetry in which the poet, instead of setting definite objects before your sight, works by creating in you the feelings that naturally accompany certain situations. It is a method that is nowhere mentioned in books of rhetoric, but it is precisely analogous to the method of Beethoven and the grand masters of symphonic music. Their music is not descriptive in the sense of cataloguing scenes and events, but produces upon the mind of the listener directly the impression which such scenes and events would necessarily produce.

Of this sort of subjective and descriptive poetry *Leaves of Grass* contains frequent examples. Here is one :

> Of the turbid pool that lies in the autumn forest,
> Of the moon that descends the steeps of the soughing twilight,
> Toss, sparkles of day and dusk—toss on the black stems that decay in the muck,
> Toss to the moaning gibberish of the dry limbs.

There are few definite points given in these lines which attract the eye. There is really no feature given us, but only a vague mystery of hinted color, and yet you at once recognize the feeling it calls into being as that which belongs to a moonlight night spent in the depth of a lonely forest.

And again, take these lines that hint of a midsummer's night. They describe nothing, but they perfectly express the physical pleasure that we feel when kissed by the warm and wandering night winds :

> I am he that walks with the tender and growing night,
> I call to the earth and sea half-held by the night.

> Press close bare-bosom'd night—press close magnetic nourishing night !
> Night of south winds—night of the large few stars !
> Still nodding night—mad naked summer night.

> Smile O voluptuous cool-breath'd earth !
> Earth of the slumbering and liquid trees !
> Earth of departed sunset—earth of the mountains misty topt !
> Earth of the vitreous pour of the full moon just tinged with blue !

Do you say that this is meaningless when each phrase is taken as a distinct statement? So is the Seventh Symphony meaningless if you try to translate it bar by bar. I claim, however, that in these verses Walt Whitman follows the method of the tone poets, and that what you call vagueness and obscurity is simply the art of the musician, the only art that transcends the art of the poet.

From a Notice in 1873.

The history of the gradual development of Walt Whitman's poems is significant, almost geologic. The author having formed his plan, commenced carrying it out by his first book at the age of thirty-five years—" in perfect health, hoping to cease not till death." Upon and around this nucleus-volume of 1855 have since been steadily formed gradual accretions, published in 1857, in 1860, in 1867, and lastly in 1872—each part of these accretions designed strictly with reference to its relative fitness as a whole—" the completed volume being best understood," as has been said, " when viewed as such a series of growths, or strata, rising out from a settled foundation or centre."

There is probably no analogous case in the history of literature where the result of a profound artistic plan or conception—first launched forth, and briefly, yet sufficiently exemplified, as in the small volume of the *Leaves* of 1855, taking for foundation Man in his fulness of blood, power, amativeness, health, physique, and as standing in the midst of the objective world—a plan so steadily adhered to, yet so audaciously and freely built out of and upon, and with such epic consistency, after that start of 1855, developed in '57, '60, and '66, in successive moral, esthetic, and religious stages, each absorbing the previous ones, but striding on far ahead of them—gradually made more and more emotional, meditative, and patriotic—vitalized, heated to almost unbearable fervency by the author's personal part in the war, composing his songs of it in actual contact with its subjects, on the very field, or surrounded by the wounded "after the battle brought in"—chanting undismayed the strong chant of the Inseparable Union, amid the vehement crises and stormy dangers of the period : and so gradually arriving at the completed book of 1871-2, and crowning all in it with the electric and solemn poems of death and immortality—has so justified, and beyond measure justified, its first ambitious plan and promise.—*John Burroughs's* NOTES.

The book is the song of Idealism. Underneath every page lurks the conviction that all we fancy we see, may be but apparitions—and that

"The real Something has yet to be known."

Its scope and purpose are, therefore, by no means merely intellectual, or imaginative or esthetic. Using the term in its late t and largest, and not at all in its dogmatic and scholastic sense, Walt Whitman's poetry is, in its intention, *philosophic*. It is beyond the moral law, and will probably therefore always appal many. The moral law, it is true, is present, penetrating every verse, like shafts of light. But the whole relentless kosmos out of which come monsters and crime and the inexhaustible germs of all the heat of sex, and all the lawless rut and arrogant greed of the universe, and especially of the human race, are also there. Strange and paradoxical are these pages. They accept and celebrate Nature in absolute faith. Then, as over and out of some unbounded sea of turmoil, and whirl and hiss of stormy waves, hurrying and tumbling and chaotic—which they largely are—still, by attempts, indications at least, rise voices, sounds of the mightiest strength and gladdest hope yet given to man, with undismayed, unfaltering faith in destiny and life.

The history of the book, thus considered, not only resembles and tallies, in certain respects, the development of the great System of Idealistic Philosophy in Germany, by the "illustrious four"—except that the development of *Leaves of Grass* has been carried on within the region of a single mind,—but it is to be demonstrated, by study and comparison, that the same theory of the essential identity of the spiritual and the material worlds, the shows of Nature, the progress of civilization, the play of passions, the human intellect, and the relations between it and the concrete universe, which Kant prepared the way for, and Fichte, Schelling, and Hegel have given expression and statement in their system of transcendental Metaphysics,—this author has, with equal entirety. expressed and stated in *Leaves of Grass*, from a poet's point of view—singing afresh, out of it, the song of the Visible and invisible worlds—renewing, reconstructing, consistently with the modern genius, and deeper and wider than ever, the promises of immortality—endowing the elements of faith and pride with a vigor and *ensemble* before unknown—and furnishing to the measureless audience of humanity the only great Imaginative Work it yet possesses, in which the objective universe and Man, his soul, are observed and outlined, and the theory of Human Personality and Character projected, from the interior and hidden, but absolute background, of that magnificent System.—*John Burroughs's* NOTES.

It will always remain, however, impossible to clearly and fully state either the theory of Walt Whitman's composition, or describe his poems, its results. They may be absorbed out of themselves, but only after many perusals. They are elusive and puzzling, like their model, Nature, and form, in fact, a *person*, perhaps a *spirit*, more than a book. They read clearest tête-à-tête, and in the open air, or by the sea, or on the mountains, or in one's own room, alone, at night. They are to be inhaled like perfumes, and felt like the magnetism of a presence. They require affinity in the tastes and qualities of the reader. There is, mainly, that in them akin to concrete objects, the earth, the animals, storms, the actual sunrise or sunset, and not to the usual fine writing or imagery of poems. Yet their subject is not abstract or irrational Nature, but

living, heart-beating humanity, with all its interests and aspirations, its sadness and its joy.

It is to be added that the whole work, as it now stands, the result of the
several accretions, singularly hinges on the late Secession war.

In the "Contemporary Review," for December, 1875, there was a long and
elaborate article by Peter Bayne on "Walt Whitman's poems," written, evidently, after some study of *Leaves of Grass.* I know nothing myself about
this Peter Bayne, and I am willing to believe that he is an able and conscientious man. According to him Walt Whitman has almost every quality that a
writer ought not to have, and not a single one that a man must have to be a
poet. He says: "If I ever saw anything in print that deserved to be characterized as atrociously bad, it is the poetry of Walt Whitman." He says that
those who praise this poetry "appear to me to be playing off on the public a
well-intentioned, probably good-humored, but really cruel hoax."

Mr. Bayne finds *Leaves of Grass* "inflated," "wordy," "foolish," its originality is a "knack," a "trick." The poems are "extravagant," "paradoxical,"
"hyperbolical," "nonsensical," "indecent," "insane," "dull," "irremedica-
bly vile," "nauseous drivel," full of "extravagant conceit" and "idiocy."
In them Walt Whitman "mumbles truisms," talks "pretentious twaddle."
Leaves of Grass abounds with "the thoughts of other men spoiled by obtuse-
ness," it is "inhumanly insolent," "self-contradictory," "venomously malignant," "mawkish." About the middle of his article he announces that Walt
Whitman "is a demonstrated quack." He might one would think have been
content to stop there, but he goes on to say that *Leaves of Grass* is "void of
significance," "brainless," "a poor piece of mannerism," "wretchedly worked," "rant and rubbish," a "jingle," "linguistic silliness," "verbiage,"
"hopelessly bad writing." In a somewhat long article these complimentary
terms are used over and over and over again, so that, by the time we finish
reading it, Mr. Bayne does not leave us in any doubt as to *his* opinion of
Leaves of Grass and of its author. But in case such doubt should remain in
the reader's mind, he closes his review as follows:

"This is the political philosophy of bedlam, unchained in these ages chiefly
through the influence of Rousseau, which has blasted the hopes of freedom
wherever it has had the chance, and which must be chained up again, with
ineffable contempt, if the self-government of nations is to mean anything else
than the death and putrescence of civilization. Incapable of true poetical
originality, Whitman had the cleverness to invent a literary trick, and the
shrewdness to stick to it. As a Yankee phenomenon, to be good-humoredly
laughed at, and to receive that moderate pecuniary remuneration which nature
allows to vivacious quacks, he would have been in his place; but when influential critics introduce him to the English public as a great poet, the thing becomes
too serious for a joke. While reading Whitman in the recollection of what
has been said of him by those gentlemen, I realized with bitter painfulness
how deadly is the peril that our literature may pass into conditions of horrible
disease, the raging flame of fever taking the place of natural heat, the raving

of delirium superseding the enthusiasm of poetical imagination, the distortions of titanic spasms caricaturing the movements, dance-like and music-measured, of harmonious strength."

From Joaquin Miller's Washington Lecture, 1876.

Here in this high capital, there was once a colossal mind; an old, and an honorable old man, with a soul as grand as Homer's—the Milton of America. He walked these streets for years, a plain, brave old man, who was kind even to your dogs. He had done great service, in an humble way, in the army; he had written great books, which had been translated in all tongues and read in every land save his own. In consideration thereof he was given a little place under the Government, where he could barely earn bread enough for himself and his old mother. He went up and down, at work here for years. You mocked at him when you saw him. At last, stricken with palsy, he left the place, leaning upon his staff, to go away and die. I saw him but the other day, dying, destitute. Grand old Walt Whitman! Even now he looks like a Titan god! Don't tell me that a man gives all his youth and all his years in the pursuit of art, enduring poverty in the face of scorn, for nothing. That man shall live! He shall live when yon mighty dome of your Capitol no longer lifts its rounded shoulders against the circles of time. No, no! We laugh too much. We laugh at each other; we laugh at art; we laugh at men whom we have placed in exalted positions. We caricature great and good men, and disgrace only ourselves. We laugh at old men and old women. If ever I grow old I shall go to Europe, that I may be respected in my age. We laugh at religion and we laugh at love. There is no reverence in us; we are a race of clowns.

LEONARD WHEELER TO WALT WHITMAN.

O pure heart singer of the human frame
    Divine, whose poesy disdains control
    Of slavish bonds! each poem is a soul,
Incarnate born of thee, and given thy name.
Thy genius is unshackled as a flame
    That sunward soars, the central light its goal;
    Thy thoughts are lightnings, and thy numbers roll
In Nature's thunders that put art to shame.
    Exalter of the land that gave thee birth,
Though she insult thy grand gray years with wrong
    Of infamy, foul-branding thee with scars
    Of felon-hate, still shalt thou be on earth
Revered, and in Fame's firmament of song
    Thy name shall blaze among the eternal stars!

The London "Daily News," March 13, 1876, had published a long and eloquent letter from Robert Buchanan, about W. W., who was then lying very ill and very poor, at Camden. Mr. B.'s letter aroused a general and exciting volley of journalistic and editorial comments, both in Great Britain and America. There were several Atlantic cable telegrams or "messages" exchanged by newspapers on the subject. Certain New York writers resented R. B.'s accusations—attacking *Leaves of Grass* and its author in a furious style. The following is a sample:

.......The conclusion here arrived at, that Whitman, in his literary life and methods, is a mere trickster, is verified by his history. There was nothing peculiar about his early career. Belonging to a respectable family of farmers on Long Island, he went to school like other boys. When he grew to be a young man, he taught school like many other young men. When the cele-brated hard-cider and coon-skin political campaign stirred up the community in 1848, Whitman was drawn into it, and spouted democracy from the stump, as it is very common for young men to do in the country. Waxing ambitious, and wishing to escape democratic labor in the country, he came to New York to get a living by his wits. Well introduced by political acquaintance, he took to the business of writing for newspapers and magazines. He wrote stories, essays, and articles of all sorts that he could sell. He got access to the "Democratic Review," then the leading literary periodical of New York, edited by Hon. J. L. O'Sullivan. His contributions to this magazine from 1840 to 1850, signed "Walter Whitman," appear among those of Whit-tier, Poe, Brownson, Hawthorne, Tuckerman, Curtis, Godwin, and Taylor. They are decorous, jejune, and commonplace, contrasting strongly with the general quality of the magazine, and deserving no attention, they attracted none. Whitman also wrote for the Sunday papers and the daily press— turning his hand to anything he could get, and, if we are not mistaken, when the Washingtonian movement rose he availed himself of the excitement, and wrote a temperance novel. He was, moreover, a pleasant gentleman, of agreeable address, and went into society as well attired as his precarious resources would allow. In short he was an entirely respectable person, with nothing marked about him, and meeting with a dubious success due to moder-ate ability, qualified by excessive indolence.

Such was Whitman's "foreground." He had a dozen or fifteen years' ex-perience of practical literature and miscellaneous journalism in the metropolis, with every opportunity to win a position and make himself known if he had been capable of it. But Whitman had an ambition, born of egregious vanity, and he was not content with the obscurity from which he had been unable to escape in the open competitions of literature. Correctly concluding that it was of no use to pursue that tack longer, and determined to became a marked man somehow, he resolved to change his tactics. If he could not win fame, he would have notoriety; if the critics would not recognize him, he must find people that would. But, whatever may have been his ratiocination in the case, he changed his manner of life, and took to consorting with loafers. Donning a tarpaulin, blouse, and red flannel shirt, conspicuously open, he snubbed conventionalities, clambered on the outside of the omnibuses, culti-vated the drivers, and soon became a hero among the roughs. Sauntering leisurely along the thoroughfares and lingering at show-windows in his jaunty, uncouth costume, with a quiet air of defying the world, he soon attracted at-tention, and began to be talked of and inquired about. He thus got recog-nition as "Walt Whitman," patron and pride of the ruder elements of so-ciety.

Coincident with this external transformation there was an internal change equally marked. He made a strike in literature from his new standpoint. He had been scribbling away for years to no purpose, and at last he charged his old carbine with smut to the very muzzle, let drive, and brought down the first of American thinkers at the first shot. More literally, he issued a " pome," so called in his new vernacular, entitled *Leaves of Grass.* Mr. Whitman had never been celebrated; he had found nobody to celebrate him, and so the first words of his new book were, " I celebrate myself." It was a performance of unparalleled audacity. In total contrast with all that he had ever done before, it was an outrage upon decency, and not fit to be seen in any respectable house. Impudent and ridiculous as the book was, it would not have been easy to get it before the public, but accident and the author's cunning favored him. He sent a copy to Mr. Emerson, who returned a very flattering, but probably hasty private note, not dreaming that any public use would be made of it. Walt printed it at once, and the weight of Emerson's name sent the book straightway into circulation. Then people made pilgrimages to see the extraordinary man with the curious aspect that had made such an astonishing book, and of whom nobody had ever heard before; and the notion was spread that he was the original genius of Nature itself, unwarped by culture, unspoiled by society, careless of conventions, because dwelling far above them in the realm of his own sublime individuality. The external evidence thus coincides with Mr. Bayne's analysis of Whitman's writings in showing that they are but an affectation and a pretence. Those may believe who will that when he entered upon the rôle of loafer, dressed up accordingly, vulgarized his name, and wrote a book filled with drivel and indecency, Mr. Whitman suddenly became the inspired poet of democracy, and, as Swinburne says, "the greatest of American voices;" but against such a view common-sense protests. If his English devotees wish to testify their appreciation of Whitman's life and labors in a substantial way, let them quietly remit their sovereigns and do so. But let us be spared their insulting telegrams. The less publicity they give to their proceedings the better.

ARRAN LEIGH (ENGLAND) TO WALT WHITMAN.

" I, thirty-six years old, in perfect health, begin,
Hoping to cease not till death."—Chants Democratic.

They say that thou art sick, art growing old,
  Thou Poet of unconquerable health,
  With youth far-stretching, through the golden wealth
Of autumn, to Death's frostful, friendly cold;
The never-blenching eyes, that did behold
  Life's fair and foul, with measureless content,
  And gaze ne'er sated, saddened as they bent
Over the dying soldier in the fold
  Of thy large comrade love:—then broke the tear!
War-dream, field-vigil, the bequeathed kiss,
  Have brought old age to thee; yet, Master, now,
Cease not thy song to us; lest we should miss
  A death-chant of indomitable cheer,
  Blown as a gale from God;—Oh, sing it thou!

From the Camden, N. J., "New Republic," April 1st, 1876.

Some idiot, or worse (undoubtedly worse), has an editorial piece in the New York "Tribune," 30th inst., telling how, years since, a family of four children lived on the salary of a clerkship in the U. S. Attorney General's office—which clerkship, at the instance of the "authors of Washington," with Mr. E. C. Stedman at "the head" of them, was taken away from the sustenance of the four children, and bestowed on (of all the men in the world!) Walt Whitman! If this story is intended as a joke, the fun of it is too deep to be fathomable. Fortunately for the "authors of Washington" and the gentleman at "the head" of them, it is so entire and absolute a falsehood that it transcends the standard even of that magnificent District. We hope, for the sanity of "the head" aforesaid, that he had nothing to do with starting so small and dirty a fiction.

Later.—Since the above, appears a special card from Mr. Stedman (see "Tribune," 31st), fully exonerating that gentleman himself, and placing him in a perfectly candid and honorable attitude in the matter, as, indeed, was to be expected, to be consistent with his whole life.

But who, or rather *what*, has been writing the big and little editorials* that have appeared in the "Tribune" during the past week? Whitman's works, now finished—and his life now near its close—are beginning to claim serious judgment. The points involved are the deepest in nationality, art, literature. Has the "Tribune" nothing to offer but these frivolous slurs, hardly up to the level of the flash papers? or to invent shameless and petty personal items? or to reprint the foppish venom and aristocratic sputter of the "Saturday Review"?

From the "Camden Post," March 29th, 1877.

WALT WHITMAN.—HE VISITS NEW YORK AFTER FIVE YEARS' ABSENCE—HIGH-TONE SOCIETY NOW TAKES HIM TO ITS BOSOM—YET HE RIDES AGAIN ATOP OF THE BROADWAY OMNIBUSES AND FRATERNIZES WITH DRIVERS AND BOATMEN.—After an absence and sickness of nearly five years, says a New York paper of March 28th, 1877, the "old gray poet" has returned temporarily to his

Mast-hemm'd Manhattan,

and, in moderation, has been all the past month visiting, riding, receiving, and jaunting in and about the city, and, in good-natured response to pressure, has even appeared two or three times in brief, off-hand public speeches.

Mr. Whitman, at present near his fifty-ninth birth-day, is better in health and appearance than at any time since his paralytic attack at Washington in 1873. Passing through many grave experiences since that period, he still remains tall and stout, with the same florid face, with his great masses of hair and beard whiter than ever. Costumed in his usual entire suit of English gray, with loose sack-coat and trousers, broad shirt-collar open at the neck and guiltless of tie, he has, through the month, been the recipient and centre of social gatherings, parlors, club meetings, lunches, dinners, and even dress receptions—all of which he has taken with steady good nature, coolness, and moderation.

As he sat on the platform of the Liberal Club on Friday night last he looked like an old Quaker, especially as, in response to the suggestion of the President, and sitting near a window-draught, he unhesitatingly put on his old white broadbrim, and wore it the whole evening. In answer to pressing requests, however, toward the close, he rose to let the audience see him more fully, and, doffing his hat, smilingly said, in response to calls for a speech, that he "must decline to take any other part than listener, as he knew nothing of the subject under debate (blue glass), and would not add to the general stock of misinformation."

At the full-dress reception of the Portfolio and Palette Clubs on the Fifth Avenue, a few nights previous, as he slowly crossed the room to withdraw, he was saluted by a markedly peculiar murmur of applause, from a crowded au-

---

* They were written by the late Bayard Taylor.

dience of the most cultured and elegant society of New York, including most of the artists of the city. It was a singularly spontaneous and *caressing* testimonial, joined in heartily by the ladies, and the old man's cheeks, as he hobbled along through the kindly applause and smiles, showed a deep flush of gratified feeling.

Mr. Whitman has been the guest, most of the month, of Mr. and Mrs. Johnston, of 113 East Tenth Street, whose parlors have been thrown open on two special occasions for informal public receptions in compliment to him, which were crowded, happy, and brilliant to the highest degree.

Nearly every fair day Mr. Whitman has explored the city and neighborhood, often as near as possible after the fashion of old times. Again he has taken rides up and down Broadway on top of the Fifth Avenue and Twenty-third Street omnibuses, and talked with his old chums, the drivers, receiving incessant salutes of raised hands as he passed and was recognized. He has been over to Brooklyn and taken the unsurpassed views again from the hills of Fort Greene, and ocean vistas from Prospect Park. Again, too, he has lingered for several trips up in the pilot-house, crossing Fulton ferry, conferring with his old comrades the pilots and deck hands. Again he has dwelt long on the picturesqueness, beauty, and unequalled show of our waters and bay.

Walt Whitman will finish his fifty-eighth year on the coming 31st May, that being his birth-day. Physically, his paralysis is still uncured, and he has serious stomachic trouble, and bad lameness, but he gets around quite a good deal, keeps always excellent spirits, believes thoroughly not only in the future world, but the present, and especially in our American part of it.

A foreign tourist and interviewer, under date of March 30th, 1877, writes: I have to-day, with two companions, just visited Walt Whitman, at Camden, New Jersey, and had a good talk with him. He takes the late English whirlwind about him and his writings very quietly. I am convinced he really cares nothing for popular or literary incense—views things mainly, I should say, from his own standpoint, and is, as the world goes, a queer, proud man. That he is poor (which he really is), that the American publishers won't publish him, that the magazines reject his MSS., that the bards of fame here ignore him, and that all the big poetic collection-books leave him out in the cold, are facts which I believe in my soul he is far more proud of than put out by. He has a clear gray eye, and his manners, though a little haughty and *pent*, combine, with entire self-possession, a wonderful warmth and magnetism. The only bitterness that escaped him was about the persistent embezzlement and theft, during his illness and helplessness of the last three years, by his agents (they sold for him on commission) of the deeply-needed income due from his New York book-sales, "which, fortunately," he added in a dry tone, "were not so large, either." He is permanently paralyzed, walks only a little, sometimes hardly at all, and suffers from a chronic affection of the stomach; but keeps up, and often gets on the river here, the Delaware, and over to Philadelphia. On my speaking of the Secession war, and at the request of one of our party, a lady, he read his poem of "The Wound-Dresser." (I have felt disposed since to fasten that name upon him.) Whitman is tall, middling heavy in build of body, with a large head and red face, very plentiful hair and beard (white as snow), talks neither much nor little, and with a strong and musical voice. Finally, I think the old fellow the most *human* being I have ever met.

19

Letter from Greenock, Scotland, 1879

I first became acquainted with *Leaves of Grass* four years ago (when I was twenty two years of age) through Rossetti's book of selections. Previously I had been familiar with Carlyle, and then with Goethe, and then with the prose and verse of Emerson. But it was more than all these my own deep experience that prepared me for receiving Walt Whitman's writings with instant and passionate acceptance. I shall never forget my sensations on reading certain parts of the prose preface to the [first] *Leaves of Grass.* I said again and again, " Here the universal mother herself is speaking,"—for example, in regard to pride and sympathy, " Neither can stretch too far while it stretches in company with the other." Then I found it said of the "greatest poet," " He is indifferent which chance happens, and which possible contingency of fortune or misfortune." It was as if I had heard speaking the very inmost spirit of Christ, and for the next few weeks I remember I was quite feverish with joy, and no wonder, for I then for the first time saw clearly. By degrees I saw what is called evil to be but immaturity, and I saw the immortal beauty of the laws of pain. I did not, at that time, dwell much upon the thought of immortality, and had not yet penetrated to Walt Whitman's conception of it, but my faith was without cloud; I knew I had " Come well, and should go well." I saw that one cannot possibly lose anything, for I saw that every condition is profitable and blessed. I saw how great it is to be subject to the eternal laws even when they maim or break us. I saw that heroism is reached when one is able to see and say triumphantly at any possible worst, " Yes, I may be broken, but the law that breaks me is righteous and immortal." Walt Whitman seemed to have bidden the cosmos lie close upon me that it might enter into me at every pore. It seemed that he had taken me by wild and rejoicing seas and hills, and transformed me from a doubter and despairer into a piece of nature capable of strength and joy. Since I have known *Leaves of Grass*, books, mere reading, is less important to me than formerly. I like best to be out in the open air, and among men and women (old and young) and children, and animals, and when I ask myself whether others can possibly feel the same delight in living that I do, I am constantly reminded that life and death might have seemed less great to me (and to how many, many more throughout the world) but for Walt Whitman.

JOAQUIN MILLER TO WALT WHITMAN.

O Titan soul, ascend your starry steep,
 On golden stair, to gods and storied men !
Ascend ! nor care where thy traducers creep.
 For what may well be said of prophets, when
A world that's wicked comes to call them good ?
Ascend and sing ! As kings of thought who stood
 On stormy heights, and held far lights to men,
Stand thou, and shout above the tumbled roar,
Lest brave ships drive and break against the shore.

What though thy sounding song be roughly set ?
 Parnassus' self is rough ! Give thou the thought,
The golden ore, the gems that few forget ;
 In time the tinsel jewel will be wrought.
Stand thou alone, and fixed as destiny,
 An imaged god that lifts above all hate ;

Stand thou serene and satisfied with fate;
Stand thou as stands the lightning-riven tree,
That lords the cloven clouds of gray Yosemite.

Yea, lone, sad soul, thy heights must be thy home;
Thou sweetest lover! love shall climb to thee
Like incense curling some cathedral dome,
. From many distant vales. Yet thou shalt be,
O grand, sweet singer, to the end alone.
But murmur not. The moon, the mighty spheres,
Spin on alone through all the soundless years;
Alone man comes on earth; he lives alone;
Alone he turns to front the dark unknown.

From " Papers for the Times"—by Frank W. Walters—*January, 1880, London, England.*

At last, he for whom we looked is come. America has found voice. The teeming life of that wonderful New World has risen into song; the infant civilization can now boast a true-born poet of its own. If Greece had its Homer, if England had its Chaucer, so, now, America has brought forth the first-born of, we believe, a long line of glorious bards such as the world has never seen before. To some, who have only heard Walt Whitman's name, or only seen him laughed to scorn by reviewers who fail to understand him, our words will seem extravagant. To us who have read and re-read his poems with ever-increased delight, it seems impossible to express our sense of their power and beauty. Their power is sometimes overwhelming, and to read some of them produces an effect similar to that of gazing upon a tempest, listening to a hurricane, or watching the lightning. Their beauty and pathos now fill the soul with rapturous joy in the perfection of the world, and now plunge one into tears over the mysteries and sufferings of human life. These poems are called *Leaves of Grass;* and the title is excellent. They are one with Nature; they are not *made,* they *grow;* they have all the characteristics of natural productions. This man wrote because the spirit moved him; necessity was laid upon him; his utterances pour forth from volcanic depths of soul. To read them is to come near to him. His personality electrifies you in every living sentence. He speaks to you, and speaks the very things you have *felt,* but could not put into words. He interprets your soul to you. He takes you by the hand; you feel the beating of his pulse. He calls you his comrade; he puts his arms around you, takes you to his breast, and you feel the beating of his heart. He invites you forth with him to sound the depths and scale the heights; and, with your hand in his, you go forth without fear, as under the protection of a strong elder brother. These poems are not part of the man, they are the man himself. They are the Incarnate Word in which he manifests the fulness of his manhood. Here is not merely the poet—here is the MAN, through and through, from .top to toe. He gives to you the unspeakable gift of himself—not merely his thoughts, but himself. You not only hear him, you see him; you not only see him, but you see through him; you not only see through him, but live in him; he possesses you.

And because this man has burst the ornamental chains of rhyme and metre, because his *Leaves of Grass* do not present a well-clipped lawn, because his wild flowers are not arranged into garden beds, because his intellectual growth is wild and rude as a primeval forest of his own America—there are some who would question his right to the title of poet. If Walt Whitman is not a poet, all the worse for poetry. If your definition of the poet will not admit this man into the sacred circle, then your definition needs revising. If these poems do not belong to what you call *art*, then your art is only *artificial*, it has lost its root in those depths of Nature out of which true art must grow—its life is gone; and in its place a nobler art shall rise, and of this new kingdom of the beautiful, Whitman shall be the earliest prophet, though he comes as a rude voice from the trackless wilderness, though he is clothed in camel's hair and leathern girdle, and feeds his mighty vigor on locusts and wild honey. If Whitman be not a poet, yet he has done something more than write poems; he has shown us that the world is God's poem. He says he has listened to the Eternal Voices, and they speak but one harmonious Truth. He has heard the tramp of the generations across the stage of time, and all the sounds rise into music. The clang of labor, the clash of battle, the shouts of joy, the groans of agony, the wailings of grief—all these are varying passages in the Music of Humanity.

We cannot wonder that Whitman lays tremendous emphasis on the body. Despised and counted unclean so long, it is time that we should proclaim, with unfaltering lips, the divinity of the flesh. Men have been too ready to take at its word the teaching of an emasculated pietism. They have said: " If this Body is utterly and hopelessly corrupt, then there is no use attempting to purify it. We will take it at the value you put on it. Its natural functions shall be regarded as shameful; its appetites and passions shall seek their fulfil-ment in dark places of the earth." Now, with all our heart, do we thank Walt Whitman for some of the poems which have been described as shame-less glorifications of the Flesh. *Sensuous*, indeed, they are, and that with a vengeance; but however they may appear to others, to us they are never *sensual.* No lustful mind need come to these severe pages thinking to gratify its morbid taste. We could mention books counted sacred, and novels reckoned polite, which will answer the vile purpose admirably—but not these *Leaves of Grass.* Whitman's offence (for so it is counted) is that he will sing the *whole* Man—not only Soul, but Body too.

It does seem to us that this is teaching which we sadly need. It is similar to the teaching of Novalis—"When I lay my hand upon human flesh, I touch God." It is the same as that fine doctrine of Paul—"Know ye not that ye are the Temple of God, and that the Spirit of God dwelleth in you? If any man defile the Temple of God, him shall God destroy; for the Temple of God is holy, whose temple ye are." Whitman emphasizes that Pauline doc-trine. He says that the Body is more than the Temple of indwelling Spirit; to him the Body is the LIVING GARMENT of the Soul—Mind and Matter are inextricably bound up together—yea they are but aspects of the one Manhood. If we could impress this doctrine of the divinity of the Body upon the young men of the present day, in the next generation our civilization would be regen-erated, and a moral reformation would pass over our plague-stricken society with grander results than all the theological reformations of the past.

He teaches the democracy of the soul; he can discover the divinity of every human being. Democracy, "the purport and aim of all the past," is the right of every man to become all that he is capable of becoming. He will not deny that Christ is divine, but his affirmation embraces every member of the race to which Christ belongs.

In regard to his religion in the depest sense it may be called the Religion of Humanity. He denies none of the faiths of the world, for all these grow out of the soul; he accepts all Bibles, for these contain the great thoughts to which the Soul has given birth. On the questions of God and Immortality he has some sphinx-like utterances. He refuses to argue about God, and he says he needs no logic to prove his Immortality. The thought of the Infinite, the sense of an Eternal Presence giving progress and perfection to the world, this to him is God. He never complains. Though he has fathomed the depths of sin, and borne a vicarious load of suffering, he yet declares that the world is perfect, that everything is in its place, that all events happen in due order. In passionate optimism he affirms that *All is Truth ;* that if we could see far enough and deep enough, all would appear very good. For the future he is at peace.

We think we have said enough to prove that this American singer brings us a veritable Gospel—a Gospel which transfigures Flesh into Spirit, changes mechanical duty into living impulse, and makes life rhythmic as the tides, pulsating as the heart, moving in its orb like a star—a Gospel which reveals Time's full atonement for all the sin and suffering of the world, which takes the darkness from mortality, and shows Death as a beauteous white-robed angel—a Gospel which baptizes our changeful existence into one perfect and abiding Life, and points for every soul to the vast heritage of immortal progress.

From the " Camden Post," January 7th, 1880.

WALT WHITMAN HOME AGAIN.—After an absence since last August Walt Whitman returned yesterday to his home in Camden, from a long and varied journey through the Central States of the Union. His travel has been mainly devoted to Colorado, Kansas and Missouri, but he has made visits to four or five other States. His objects of especial attention have been the Rocky Mountains, the Great Plains, and the Mississippi River, with their life, scenery and idiosyncrasies. Of the West generally he says not the half has been told. He is in love with Denver City, and speaks admiringly of Missouri and Indiana.

Going and coming, largely by different routes and with side excursions, Mr. Whitman has travelled over 5000 miles. After some pretty rugged experiences, and a tedious fit of sickness, he returns to Camden in his average health, and with strength and spirits " good enough to be mighty thankful for," as he expresses it.

From the " Philadelphia Press," May 26th, 1880.

To the Editor :—Your report in to-day's paper of Colonel Ingersoll's Tuesday evening's lecture, on " What Shall I Do to be Saved? " is interspersed every second or third paragraph with " Amen from Walt Whitman," the poet's name appearing in this manner in the long report and introduction some eight or ten times. It was at my invitation that Mr. Whitman went to the lecture, and I sat at his side throughout its delivery. He neither uttered the " Amen " which the reporter puts so often in his mouth, nor once made any sign whatever, either by voice or hand, of approval or disapproval, but maintained his usual undemonstrative manner throughout. (The " Amens " were uttered by a person immediately to the left of Mr. Whitman; the mistake was therefore a natural one.)

While I am about it, would you give me room to correct " The Genesis of Walt Whitman " in " Appleton's Journal "—not the malignance and falsehood of the whole article, but a small specimen brick. The " Journal " speaks of Walt Whitman as habitually wearing, while living in New York, a red flannel shirt, a blouse and a tarpaulin hat. It doesn't seem to me to matter if he did;

but the fact is, he never in his life donned either of these articles. Whitman always dressed about the same as he does now.

One might say that such mistakes are not important, and at all events get rectified in time. But they don't; they often make so-called history. Walt Whitman himself laughs at them as merely amusing, but they are painful to his friends, who are more in number than perhaps is generally suspected, and as one of these I write you this letter, which I hope you will have the kind-ness to insert.   R. M. B.

From " The Truthseeker," September, 1880.

There are positively awful passages in praise of even the fiercest bodily passions—terrific shouts and cries for absolute abandonment to these. In some passages, this fierce outcry is changed for deliberate descriptions of equally appalling coolness; and both are alike utterly amazing and unquot-able—absolutely unlike anything anywhere else in the English language. Few will be able to picture a world and a state of society in which all this could be anything but wild and brutal excess, to be forcibly repressed or vig-orously struck at and killed. Alas! it is this that makes it impossible to put his complete writings into every one's hands. Taking the world as it is, it is all wrong; but it is not impossible to imagine a world, and a better world too, where it would be all right. The world as it is, is, and has to be, a world of restraints, delicacies, and reticences, as to the body and the body's functions; but in a purer world there might be absolute openness, innocent unconscious-ness of uncleanness and wrong, and beautiful natural abandonment: and, though only the minority will see this, we believe that Walt Whitman belongs far more to that world than to this, where many of his utterances will be de-nounced as dangerous or even detestable: and dangerous perhaps they are. In a tremendous sense he realizes and carries out the divine word,—" What God hath cleansed, that call not thou unclean:" only he would say,—" What God hath created, that call not thou unclean." His glorification and mi-nute praise of the human body, and of every fibre and use of it, is simply overwhelming.

He knows all the significance of his work. He says of the way to himself, "the way is suspicious,—the result uncertain, perhaps destructive." He does not beseech you to go with him; rather he dissuades you : " Therefore release me now," he says. " Let go your hand from my shoulders. Put me down, and depart on your way." " Nor will my poems do good only," he says; " they will do just as much evil, perhaps more." Why, then, does he give forth these poems? He would say,—I cannot help it. The free birds sing: and I must speak—or die. His poems are the outbursting of his strong, free, boundlessly sensitive self.

Mark well again, then,—he is the poet of a fresh, free, unbound, natural, new-made world,—the poet of the earth newly-turned-up, of the primeval woods newly explored, of wharves and docks and busy towns, and the strong flood of life all new and strange—nothing stale, flat, commonplace, familiar; in a word, the poet who is most like a child-man, opening his wide wonder-ing eyes, brimming over with joy, and feeling the mystery and beauty and de-light of bodily sensations in a world of boundless animation, vigor, and ever fresh surprise.

Motto suggested by a lady for this Volume, from Tennyson's " Idyls."

. . . . . . " Now I know thee, what thou art;
Thou art the highest, *and most human too."*

From "The Long Islander," August 5th, 1881.

WALT WHITMAN IN HUNTINGTON.—After more than forty years' absence, the author of *Leaves of Grass*, and founder of this paper, has been visiting our town the past week in company with Dr. R. M. Bucke, of London, Canada, who is engaged in writing a life of "the good gray Poet." They put up at the Huntington House, and spent several days in calls and explorations at West Hills, on and around the old Whitman homestead and farm (now owned and occupied by Philo R. Place), and also down to the house where, in 1819, Walt was born (the farm now of Henry Jarvis), and the adjacent parts of the country for several miles. They were especially interested in the old Whitman burial hill and cemetery, containing the poet's ancestors for many generations, dating more than two hundred years back, with its rows of ancient moss covered graves. The poet and Dr. Bucke also went over to the Van Velsor homestead, adjacent to Cold Spring, the birthplace of Mr. Whitman's mother, Louisa, daughter of Major Cornelius Van Velsor. The house, barn, and other buildings were all gone, and the ground ploughed over. But about a hundred rods off was the old Van Velsor burial ground, on a hill in the woods, and one of the most significant and picturesque spots of the kind it is possible to conceive.

Mr. Whitman was called upon during his brief stay in Huntington by many old and some new friends, among others, the following: Charles Velsor, of Cold Spring; Benjamin Doty, of same place; in West Hills, Lemuel Carll, John Chichester, Miss Jane Rome, William May, and Samuel Scudder; in Huntington, Henry Lloyd, Lawyer Street, Albert Hopper, Smith Sammis, Thomas Rogers, John Fleet, Ezra Prime, Henry Sammis, Thomas Aitkins, Charles E. Shepard, Messrs. Wood and Rusco, and Fred Galow.

LINN PORTER TO WALT WHITMAN.

Hawthorne Rooms, Boston, April 15th, 1881.

I knew there was an old, white-bearded seer
    Who dwelt amid the streets of Camden town;
    I had the volumes which his hand wrote down—
The living evidence we love to hear
Of one who walks reproachless, without fear.
    But when I saw that face, capped with its crown
    Of snow-white almond-buds, his high renown
Faded to naught, and only did appear
    The calm old man, to whom his verses tell,
All sounds were music, even as a child;
    And then the sudden knowledge on me fell,
For all the hours his fancies had beguiled,
    No verse had shown the Poet half so well
As when he looked into my face and smiled.

From the (Boston) "Literary World," December 3d, 1881.

.   I was very glad to read your notice of Whitman's stuff. The original *Leaves of Grass* is the dirtiest unsuppressed book ever published in this country. I should judge that the new edition has not been purified.—*Concord, Mass.*

. . . I want to tell you also how much I liked that notice of Walt Whitman's *Leaves of Grass* in your last. It was the right thing to say, strongly and rightly said.—*Newport, R. I.*

. . . You may be sure of the sympathy and thanks of most of your readers when you call a spade a spade, and give the right name to the indecency of Walt Whitman. . . . It is a comfort to find a newspaper, that has a reputation for intelligence and honesty, willing to speak the plain truth. You did the same thing some months since of a book of Heine's. . . . I hope you will continue to remind your readers that no brilliancy of intellect can atone for a want of common decency.—*Philadelphia.*

From the " *Boston Herald*," *April 18th, 1881.*

Walt Whitman is now on his second visit to Boston. He came quietly, but he finds himself the subject of an ovation given with such hearty cordialness as to prove with what a real affection he has come to be regarded. At about the time when the St. Botolph Club was organized, a few of the young fellows happening to speak of Lincoln, it was suggested by one of them that they ought to have Walt Whitman here to read his commemoration essay on the great President, a service that he reverently performs every year on the anniversary of Lincoln's death. The idea took root at once, and the arrangements were made that have resulted in the present occasion. It was a pleasant sight at the Hawthorne Rooms on Friday evening; the fine audience representing the best side of Boston literary activity, and the poet, with venerable hair and beard, but sturdy presence, reading his fine essay with the native eloquence born of sincere feeling—just as if reading to a few personal friends—but with none of the tricks of the elocutionizing trade.

He has been welcomed to Boston with open arms. Old and young, old friends and new, have gathered around him. The young men have taken to him as one with themselves, as one of those fresh natures that are ever youthful; the older ones, many of whom might once have been disposed to regard him with disfavor, now have grown to see the real core of the man in its soundness and sweetness, and are equally hearty in their welcome. " He is a grand old fellow " is everybody's verdict. Walt Whitman has in times past been, perhaps, more ignorantly than wilfully misunderstood, but time brings about its revenges, and his present position goes to prove that, let a man be true to himself, however he defies the world, the world will come to respect him for his loyalty. Perhaps frankness may be said to be the keynote of Walt Whitman's nature. He glows with responsive cordiality. He is not afraid to be himself, and he asserts it with ideal American unconventionality,—that is, he is thoroughly individual in his personal ways and expressions, and all without offence to the individualism of others. He looks it in his strong features, full of the repose of force in reserve; his clear, friendly blue eyes, the open windows of a healthy brain; the pleasant, sympathetic voice ; the easy suit of pleasant gray, and the open shirt with rolling collar; the broad, black felt hat contrasting with his white hair. All express the large-hearted, large-minded man. His ruddy face and powerful frame indicate good health, and it is only when he rises that one sees in his slow walk the invalid that he now is,—" a half-paralytic," he calls himself. He is hearty in speaking of his contemporaries, and he thinks America is to be esteemed fortunate in having felt the influence of four such clean, pure and healthful natures as Emerson, Bryant, Whittier, and Longfellow. As his frank comments on others are without reserve, so his free talk of himself is without egotism, as can well be the case with a man of such large personality.

When in Washington, he was astonished to receive a letter from Tennyson, wonderfully cordial and hearty, inviting him to come to see him in England, and full of friendly interest. It was not so much about his book as it was a personal tribute, which seemed the more amazing coming from Tennyson, who never goes out of his way, even for kings. This was the beginning of a group of devoted admirers in England, and, until recently, the poet has received the most of his support from the British isles, where he has sold the greater number of his books.

One of the latest articles on Walt Whitman was that of Stedman's in a recent number of " Scribner's." It is an appreciative and fine feeling paper, full of friendly recognition. In parts, however, it seems as if he failed to grasp the true significance of his subject. He makes, for instance, a most mistaken comparison between Whitman and William Blake. Whitman, in fact, had probably never heard of William Blake until Stedman's article appeared. And it seems difficult, indeed, to find any similarity between the grand healthiness of Whitman and the morbid, diseased thoughts of the half-crazy Englishman. Regarding Stedman's characterization of certain passages in Whitman's poems as false to art, since Nature was not to be seen in her nakedness, for she always took care to cover up her naked places with vegetation, a great poet said to the writer that there were times when Nature was to be seen when she was in all her nakedness, and that it was proper that she should thus be seen; a great artist could so present her, and thereby there would be no violation of the laws of art. Concerning these passages, Walt Whitman says that, after much thinking it over, he feels that he was right in writing them, and that he would not have them otherwise. There is something way back of logic, back of reason, that prompts us, and this feeling tells him that he was right.

From the Philadelphia "Progress," April 30th, 1881.

WALT WHITMAN'S LATE LECTURE IN BOSTON.—There is a mixture of pensiveness, fitness, and of his own individuality—perhaps obstinacy—in Walt Whitman's determination to keep in his own way every recurrence of the anniversary of President Lincoln's death. " Oft as the rolling years bring back this hour," he said in his discourse last week in Boston, " let it again, however briefly, be dwelt upon; for my own part, I hope and intend, till my own dying day, whenever the 14th or 15th of April comes, to annually gather a few friends, and hold its tragic reminiscence."

Twice before has he read his notes on this theme; once, in 1879, in New York city, and in 1880 in Philadelphia. This time it was in Boston, where he had been invited by the young journalists, artists, and by the St. Botolph Club. The old " Evening Traveller " of next day, April 16th, 1881, in an editorial leader thus describes the speaker and the speech :

" There was a theme for poet or painter in the scene at the Hawthorne Rooms last evening, when Walt Whitman read to a fascinated group of auditors his reflections upon the death of Abraham Lincoln. As he entered, unattended and unannounced, and made his way painfully along the narrow aisle, supported by his stout stick, to the desk behind which looked out the face of the martyr President, and sitting in the broad oaken armchair, his clear, resonant voice filling every part of the room, the venerable prophet of Democracy presented a picturesque figure. He was clad in his customary suit of light gray, his fresh and striking countenance set off by waves of snow-white hair and beard, the ' copious blanchness ' of his linen adding yet another element to the chaste simplicity of his attire; while in the audience before him were many eminent in art and letters, who had come to pay homage to one who is already fast being regarded as the typical citizen of the republic. There was something of poetic justice, too, in thinking of the reception of this man who had been scorned as a barbarian rhymester, whose burning lines, surcharged with the future, had long fallen unheeded upon the indifferent ears of his country. men, and whose very presence was now felt almost as a benediction.

" The scenes in that mighty drama which those present were gathered to commemorate were painted by Whitman in a series of bold, masterly strokes. The great incidents leading up to the culminating tragedy were swiftly enu. merated; then the scenes of that wild and eventful April night, in clear-cut, well-chosen words, every epithet bearing its weight of meaning; and then the speaker went on in prophetic strains to foretell the significance of this great event, and its influence upon the art, history, and literature of the nation. The lecture closed with the recitation by the author of his grandly pathetic lament, ' O Captain, my Captain,' the lines gaining new grandeur and pathos as they came from his lips.

" It was a scene which those present will long remember as pregnant with meaning to their whole after lives."

From the "Boston Globe," August 24th, 1881.

In a small inner room connected with the printing establishment of Rand, Avery & Co., Walt Whitman, the poet, was reading by a table yesterday. Near by was a pile of corrected proof-sheets bearing the heading *Leaves of Grass.* His ruddy features were almost concealed by his white hair and beard. When he laid down his book on the intrusion of the writer, his eye, still bright and keen, glowed with a genuine good nature. No, he had no objections to entering into a conversation which should be given to the public, provided there was any interest in what he might say. He was here, he said, to look over the proofs of his new *Leaves of Grass,* which James R. Osgood & Co. are to issue.

" It is a long time," remarked the reporter, " since the book by that name was first given to the world." " Yes," replied the poet, leaning back com- fortably in his chair, and looking reflectively across the table at the writer, who had seated himself opposite, " it is now, I believe, twenty-six years since I began to work upon the structure; and this edition will complete the design which I had in my mind when I began to write. The whole affair is like one of those old architectural edifices, some of which were hundreds of years building, and the designer of which has the whole idea in his mind from the first. His plans are pretty ambitious, and, as means or time permits, he adds part after part, perhaps at quite wide intervals. To a casual observer it looks in the course of its construction odd enough. Only after the whole is com- pleted, one catches the idea which inspired the designer, in whose mind the relation of each part to the whole had existed all along. That is the way it has been with my book. It has been twenty-six years building. There have been seven different hitches at it. Seven different times have parts of the edifice been constructed,—sometimes in Brooklyn, sometimes in Washington, sometimes in Boston, and at other places. The book has been built partially in every part of the United States; and this edition is the completed edifice.

" Then I do not know whether it will appear to the casual reader, but to myself my whole book turns on the Secession War. I desired to make it the poem of the War—not in a way in which the old war poems, such as the ' Iliad,' were war poems, but in entirely a new way. This came to me after the second part was composed, and has readily fused in with the other parts of my plan, and even dominated them."

From the Springfield (Mass.) "Republican," November 10th, 1881.

It was a great age, men will say hereafter, and a grand country, that could produce in one generation three figures for posterity to gaze on, like John Brown, Abraham Lincoln, and Walt Whitman—men unlike each other and unlike all others, such as no other land produced or could produce; embodied heroism, embodied sense and sensibility, embodied imagination. So I view the three men, in the mass of their character—not considering the loose and trivial details which to many eyes have seemed to be the whole character. If it were possible to see the genius of a great people throwing itself now into this form, now into that—as the prairie wheatfield takes the quick shape of the passing wind—it would be just to say that we had seen this mystery in the "plain heroic magnitude of mind" with which Brown met death,—in the broad and patient wisdom of Lincoln,—and in the immense landscape of Whitman's teeming imagination. His *Leaves of Grass*, as he has now published them, complete the vast picture of his mind, and bring out not merely the confusion of details, which we could only see at first by the light of poetic flashes—but the broad unity of the piece. It is as if the ancient seamen had found their ocean-god slumbering along his shores, and upon near view could only see a hand here, an eyebrow there, a floating mass of beard elsewhere—but when they stood back from the strand, or best if they climbed a hill of prospect, the symmetry and articulation of the mighty frame plainly appeared, and they knew by sight their unconscious divinity, Neptune.

There is in Whitman's verse, more than in any other modern poet's, what Keats called "that large utterance of the early gods"—an indistinct grandeur of expression not yet moulded to the melody of Shakespeare, Lucretius, and Æschylus, but like what Keats again calls "the overwhelming voice of huge Enceladus."

It is when he speaks of Lincoln and the Civil War that Whitman is least indistinct. And no other of our poets—no, nor all of them together—has so well caught and rendered the spirit of that struggle as he has done it.

From the "New York Tribune," November 19th, 1881.

After the dilettante indelicacies of William H. Mallock and Oscar Wilde, we are presented with the slop-bucket of Walt Whitman. The celebrity of this phenomenal poet bears a curious disproportion to the circulation of his writings. Until now, it cannot be said that his verses have ever been published at all. They have been printed irregularly and read behind the door. They have been vaunted extravagantly by a band of extravagant disciples; and the possessors of the books have kept them locked up from the family. Some have valued them for the barbaric "yawp," which seems to them the note of a new, vigorous, democratic, American school of literature; some for the fragments of real poetry floating in the turbid mass; some for the nastiness and animal insensibility to shame which entitle a great many of the poems to a dubious reputation as curiosities. Now that they are thrust into our faces at the bookstalls there must be a re-examination of the myth of the Good Gray Poet. It seems to us that there is no need at this late day to consider Mr. Whitman's claims to the immortality of genius. That he is a poet most of us frankly admit. His merits have been set forth many times, and at great length, and if the world has erred materially in its judgment of them the error has been a lazy and unquestioning acquiescence in some of the extreme demands of his vociferous partisans. The chief question raised by this publication is whether anybody—even a poet—ought to take off his trousers in the market-place. Of late years we believe that Mr. Whitman has not chosen to be so shocking as he was when he had his notoriety to make, and many of his admirers—the rational ones—hoped that the *Leaves of Grass* would be weeded before he set them out again. But this has not been done : and indeed Mr. Whitman could hardly do it without falsifying the first principle of his philosophy, which is a belief in his own perfection, and the second principle, which is a belief in the preciousness of filth. " Divine am I," he. cries, " Divine am I inside and out, and I make holy whatever I touch or am touched from. The scent of these arm-pits aroma finer than prayer, This head more than churches, Bibles, and all the creeds." He knows that he is " august." He does not care for anybody's opinion. He is

> Walt Whitman, a kosmos, of Manhattan the son,
> Turbulent, fleshy, sensual, eating. drinking, and breeding,
> No sentimentalist, no stander above men and women or apart from them,
> No more modest than immodest.

There is nothing in the universe better than Walt Whitman. That is the burden of the " Song of Myself," which fills fifty pages of the present volume:

> I dote on myself, there is that lot of me, and all so luscious.

Nothing is obscene or indecent to him. It is his mission to shout the for-bidden voices, to tear the veil off everything, to clarify and transfigure all that is dirty and vile, to proclaim that garbage is just as good as nectar if you are only lusty enough to think so. His immodesty is free from glamour of every sort. Neither amatory sentiment nor susceptibility to physical beauty appears to have anything to do with it. It is entirely bestial; and in this respect we know nothing in literature which can be compared with it. Walt Whitman, despising what he calls conventionalism, and vaunting the athletic democracy, asks to be accepted as the master of a new poetical school, fresh, free, stal-wart, " immense in passion, pulse, and power," the embodiment of the spirit of vigorous America. But the gross materialism of his verses represents art in its last degradation rather than its rude infancy.

From the "Boston Transcript."

Now when every legitimate leaf of grass is looking its freshest and green-est, the sun of adversity seems to have wilted—permanently, let us hope—those " leaves " which twenty-five years ago sprouted from our literary soil under the auspices of Walt Whitman. The attorney-general of the Common-wealth notified the publishers of *Leaves of Grass* that certain changes must be made in the contents of the book, or its sale must cease. The publishers manifest perfect willingness to accede to the demand, but the author stubbornly refuses to omit a word or change a line. A great many people who know nothing about the book will wonder at Whitman's refusal to re-edit it, but to tell the honest, shameful truth, the very portions objected to are all that have made the book sell. It is now nearly thirty years since Whitman uttered his literary " yawp." It was at a peculiar period in American literature. None of our great poets had then developed their full strength. There was a lack of that brawny, unconventional vigor in American poetry which the popular mind yearned for, and which was felt by right to belong to it: The very audacity and lawlessness of *Leaves of Grass* did for the moment what no amount of merit could have done, and many enthusiastic critics saw in it promises of the coming man. In England the volume was received as a work of special inspiration by the pre-Raphaelites, and an edition was brought out by Rossetti in 1868. An Irish critic demanded for the author a place by the side of Æschylus, Homer, Dante, and Shakespeare, intimating that he would not suffer by comparison with any one of the four.

From the Springfield (Mass.) "Republican," May 23d, 1882.

LETTER FROM R. M. BUCKE.

I desire briefly to call your attention to the fact that in this country, which boasts of its liberty, and especially of its free press, the publication of perhaps the best book which has so far been produced in it has been stopped by legal interference. I allude to the interdiction of the issue of *Leaves of Grass* by a notice served upon James R. Osgood & Co., its publishers, by District Attorney Oliver Stevens in March last; which notice was to the effect that unless the issue of the book at once ceased the firm would be prosecuted "in pursuance of the public statutes respecting obscene literature."

It is not easy for me, who for the last sixteen years have made this book a constant companion, and have received (as have so many others) unspeakable benefit from it, to speak of this action in terms of moderation; but I shall, nevertheless, try to do so. It seems, then, that this is the outcome of the boasted freedom of America toward the end of the nineteenth century, that the publication of a book, the most honest, pure, religious and moral, of this or of almost any other age, can be stopped, and is stopped by the law. That this could happen would be bad enough if the book were, for instance, comparable to Byron's "Don Juan," Sterne's "Tristram Shandy," Fielding's "Tom Jones," or hundreds of other really great books of the same kind, which, though shunned by prudes, are the joy and delight of all the rest of the world. If it were a book in which sensual pleasures were pictured and praised for their own sake, or in which some of the fundamental principles of morality were attacked, it would still be wrong, inexpedient, and contrary to the spirit of this age and country to suppress it by legal interference; for the Americans of this generation are, I take it, grown up men and women, and require no district attorney or other official to instruct them as to what books are, and what not, proper to be read, but are perfectly able to decide (each one of them) such matters for themselves.

But *Leaves of Grass* does not stand in the same category with either the books mentioned or those alluded to, nor does it advocate acts or practices which are considered by any sane person to be immoral or wrong; the whole crime of its author is that he believes in the grandeur and goodness of humanity in all its parts and relations; that he, being himself pure, sees that man is so in his essential nature, in spite of any and all appearances to the contrary; that all his parts and all his functions are well made and divinely appointed; that man, in fact, is the work of a wise and good God—not his head and hands, his eyesight and intellect merely, but also all the rest of his body and his instincts, including the sexual passion, and the organs and the acts by and through which this passion (for the greatest of all ends) seeks and finds its gratification:

> The very head and front of (his) offending
> Hath this extent, no more.

He simply, like Milton, "asserts (universal) providence, and *justifies the ways of God to man*," his crime being that, as he has absolute, not partial faith, so he justifies *all* God's ways, not a selected few of them.

If even, his intention being pure, he had so failed in the carrying of it out that while aiming to strengthen virtue the book unawares stimulated vice, it would then undoubtedly be a proper subject for hostile criticism, but not for the interference of the law, which in such a case could only be appealed to by persons who felt that the ends they sought could not be attained by reason. But it has not been and cannot be shown that the book is of the character supposed, for it was not only intended to contain, but it does contain, no page, line, or word calculated to arouse or capable of arousing any improper or immoral emotion whatever, but, on the contrary, its invariable tendency is toward purity in thought, word, and deed. Walt Whitman says, and rightly, that, "If anything is sacred the human body is sacred" (not part of the body, mind, but all of it), and as a logical deduction from that proposition (which even Oliver Stevens will hardly deny) he continues:

O my body! I dare not desert the likes of you in other men and women, nor the likes of the parts of you.
I believe the likes of you are to stand and fall with the likes of the soul (and that they are the soul).

He therefore goes on to praise in detail all the various parts, organs, and functions of the body, and this is done in an absolutely chaste manner. There is no make-believe about all this on the part of the poet; all parts of the body are praiseworthy and admirable to him (as they ought to be to us all, for they are so in reality), and *Leaves of Grass*, properly read, is to make us see the universe in all its parts, including man, as he sees it, and feel toward it as he feels toward it, *i. e.*, to see and feel that the world and humanity are not half God's work and half the devil's, but that they are all God's work, and all perfect; that "not an inch or a particle of an inch is vile."

If so to feel toward and so to treat the earth and its inhabitants is a crime deserving the interference of the law, then (I say it in all reverence) the teaching of Christ was immoral, and the Pharisees had the best of the argument, for this was the basis of all his teaching: "These people and these things that you Pharisees think vile are not so in fact—these publicans, these prostitutes are the children of God; these acts that seem to you to need condemnation and punishment, need instead pity and forgiveness; these things that seem to you trivial and worthless have an eternal and sublime significance, if you could only see it." Has the world learned the lesson? Ought it no longer to be insisted upon? Are we all (now at last) good enough, wise enough? Do we all fully realize the whole grandeur and beauty of the world and of man? Are our feelings towards these always and under all circumstances what they should be? *Are they ever what they should be?* If man is already perfect, of course he wants no more teachers, so let us suppress all books (and all men too) that are above our own level; or, it being admitted that man is not quite perfect, shall we say that he is not capable of ever being nearer so than he is at present, and that therefore all teaching intended to elevate him is useless? If this is the case then certainly books like *Leaves of Grass* have no value. However, the point to be kept in view at present is not so much the value or no value of this despised and interdicted book, but the question whether any honestly written book may, simply because of the mention in it of things not usually talked about, be suppressed by any man who, perhaps not understanding it, happens not to like it. It is no use to seek to justify the suppression by saying that it was effected by means of and in accordance with law, for the worst crimes ever committed, the burning of witches, the butcheries of Jeffries, the execution of early Christians by pagans, and of later Christians by one another for religious error, yes, even the Crucifixion itself, were all legal. The question is not whether Oliver Stevens's act is legal, but whether it is right. The suppression (even for the moment) of *Leaves of Grass* is a serious matter from several points of view, but the general question involved in the act is far more serious. But upon this point Oliver Stevens has now expressed his opinion: it remains to be seen what the American people will think of it.

From the " Boston Herald," May 28th, 1882.

Suppressing Walt Whitman's poems is like putting the Venus of Milo in petticoats.   A few years ago a dealer in New Bedford was prosecuted for exposing a copy of the statuette of Narcissus in his window.   This is prurient prudery.   We expect it in untravelled country people, but city lawyers ought to know better.   We presume it is not Dist.-Attorney Stevens, or Atty.-Gen. Marston, to whom the credit of this small bigotry belongs, but Anthony Comstock, the narrow apostle of drapery.   If Walt Whitman's poems are obscene, what shall be said for Shakespeare, Montaigne, Swedenborg, and the Bible? On what principle can " the good gray poet" be condemned, and these exalted?   It is reported that Anthony Comstock has promised not to prosecute the classics " unless they are specially advertised."   Such a glimpse of bigotry is enough to make one shudder.   We regret that such facile legal tools were found in Massachusetts, and that the publishers did not have the courage to stand a prosecution for the sake of truth and art, and truth in art.

From the " Chicago Herald," October 16th, 1882.

Mr. George Chainey, of Boston, delivered a lecture last evening in Hershey Hall upon Walt Whitman's suppressed book, *Leaves of Grass.*   The audience was small and very appreciative.   Mr. Chainey is a tall, round-shouldered, smooth-faced gentleman, with flowing black hair, very large dark eyes, and a strong tendency toward epigrammatic and poetic expression.   He appears to be about forty years old.   He said that Walt Whitman is pre-eminently the poet of to-day.   Perhaps he might more justly be called the poet of the future. No poet of our time has been so coldly received—and yet there is no heart that beats so responsive to the voice of humanity as that of Walt Whitman. The critics refused to acknowledge him a poet, because he failed to write according to any of their rules of rhyme.   He read his lines in the book of Nature.   To express one's thoughts musically is a most valuable gift, but it is necessary for the poet to have something to reveal.   The heart of to-day seeks to express itself in its own way.   Millions still wear the manacles of yesterday, but it is without enthusiasm.   The devotees of the church are bound by a law which does not satisfy their desires.   They preach a salvation from hell. What they preach is hell.   Bondage is hell; freedom is heaven.   Shakespeare was the Pacific Ocean of poetry; Whitman is the Atlantic.   The one carries the freight of kings and queens, and the romance of the past; across the other come the steamships of to-day's commerce.   Other poets have sung of the pomps and romances of high life, but Walt Whitman has taken up the commonest things of earth, and shown their relation to the highest human life.   To him all the bibles, religions, philosophies of the past are as the grass of yesterday. They have fed the world, but are not food for the present.   All the first part of *Leaves of Grass* is taken up with this thought.   If men and women would listen to the teachings of this true poet they would save themselves much pain and error. It is our right to enjoy ourselves in our own way, provided we interfere with the rights of no other person.   Whitman is as original in matter as in manner. He is the first poet of true Democracy.   All through his book he pleads the cause of the despised and down-trodden.   He demolishes all distinctions drawn by church and state.   Walt Whitman cannot come to his own to-day because the church has preëmpted the land which he could profitably occupy. He can afford to wait until, as he says, there shall be no more priests.   His idea of Democracy is different from that of the politicians.   It means that the wise and strong are to use their wisdom and strength for the benefit of all.   Democracy means equality of opportunity and right. Air, water and land should be common to all under a wise management. Absolute possession of land will some day be looked at in the same light as absolute possession of men and women. Neither should to day be permitted to put claims on to-morrow. It should be held a crime to bequeath fortunes to perpetuate a political or religious creed. Woman must become in law as she is in fact the equal of man before the true Democracy can be had.

The lecturer read Whitman's poem addressed to a Common Prostitute, and said that on account of his publishing that poem in his paper he was greatly annoyed by Postmaster Tobey of Boston. He claims that the lines are pure and chaste when read understandingly in connection with the whole book. For this charity of Whitman's toward all Magdalens he has been persecuted in business and person, and classed with those who secretly corrupt the virtue of youth. He finds it necessary to treat of sex. In writing of this subject he uses some expressions which are objected to. He says that there have been two ways of treating these subjects, one the conventional method of absolute silence, the other in the vulgar words which come from masculine mouths. The speaker here interpolated a story of his first loss of faith in the purity of the Christian Church when he found himself in the company of three ministers who regaled each other for an entire evening with smutty stories. In camp-meeting while part of the preachers are thundering to better men than themselves to repent or be damned, the others are regaling each other in this delicate fashion in the privacy of their tents.

In closing, the speaker said that there were some passages in *Leaves of Grass* which he had not and could not read to the audience, not because the poetry was impure, but because the minds of his hearers were in such a condition that the poet's words would raise impure thoughts.

From the Philadelphia " Progress," November 11, 1882.

WALT WHITMAN'S LATE ILLNESS.—Dressed in a plain but handsome new suit of iron gray, all of a piece, loose and old-fashioned, yet a certain dashy style of its own, " the poet of future Democracy," as Thoreau once termed him—up again from his recent severe sickness—resumed, last week, his occasional mid-day saunters along Chestnut street. The whole rig, and the generous-crowned light hat of soft French beaver, that always surmounts its stalwart six-feet height, showed that free and large physique not unbecomingly.

It is not generally known that Walt Whitman's frequent spells of paralysis and sickness, the last fifteen years, are legacies from his overstrained labors in the Secession War. Never was there a grander and more perfect physique than he threw into that contest in 1862, with all the ardor of his nature, and continued till 1865, not as the destroyer of life, but its saviour, as volunteer army nurse and missionary, night and day, through the whole of three unintermitted years, always tending the Southern wounded just the same as the Northern. Well has it been claimed for him that behind his books stand the unrivalled deeds of his personal career.

He told me last week that in the two Philadelphia volumes just issued, the one comprising his entire poetic *Leaves*, and the other, *Specimen Days*, giving his autobiography and collected prose writings—both volumes printed solely under his own eye and direction—he has put himself on record for the future, " for good or bad, hit or miss," as he phrased it; and that he shall bother himself about the whole matter no further.

· *William Sloane Kennedy, Massachusetts. (Excerpts).*

Walt Whitman is not a man who can be described by comparison or by antithesis. No genius can be so described. If you will give me an adequate account of a cubic mile of sea-water or blue ether, measure the work of the sun, the beauty of the morning star, or the influence of the starry midnight upon the soul, then I will give you an adequate account of this man. He is not immoral, but unmoral, as a faun or a satyr; a dynamic force, an animate fragment of the universe, a destroyer of shams, a live fighter upon the stage ("im Hintergrund wimmelt's von gemalten Soldaten.").

Don't go to him expecting everything of him. Don't *expect* to find an artist. Don't ask for music. Be satisfied with the grand thought, the manly faith in democracy, the occasional majestic rhythm and poetry, the subtle spirituality, the antique strength and fresh savagery, the handling of vast masses of matter and spanning of gulfs of space and time with an ease and sureness never exhibited by any other poet. If you are inclined to laugh at Whitman's weaknesses and absurdities, do so by all means; it is right that you should. But if you are inclined to underrate his real strength, just attempt to draw his bow, and see how ridiculous will be your failure. There is not a man living who can write anything that will come within a thousand miles of such compositions as Whitman's "Song of Myself," "Crossing Brooklyn Ferry," "Burial Hymn of Lincoln," "Calamus," "Eidólons," his sea pieces, etc.; and no one but Carlyle could write such prose as the best of Whitman's. For my part, I despair of being able to completely analyze him, so revolutionary is he, so infinitely suggestive. A man, who, in his philosophy, has oriented himself by the perihelion and aphelion of the earth's orbit; who has taken the parallax of stars sunken deep beyond the vision of others' eyes, and whose diameters of faith span all gulfs of despair,—this is one whom I can trust and respect, but can with difficulty fathom.

It is the few men of tremendous native force of character, appearing at long intervals in history, that redeem literature from its vapidity and chaffiness. The value of Whitman in literature is, that in among the idiotic dandies and dolls of book characters he has placed A LIVE MAN, with all his sins and crudities, his brawn and blood, sexuality and burliness, as well as his noble and refined qualities. The effect and the shock of this upon the morbid mental condition of the popular mind of the day, is like that which would be produced by suddenly producing a nude figure of Angelo's, or an undraped Bacchus, in a ladies' sewing circle of a Methodist church.

As the author of *Leaves of Grass* himself says, in his article in the "North American Review," for June, 1882, the cosmical completeness of his work would have been injured by his omission to present the matter of sex. There is architectural proportion in the plan of his writings. As in antique sculpture all parts of the body are faithfully reproduced, so in Whitman's writings is all Nature reflected, and in proper proportion. Sexuality, fatherhood, and motherhood are themes which he treats only in two or three of his earlier poems; and, unquestionably, they should have been sung by so universal a poet—only in a more delicate way.

Let me close this topic by quoting the following passage from H. R. Haweis's excellent work on "Music and Morals:" "In some of the Gothic cathedrals we may have noticed strange figures hiding in nooks and corners, or obtrusively claiming attention as water-spouts. Some of them are revolting enough, but they are not to be severed from their connection with the whole building. *That* is the work of art; these are but the details, and only some of the details. How many statues are there in all those niches?—let us say a thousand. You shall find seventy pure virgins praying in long robes, and forty monks and apostles and bishops, and angels in choirs, and archangels standing high and alone upon lofty façade and pinnacle and tower ; and around the corner of the roof shall be two devils prowling, or a hideous-looking villain in great pain, or (as in Chester cathedral), there may be a proportion—a very small propor-tion—of obscene figures, hard and true and pitiless. ' What scandalous subjects for church decoration !' some may exclaim; yet the whole impression produced is a profoundly moral one. The sculptor has given you the life he saw ; but he has given it from a really high standpoint, and all is moral because all is in healthy proportion. There is degradation, but there is also divine beauty; there is passionate and despairing sin, but there is also calmness and victory; there are devils, but they are infinitely outnumbered by angels; there lurks the blur of human depravity, but as we pass out beneath groups of long-robed saints in prayer the thought of sin fades out before a dream of divine purity and peace. We can see what the artist loved and what he taught; that is the right test, and we may take any man's work as a whole, and apply that test fearlessly.''

And what a diction he has! His monosyllabic Saxon epithets somehow have imparted to them the crisp and crude freshness of the natural objects themselves to which they are applied. And his style is by no means sponta-neous. I have personal knowledge that he has always kept in view the advice given by Béranger to a brother poet, namely, that he should keep clear of all hack writers, and study words, words, words. Whitman's words are alive. His pages snap and crackle with vitality. Like Homer, he gives us actions, and not descriptions of actions. Something in the movement of his periods, like the blind resistless *trieb* of growing wood fibre, the erratic and ponderous push of writhen oak knots.

If there remains anything to be said it is this : Throw aside the present ar-ticle, and all articles about this great man, and go read his books. One result will be inevitable—you will discover your own limitations.

From "*The Herald,*" *Boston, October 15th, 1882.*

THE PROSE WRITINGS OF THE " GOOD GRAY POET." A TWIN VOLUME TO "LEAVES OF GRASS."—Walt Whitman's new book, with the odd, but thoroughly characteristic and descriptive title, *Specimen Days and Collect,* is a prose companion to *Leaves of Grass,* being a complete collection of the author's prose writings, as the former comprises all his verse. It is a meaty, compact volume, and is more directly comprehensible to the understanding of the multitude than the greater and more famous work. And yet this is as much Whitman as his verse is, and the same characteristics pervade it : grand healthiness of tone, largeness of view, universal reach, and, at the same time, delicate perception and sensitiveness, and identity with Nature, indissoluble and knit through and through with its fabric. Had *Leaves of Grass* never been written, this book alone would be enough to establish the author's fame as a great poet.

In a personal letter, Whitman writes: " It is a great jumble (as man him-self is)—an autobiography after its sort—(sort o' synonymous with Mon-taigne, and Rousseau's ' Confessions,' etc.)—is the gathering up and formula-tion and putting in identity of the wayside itemizings, memoranda, and per-sonal notes of fifty years—a good deal helter-skelter, but, I am sure, with a certain sort of orbic compaction and oneness as the final result. It dwells long on the Secession War, gives glimpses of that event's strange interiors, especially the army hospitals; in fact, makes the resuscitation and putting on record of the emotional aspect of the War of 1861–65 one of its principal features."

Indeed, too much stress cannot be laid upon this latter phase of the book. No history or description of the war that has yet been written probably gives such vivid and graphic pictures of its events—its heroism, its horror, its sadness, the pathetic tenderness of countless of its incidents, and, above all, its grand significance. For this reason it ought to be dear to every soldier.

During the years from 1873 to the present date, Whitman has been a partial paralytic. Very much of his days (and nights, also, it appears) he has spent in the open air down in the country in the woods and fields, and by a secluded little New Jersey river. His memoranda, on the spot, of these days and nights, fill a goodly portion of the volume.

Then comes the "Collect," embodying "Democratic Vistas," the noble prose Preface to *Leaves of Grass* of the edition of 1855, and much other prose, together with a number of youthful efforts in prose and poetry, which, in a note, the author explains he would have preferred to have them quietly dropt in oblivion, but, to avoid the annoyance of their surreptitious issue, he has, with some qualms, here tacked them on.

The whole volume, in its arrangement, is pregnant with Whitman's personality, and it seems more a part of its author than paper and printers' ink usually do. It also exhibits, as far as possible for any public record, that most wonderful and intricate of processes, the workings of a poet's mind, and affords an insight into the mysterious interior depths and rambling galleries and chambers of the cosmic sphere whose large and rugged exterior is clothed with the fresh beauty of "leaves of grass."

From "The Press," Philadelphia, March 18th, 1883.

Ralph Waldo Emerson's cordial letter to Walt Whitman "at the beginning of a great career," has become familiar in American literature. Of scarcely less interest is Emerson's frank personal estimate of the new poet in a letter written to Carlyle in 1856, when the flat, thin quarto was unknown to the general, or for that matter, to any reader. "One book came out last summer in New York," Emerson writes, "a nondescript monster, which yet had terrible eyes and buffalo strength, and was indisputably American. It is called *Leaves of Grass*. After you have looked into it, if you think, as you may, that it is only an auctioneer's inventory of a warehouse, you can light your pipe with it."

It would not be easy to improve on this to-day as the transcription of a first impression. "Nondescript" and a "monster" *Leaves of Grass* unquestionably was by all literary canons with which either Carlyle or Emerson were familiar; but the keen critical spirit of the Concord philosopher felt, rather than saw, the coming power looming great through the mist of forms strange and new in literature. For the rest, the neat suggestion that Carlyle would be opaque to the new light is admirable.

From the Sydney, Australia, "Evening News," March 21st, 1883.

AMERICAN FREETHOUGHT AND FREETHINKERS.—On Monday evening a crowded audience assembled in the Masonic Hall to hear a lecture by Mr. Charles Bright on "American Freethought and Freethinkers." Some fifteen months ago he took a trip to America for the benefit of his health, and he has returned to Sydney with a considerably augmented knowledge of the progress of thought in the Great Republic. He spoke for nearly two hours, and gave a deal of interesting information concerning the advanced thinkers of the country, and the influence they exercise on the progress of thought in the direction of mental liberty. Of the many freethinkers he had met he ranked Walt Whitman, the poet, highest. Whitman was the grandest and best man in every sense, morally, intellectually, and physically, he had ever met in his life—a prophet poet, who was as far in advance of other writers and thinkers in the present day as Isaiah and Jeremiah were in advance of their contemporaries

ROBERT BUCHANAN TO WALT WHITMAN.

From " Faces on the Wall."

Friend Whitman! wert thou less serene and kind,
  Surely thou mightest (like the Bard sublime,
Scorned by a generation deaf and blind),
  Make thine appeal to the avenger TIME;
For thou art none of those who upward climb,
Gathering roses with a vacant mind.
  Ne'er have thy hands for jaded triflers twined
  Sick flowers of rhetoric and weeds of rhyme.
Nay, thine hath been a Prophet's stormier fate.
While LINCOLN and the martyr'd legions wait
  In the yet widening blue of yonder sky,
On the great strand below them thou art seen,
Blessing, with something Christ-like in thy mien,
  A sea of turbulent lives, that break and die.

ENGLISH CRITICS

ON

WALT WHITMAN

EDITED BY

EDWARD DOWDEN, LL.D.,

PROFESSOR OF ENGLISH LITERATURE, TRINITY COLLEGE, DUBLIN.

ENGLISH CRITICS ON WALT WHITMAN.

HAVING heard from Dr. Bucke that it was his wish to add a fuller account of the history of opinion in England with reference to Whitman's writings than that contained in the first edition of his " Walt Whitman," as printed in America, I have compiled what follows, and add it here with the permission of Dr. Bucke's publishers. To prevent misapprehension, I desire to state that I am in no sense editor of this English edition of Dr. Bucke's work; his estimate of Whitman's position in literature differs in important respects from mine; but with him I recognize in Whitman a man of rare nobility of character, and an inspiring influence in literature. I have included in my record all the facts of interest that I have been able to ascertain, but I have not thought it worth while to notice short unsigned reviews—indeed, only one article by an author unknown to me by name is here noticed, that in *The Scottish Review*, which is a substantial contribution to criticism. Where the criticism has been wholly adverse to Whitman I have represented it as frankly as where it has been wholly favourable. Where the central feeling of the writer was one of admiration, but this was qualified by admissions to Whitman's disadvantage, whether from an ethical or artistic point of view, I have thought it fair to express the writer's central feeling in my brief extract. But wrong will be done to some of the writers—I may name, for example, Mr. Saintsbury, Dr. Todhunter, Mr. Stevenson, and the contributor to *The Scottish Review*—unless it is borne in mind that their admiration for Whitman's writings is qualified by considerations (sometimes gravely, sometimes smilingly expressed) of an unfavourable kind. This record of opinion in the main, but not invariably, follows a chronological order.

EDWARD DOWDEN.

THOMAS DIXON.

[Mr. Thomas Dixon was a working cork-cutter of Sunderland, to whom Mr. Ruskin addressed the twenty-five letters on the laws of work published in 1867 under the title "Time and Tide by Weare and Tyne."]

Mr. William Bell Scott permits me to publish the following letter :—

92 Cheyne Walk, Chelsea,
22nd January, 1884.

My dear Professor Dowden,—Not long before Thomas Dixon of Sunderland's death, when the question even in America of the earliest reception of Walt Whitman's *Leaves of Grass* was exciting some attention, I thought it worth while to write to him to learn how the copies of the first edition of that book, which could scarcely be said to have been published in the ordinary way, had so quickly come to this country, the title-page bearing no imprint save "Brooklyn, New York, 1855," while I was furnished with several copies by T. Dixon so soon as in the summer of the following year, 1856. I may quote from his reply :—

"I will tell you willingly how the first copies of the *Leaves of Grass* reached this country. They are still dear to me from association with the man who brought them, and because I knew you, by whom Walt Whitman has been valued. There is a plan of dealing called hand-selling, which is selling by a kind of auction, the dealers who adopt this plan not being lawfully qualified as auctioneers. The value of the book offered is gradually reduced till some one takes it. Say it starts at five shillings : he reduces the price, less and less, till it reaches a shilling or sixpence. A man arrived here at that time, summer of 1856, James Grindrod by name, following this trade with a stock of books that had missed their market, or had never been really published at all. He had a number of the *Leaves of Grass*, of which you had three.

"He soon disappeared, but came again to Sunderland after the American War was finished, and recommenced the same kind of bookselling. [He left Sunderland again, after having set up his wife in a shop of her own well stocked. Mr. Dixon continues :] I was very sorry for this, because he had such lots of wonderful, curious books that could not be seen elsewhere. He came and took tea with me cn Sunday afternoons, and then I found he had been in the thick of the American War, as well as Whitman,—was with Sherman at the taking of Atlanta, and then got his discharge with others who had done the same hard service. . . . I may as well tell you his end. He went into Lancashire, his own county originally, and was killed in a railway collision in a tunnel a year or two afterwards."

This is, I think, worthy of record, as no publisher being interested in this first edition of the book it might have been long enough before reaching this country, but for the travelling James Grindrod with his Dutch auction. Besides, his having a number of copies in his miscellaneous pack shows the small value of the book in America at its first appearance. . . . .

Ever yours,

WILLIAM BELL SCOTT.

WILLIAM BELL SCOTT.

The attitude of Mr. W. B. Scott, towards Whitman is apparent from the preceding letter, and from the following passage in Mr. W. M. Rossetti's dedication to Mr. Scott of "Poems by Walt Whitman, selected and edited" (Hotten, 1868) :—

"To William Bell Scott. Dear Scott,—Among various gifts which I have received from you, tangible and intangible, was a copy of the original quarto edition of Whitman's *Leaves of Grass*, which you presented to me soon after its first appearance in 1855. At a time when few people on this side of the Atlantic had looked into the book, and still fewer had found in it anything save matter for ridicule, you had appraised it, and seen that its value was real and great. A true poet and strong thinker like yourself was indeed likely to see that."

See also the next entry in this compilation under the heading William M. Rossetti.

W. M. ROSSETTI.

Mr. William Bell Scott writes to me in the letter quoted above, under the heading "Thomas Dixon," as follows :—

"One of my copies [of *Leaves of Grass*] I forthwith sent to my friend William M. Rossetti, then the centre of a literary circle of influence and judgment. I find him writing to me under date December, 1856: 'Many thanks for the *Leaves of Grass*, which I have not yet received from W., but shall be eager to read as soon as I get it. W. and others denounce it in the savagest terms, but I suspect I shall find a great deal to like, a great deal to be surprised and amused at, and not a little to approve—all mingled with eccentricities. . . The *Leaves of Grass* has come to hand. My best expectations are more than confirmed by what little I have read as yet, and Gabriel [Dante Gabriel Rossetti] tends now even towards enthusiasm. You could have given me nothing I could better like to receive.'"

In 1867, or perhaps 1866, Mr. Rossetti printed in *The Chronicle* an article on Whitman, which furnished the basis of his volume of "Selected Poems."

In 1868 appeared Mr. Rossetti's volume of "Selected Poems by Walt Whitman." The estimate of Whitman expressed by Mr. Rossetti in the Prefatory Notice to this volume, is reaffirmed in the Preface to "American Poems Selected and Edited by William Michael Rossetti" (Moxon & Co.), a volume "Dedicated with Homage and Love to Walt Whitman." Mr. Rossetti there writes as follows :—

"I conceive Walt Whitman to be beyond compare the *greatest* of American poets, and indeed one of the greatest now living in any part of the world. He is just what one could conceive a giant to be, if all the mental faculties and aspirations of such a being were on the same scale with his bodily presence. We should expect his emotions and his intellectual products to be colossal, magnificent, fervid, far-reaching, many-sided,—showing the most vivid perceptions and the strongest grasp. . . This is what we find in Whitman. He is not insensible to grace, nor yet to art, for his mind, besides all its other large endowments, is distinctly that of a poet ; but the scale of his intuitions, his sympathies, and his observation, is so massive, and his execution has so wide a sweep, that he does not linger over the forms or the finish of his work—not at least over forms and finish of such sort as most poets delight in, though he has his own standard of performance which he willingly and heedfully observes."

DANTE G. ROSSETTI.

In the preceding notice ["W. M. Rossetti,"] a passage from a letter of Mr. W. M. Rossetti is quoted :—"Gabriel [Dante G. Rossetti,] tends now [December 1856,] even towards enthusiasm."

Mr. W. M. Rossetti permits me to print the following passage from a letter addressed by him to me, and dated 17th January, 1884 :—

"My brother never wrote for publication anything about Whitman. Towards 1865-6, when he saw Swinburne constantly, and when Swinburne (since then considerably cooled about Whitman, I suspect,) admired him fervently, my brother also set a high value on Whitman—most especially the Dirge for Lincoln. Even at that time I question whether my brother read in full the most characteristic and stirring poems of Whitman; and since then, I think, he hardly opened his books. In this state of things his feeling towards Whitman gradually changed; and his tone was one of impatience against professed poetry in which recognised poetic form bore so small a part. He said to me more than once that Whitman is nothing but "sublimated Tupper;" and seriously contended that Whitman must certainly have read Tupper's book before undertaking his own. Yet, spite of all this, my brother had a real deep-lying sense of Whitman's greatness of scale and powerful initiative."

G. H. LEWES.

Mr. W. M. Rossetti permits me to print the following passage from a letter of his addressed to me, and dated 17th January, 1884 :—

"G. H. Lewes was, I fancy, the very first Englishman to put into print something about Whitman. *Leaves of Grass* came out, I think, in 1855, and Lewes was then editor of a weekly review named *The Leader,* and wrote in it something discerning about Whitman. I can't *assert* that Lewes's name was signed to the article, but am sure I am not mistaken in saying that the article was generally accepted as being his."

This article I have not seen.

GEORGE ELIOT.

"George Eliot read but little contemporary fiction, being usually absorbed in the study of some particular subject. 'For my own spiritual good I need all other sort of reading,' she says, 'more than I need fiction . . . My constant groan is that I must leave so much of the greatest writing which the centuries have sifted for me unread for want of time.' For the same reason, on being recommended by a literary friend to read Walt Whitman, she hesitated on the ground of his not containing anything spiritually needful for her, but, having been induced to take him up, she changed her opinion, and admitted that he *did* contain what was good for her soul."

"George Eliot" by Mathilde Blind (1883), p. 210.

W. J. FOX.

Mr. Rossetti writes in the Prefatory Notice to his "Poems by Walt Whitman, Selected and Edited" (1868) : "Some English critics, no doubt, have been more discerning,—as W. J. Fox, of old, in the *Dispatch,* the writer of the notice in the *Leader,* and of late two in the *Pall Mall Gazette* and the *London Review;* but these have been the exceptions among us."

I have not seen Mr. Fox's article.*

---

* The articles in the *Pall Mall Gazette* I read many years ago, and heard them attributed to the late Viscount Strangford. If my memory does not mislead me, they dwelt on the resemblances between Whitman's writings and Oriental poetry, to which Mr. Moncure Conway also called attention.

ALGERNON C. SWINBURNE.

In "Songs before Sunrise" (1871), Mr. Swinburne addresses a poem "To Walt Whitman in America," beginning

" Send but a song oversea for us,
    Heart of their hearts who are free !
    Heart of their singer, to be for us
    More than our singing can be."

In Mr. Swinburne's "William Blake : a Critical Essay" (1868), pp. 300-302, a comparison is instituted between Blake and Whitman. "In externals and details the work of these two constantly and inevitably coheres and coincides. A sound as of sweeping wind ; a prospect as over dawning continents at the fiery instant of a sudden sunrise ; an expanse and exultation of wing across strange spaces of air and above shoreless stretches of sea ; a resolute and reflective love of liberty in all times and in all things where it should be ; a depth of sympathy and a height of scorn which complete and explain each other, as tender and as bitter as Dante's ; a power, intense and infallible, of pictorial concentration and absorption, most rare when combined with the sense and the enjoyment of the widest and the highest things; an exquisite and lyrical excellence of form when the subject is well in keeping with the poet's tone of spirit ; a strength and security of touch in small sweet sketches of colour and outline, which bring before the eyes of their student a clear glimpse of the thing designed—some little inlet of sky lighted by moon or star, some dim reach of windy water, or gentle growth of meadow-land or wood ; these are qualities common to the work of either. . . . . Whitman has seldom struck a note of thought and speech so just and so profound as Blake has now and then touched upon ; but his work is generally more frank and fresh, smelling of sweeter air, and readier to expound or expose its message, than this of the Prophetic Books. Nor is there among these [*i.e.*, Blake's Prophetic Books] any poem or passage of equal length so faultless and so noble as his 'Voice out of the Sea,' or as his dirge over President Lincoln—the most sweet and sonorous nocturn ever chanted in the church of the world."

In " Under the Microscope" (1872), pp. 45-55, Mr. Swinburne alleges that injury has been done to Whitman's art by his doctrinaire method of preaching in verse. He writes : "By far the finest and truest thing yet said of Walt Whitman has been said by himself, and said worthily of a great man. ' I perceive in clear moments,' he said to his friend Dr. Burroughs, 'that my work is not the accomplishment of perfections, but destined, I hope, always to arouse an unquenchable feeling and ardour for them.' A hope surely as well grounded as it is noble."

MONCURE D. CONWAY.

Mr. Conway contributed an article called "Walt Whitman" to the *Fortnightly Review* for October 15, 1866. He introduces Whitman to his readers as "a singular genius, whose writings, although he certainly had no acquaintance with Oriental literature, have given the most interesting illustration of it [the Oriental tendency of the Occidental mind], besides being valuable in other respects." The article is chiefly occupied with personal reminiscences. "It was impossible," he writes, "not to feel at every moment the *reality* of every word and movement of the man, and also the surprising delicacy of one who was even freer with his pen than modest Montaigne. . . . . He had so magnetized me, so charged me, as it were, with something indefinable, that for the time the only wise course of life seemed to be to put on a blue shirt and a blouse and loaf about Mana-hatta and Paumonok—"loaf and invite my soul," to use my new friend's phrase.

ROBERT BUCHANAN.

As early as 1867, in an article which was printed in *The Broadway* and reprinted in *The New York Citizen* for November 2nd of that year, Mr. Buchanan recognised Whitman's "ministry" as "a genuine ministry, large in its spiritual manifestations, and abundant in capability for good." "In actual living force," wrote Mr. Buchanan, "in grip and muscle, he has no equal among contemporaries." In 1872, Mr. Buchanan published "The Fleshly School of Poetry and other Phenomena of the Day" (Strahan & Co.) It contains a note (pp. 96-97) on Walt Whitman in which he wrote: "There is at the present moment living in America a great ideal prophet, who is imagined by many men on both sides of the Atlantic to be one of the sanest and grandest figures to be found in literature, and whose books, it is believed, though now despised, may one day be esteemed as an especial glory of this generation. . . . Whitman is in the highest sense a spiritual person; every word he utters is symbolic; he is a colossal mystic." After condemning some fifty lines of *Leaves of Grass* as offending against decency, and disclaiming sympathy with Whitman's "pantheistic ideas," Mr. Buchanan proceeds—"My admiration for this writer is based on the wealth of his knowledge, the vast roll of his conceptions (however monstrous), the nobility of his *practical* teaching, and (most of all, perhaps) on his close approach to a solution of the true relationship between prose cadence and metrical verse. Whitman's style, extraordinary as it is, is his greatest con-tribution to knowledge."

CHARLES KENT.

Mr. W. M. Rossetti writes to me as follows :—

"When my book came out (I think 1868) Charles Kent was Editor of *The Evening Sun*. He wrote in that paper a long and most enthusiastic review—about the most affectionate and overflowing tribute to Whitman's great gifts that I have ever seen in print. Kent's name was not signed to this article, but I know it to be his."

Mr. Kent's article I have not seen.

ARCHBISHOP TRENCH.

In the first edition of Trench's "A Household Book of English Poetry" (1868), appeared Whitman's "Come up from the field, Father," to which the following note was appended. Both poem and note disappear from later editions.

"A selection of Walt Whitman's poetry has very lately been published in England, the editor of this declaring that in him American poetry properly so-called begins. I must entirely dissent from this statement. What he has got to say is a very old story indeed, and no one would have attended to his version of it, if he had not put it more uncouthly than others before him. That there is no contradiction between higher and lower, that there is no holy and no profane, that the flesh has just as good rights as the spirit,—this has never wanted prophets to preach it, nor people to act upon it; and this is the sum-total of his message to America and to the world. I was glad to find in his 'Drum-taps' one little poem which I could quote with real pleasure,"

MRS. GILCHRIST.

Mrs. Gilchrist's letters to Mr. W. M. Rossetti with reference to Whitman, dated June and July, 1869, were published under the title, "A Woman's Estimate of Walt Whitman. [From late letters by an English lady to W. M. Rossetti]" in an American periodical, "The Radical," for May, 1870. Dr. Bucke has given some quotations on p. 204-206. I add, with Mrs. Gilchrist's permission, the following :—

. . . The song of the soul's triumphant mastery of life, destiny, nature, called the "Poem of Joys," kindles the spirit like martial music. I used to think it was great to disregard happiness, to press on to a high goal, careless, disdainful of it. But now I see that there is nothing so great as to be capable of happiness; to pluck it out of "each moment and whatever happens;" to find that one can ride as gay and buoyant on the angry, menacing, tumultuous waves of life as on those that glide and glitter under a clear sky; that it is not defeat and wretchedness which come out of the storm of adversity, but strength and calmness.

See, again, in the pieces gathered together under the title "Calamus," and elsewhere, what it means for a man to love his fellow-man. Did you dream it before? These "evangel-poems of comrades and of love" speak, with the abiding, penetrating power of prophecy, of a "new and superb friendship;" speak not as beautiful dreams, unrealizable aspirations to be laid aside in sober moods, because they breathe out what now glows within the poet's own breast, and flows out in action toward the men around him. Had ever any land before her poet, not only to concentrate within himself her life, and, when she kindled with anger against her children who were treacherous to the cause her life is bound up with, to announce and justify her terrible purpose in words of unsurpassable grandeur (as in the poem beginning, "Rise, O days, from your fathomless deeps"), but also to go and with his own hands dress the wounds, with his powerful presence soothe and sustain and nourish her suffering soldiers,—hundreds of them, thousands, tens of thousands,—by day and by night, for weeks, months, years?

"I sit by the restless all the dark night; some are so young,
Some suffer so much : I recall the experience sweet and sad.
Many a soldier's loving arms about this neck have crossed and rested,
Many a soldier's kiss dwells on these bearded lips :—"

Kisses, that touched with the fire of a strange, new, undying eloquence the lips that received them ! The most transcendent genius could not, untaught by that "experience sweet and sad," have breathed out hymns for her dead soldiers of such ineffably tender, sorrowful, yet triumphant beauty.

But the present spreads before us other things besides those of which it is easy to see the greatness and beauty; and the poet would leave us to learn the hardest part of our lesson unhelped if he took no heed of these; and would be unfaithful to his calling, as interpreter of man to himself and of the scheme of things in relation to him, if he did not accept all—if he did not teach "the great lesson of reception, neither preference nor denial." If he feared to stretch out the hand, not of condescending pity, but of fellowship, to the degraded, criminal, foolish, despised, knowing that they are only laggards in "the great procession winding along the roads of the universe," "the far-behind to come on in their turn," knowing the "amplitude of Time," how could he roll the stone of contempt off the heart as he does, and cut the strangling knot of the problem of inherited viciousness and degradation? And, if he were not bold and true to the utmost, and did not own in himself the threads of darkness mixed in with the threads of light, and own it with the same strength and directness that he tells of the light, and not in those vague generalities that everybody uses, and nobody means, in speaking on this head,—in the worst, germs of all that is in the best ; in the best, germs of all that is in the worst,—the *brotherhood* of the human race would be a mere flourish of rhetoric. And brotherhood is naught if it does not bring brother's love along with it. If the poet's heart were not "a measureless ocean of love" that seeks the lips and would quench the thirst of all, he were not the one we have waited for so long. Who but he could put at last the right meaning into that word "democracy," which has been made to bear such a burthen of incongruous notions ?

"By God ! I will have nothing that all cannot have their counterpart of on the same terms ! "

flashing it forth like a banner, making it draw the instant allegiance of every man and woman who loves justice. All occupations, however homely, all developments of the activities of man, need the poet's recognition, because every man needs the assurance that for him also the materials out of which to build up a great and satisfying life lie to hand, the sole magic in the use of them, all of the right stuff in the right hands. Hence those patient enumerations of every conceivable kind of industry :—

"In them far more than you estimated—in them far less also."

Far more as a means, next to nothing as an end ; whereas we are wont to take it the other way, and think the result something, but the means a weariness. Out of all come strength, and the cheerfulness of strength. I murmured not a little, to say the truth, under these enumerations, at first. But now I think that not only is their purpose a justification, but that the musical ear and vividness of perception of the poet have enabled him to perform this task also with strength and grace, and that they are harmonious as well as necessary parts of the great whole.

. . . . Out of the scorn of the present came skepticism ; out of the large, loving acceptance of it comes faith. If *now* is so great and beautiful, I need no arguments to make me believe that the *nows* of the past and of the future were and will be great and beautiful too.

"I know I am deathless.
I know this orbit of mine cannot be swept by the carpenter's compass.
I know I shall not pass, like a child's carlacue cut with a burnt stick at night.
I know I am august.
I do not trouble my spirit to vindicate itself or be understood.

"My foothold is tenoned and mortised in granite :
I laugh at what you call dissolution,
And I know the amplitude of Time."

"No array of terms can say how much I am at peace about God and Death."

One of the hardest things to make a child understand is, that down underneath your feet, if you go far enough, you come to blue sky and stars again ; that there really is no "down" for the world, but only in every direction an "up." And that this is an all-embracing truth, including within its scope every created thing, and, with deepest significance, every part, faculty, attribute, healthful impulse, mind, and body of a man (each and all facing towards and related to the Infinite on every side), is what we grown children find it hardest to realize too. Novalis said, "We touch heaven when we lay our hand on the human body :" which, if it mean anything, must mean an ample justification of the poet who has dared to be the poet of the body as well as of the soul,—to treat it with the freedom and grandeur of an ancient sculptor.

"Not physiognomy alone, nor brain alone, is worthy of the muse :—I say
the form complete is worthier far.

"These are not parts and poems of the body only, but of the soul.

"O, I say now these are soul."

But while Novalis—who gazed at the truth a long way off, up in the air,
in a safe, comfortable fashion—has been admiringly quoted by high authorities, the great American who has dared to rise up and wrestle with it, and
bring it alive and full of power in the midst of us, has been greeted with a
very different kind of reception, as has happened a few times before in the
world in similar cases. Yet I feel deeply persuaded that a perfectly fearless,
candid, ennobling treatment of the life of the body (so inextricably inter-
twined with, so potent in its influence on the life of the soul) will prove of
inestimable value to all earnest and aspiring natures, impatient of the folly
of the long prevalent belief that it is because of the greatness of the spirit
that it has learned to despise the body, and to ignore its influences ; knowing well that it is, on the contrary, just because the spirit is not great enough,
not healthy and vigorous enough, to transfuse itself into the life of the body,
elevating that and making it holy by its own triumphant intensity ; knowing,
too, how the body avenges this by dragging the soul down to the level
assigned itself. Whereas the spirit must lovingly embrace the body, as the
roots of a tree embrace the ground, drawing thence rich nourishment,
warmth, impulse. Or, rather, the body is itself the root of the soul,—that
whereby it grows and feeds. The great tide of healthful life that carries all
before it must surge through the whole man, not beat to and fro in one
corner of his brain.

"O the life of my senses and flesh, transcending my senses and flesh !"

For the sake of all that is highest, a truthful recognition of this life, and
especially of that of it which underlies the fundamental ties of humanity,—
the love of husband and wife, fatherhood, motherhood,—is needed. Religion
needs it, now at last alive to the fact that the basis of all true worship is comprised in "the great lesson of reception, neither preference nor denial,"
interpreting, loving, rejoicing in all that is created, fearing and despising
nothing.

"I accept reality, and dare not question it."

The dignity of a man, the pride and affection of a woman, need it too.
And so does the intellect. For science has opened up such elevating views
of the mystery of material existence that, if poetry had not bestirred herself
to handle this theme in her own way, she would have been left behind by
her plodding sister. Science knows that matter is not, as we fancied, certain
stolid atoms which the forces of nature vibrate through and push and pull
about ; but that the forces and the atoms are one mysterious, imperishable
identity, neither conceivable without the other. She knows, as well as the
poet, that destructibility is not one of nature's words ; that it is only the
relationship of things—tangibility, visibility—that are transitory. She knows
that body and soul are one, and proclaims it undauntedly, regardless, and
rightly regardless, of inferences. Timid onlookers, aghast, think it means
that soul is body,—means death for the soul. But the poet knows it means
body is soul,—the great whole imperishable ; in life and in death continually
changing substance, always retaining identity. For, if the man of science is
happy about the atoms, if he is not baulked or baffled by apparent decay or
destruction, but can see far enough into the dimness to know that not only
is each atom imperishable, but that its endowments, characteristics, affinities,
electric and other attractions and repulsions—however suspended, hid, dor-

mant, masked, when it enters into new combinations—remain unchanged, be it for thousands of years, and, when it is again set free, manifest themselves in the old way, shall not the poet be happy about the vital whole? shall the highest force, the vital, that controls and compels into complete subservience for its own purposes the rest, be the only one that is destructible? and the love and thought that endow the whole be less enduring than the gravitating, chemical, electric powers that endow its atoms? But identity is the essence of love and thought,—I still I, you still you. Certainly no man need ever again be downcast at the "dark hush" and the little handful of refuse.

"You are not scattered to the winds—you gather certainly and safely around yourself."

"Sure as Life holds all parts together, Death holds all parts together."

"All goes onward and outward : nothing collapses."

Science knows that whenever a thing passes from a solid to a subtle air, power is set free to a wider scope of action. The poet knows it too, and is dazzled as he turns his eyes toward "the superb vistas of death." He knows that "the perpetual transfers and promotions" and "the amplitude of time" are for a man as well as for the earth. The man of science, with unwearied, self-denying toil, finds the letters and joins them into words. But the poet alone can make complete sentences. The man of science furnishes the premises ; but it is the poet who draws the final conclusion. Both together are "swiftly and surely preparing a future greater than all the past." But, while the man of science bequeaths to it the fruits of his toil, the poet, this mighty poet, bequeaths himself—"Death making him really undying." He will "stand as nigh as the nighest" to these men and women. For he taught them, in words which breathe out his very heart and soul into theirs, that "love of comrades" which, like the "soft-born measureless light," makes wholesome and fertile every spot it penetrates, lighting up dark social and political problems, and kindling into a genial glow that great heart of justice which is the life-source of Democracy. He, the beloved friend of all, initiated for them a "new and superb friendship ;" whispered that secret of a godlike pride in a man's self, and a perfect trust in woman, whereby their love for each other, no longer poisoned and stifled, but basking in the light of God's smile, and sending up to him a perfume of gratitude, attains at last a divine and tender completeness. He gave a faith-compelling utterance to that "wisdom which is the certainty of the reality and immortality of things, and of the excellence of things." Happy America, that he should be her son ! One sees, indeed, that only a young giant of a nation could produce this kind of greatness, so full of the ardour, the elasticity, the inexhaustible vigour and freshness, the joyousness, the audacity of youth.

ALFRED AUSTIN.

In Mr. Alfred Austin's early critical volume, "The Poetry of the Period" (1870), which dealt swashing blows among the poets,—Tennyson, Browning, Swinburne, and others,—is a chapter on Whitman entitled "The Poetry of the Future." "He recognizes," wrote Mr. Austin, "no shame, no law, no forms, no good, no evil, no beauty, no ugliness, no distinctions, differences, or limitations. This, of course, will account for the disconnectedness of his utterances, and the utter disorder of his language. . . As Mr. Rossetti reminds us, it has been said of Mr. Whitman by one of his warmest admirers, 'He is Democracy.' I really think he is—in his compositions, at least ; being like it ignorant, sanguine, noisy, coarse and chaotic."

EDWARD DOWDEN.

Professor Dowden contributed to the *Westminster Review* for July 1871, an article entitled, "The Poetry of Democracy—Walt Whitman." It is reprinted with a few additions and alterations in his "Studies in Literature, 1789-1877" (Kegan Paul & Co.) Whitman is studied as a representative poet of America and modern Democracy. In *The Academy* for November 18, 1882, Professor Dowden reviewed Whitman's "Specimen Days and Collect," of which he says :—"In the main these 'Notes of a Half-Paralytic' are sweet and sane and nourishing, more perhaps than their writer knows or can know. No diary of an invalid is wholesomer reading than this ; never a groan or a growl, never a word of complaint ; but every bright hour, every breeze of health, every delight in flower and bird and stream and star, and in the kind voice or hand of a friend, remembered and recorded." In a review of the American edition of Dr. Bucke's "Walt Whitman" in *The Academy* for September 8, 1883, Professor Dowden writes :—"If I were to put it in my own way, I should say that Whitman's feeling for the spiritual, as involved in and emerging out of what is natural and even material, gives their peculiar quality to his writings."

H. BUXTON FORMAN.

In Mr. Forman's volume, "Our Living Poets" (1871), writing of Mr. W. Bell Scott's poem "Death," he says :—

"There is a largeness here not noticeable in contemporary verse, and a form that is at once without finish and beyond the need of finish : the absolute scientific truth and philosophic insight of the second verse is comparable with the higher flights of Walt Whitman. . . It is a fact worthy of record that the only poet among us who has anything in common with the great American is one whose works are best classed among the highly cultivated results of the Preraphaelite movement. Whitman's 'return to nature' has been far more decided and marked than any return that has ever yet been made in art : he 'strikes up for a new world' in the most absolute sense, ignoring all that we have been in the habit of recognizing as appurtenances to the art of song ; while the Preraphaelites, getting their best strength from movements in the same direction, yet retain so much of the hereditary artificial elements of European poetry as are indispensable under our definitely European conceptions of song." (Pp. 302-303.)

THE HON. RODEN NOEL.

Mr. Noel contributed two articles entitled "A Study of Walt Whitman, the Poet of Modern Democracy," to "The Dark Blue" for October and November, 1871. The first article treats of Whitman generally, the second of Whitman as teacher and prophet. "To me, then, I will begin by owning at the outset Walt Whitman appears as one of the largest and most important figures of the time. . . I think that what delights and arrests one most is the general impression he gives of nature, strength, health, individuality—his relish of all life is so keen, intense, catholic—the grasp of his faith is so nervous and tremendous—as he says, 'My feet are tenon'd and mortis'd in granite.' One of the notes of a man of genius is, that through life he remains a child ; and there is something eminently childlike in Whitman. He is full of naïf wonder and delight—each thing, every time he looks upon it flashes upon him with a sense of eternal freshness and surprise ; nor is anything to him common or unclean ; but an aerial glory, as of morning, utterly insensible to vulgar eyes, bathes and suffuses all. . . As Mr. Buchanan has already remarked, he is more prophet than artist. He very seldom retires to create deliberate imaginative wholes, in whose many diverse forms may be deposited the truths he sees and must utter, the mastering emotions which dominate his soul. You never cease to see this man Walt Whitman. But then it is a very noble, and I contend, a very poetic, personality you see—one in which, as in a magic crystal, all these men and women of the world, all the sights of city and of landscape, find themselves mirrored with most astonishing dis-tinctness."

LORD TENNYSON.

Mr. John Burroughs writes in a letter "To the Editor of the Tribune," dated "Esopus, N. Y. March 30, 1876": "The attitude of Tennyson towards him is eminently cordial and sympathetic." In a letter of January 18, 1872, Mr. Whitman writes: "Tennyson has written to me twice—and very cordial and hearty letters. He invites me to become his guest."

JOHN ADDINGTON SYMONDS.

"Strange as it may seem Walt Whitman is more truly Greek than any other man of modern times. Hopeful and fearless, accepting the world as he finds it, recognizing the value of each human impulse, shirking no obliga-tion, self-regulated by a law of perfect health, he, in the midst of a chaotic age, emerges clear and distinct, at one with nature, and therefore Greek."— 1873. "Studies of the Greek Poets." Note, p. 422.

JAMES THOMSON,
Author of " The City of Dreadful Night," etc.

Mr. Thomson contributed, in the year 1874, articles on Whitman to *The National Reformer* of July 26, August 2, August 9, August 16, August 23, August 30, Sept. 6; and subsequently articles on Whitman to "Cope's Tobacco Plant" of May, June, August, September, December, 1880. The latter paper ceased to appear before Mr. Thomson's series of articles was completed. Both series of articles are more biographical than critical, but criticism predominates in the numbers of *The National Reformer* for August 30, and Sept. 6, 1874. I quote the closing sentences of the number of Sept. 6 :—

"In conclusion, I will simply commend him to all good readers, and especially young readers, whose intelligence and character are still plastic to influences from without and effluences from within, as one of the most power-ful and cordial and wholesome writers they can become acquainted with ; as a modern of the moderns, to counterprise yet harmonise with the august ancients ; and (if we consider Emerson as in large measure the result of old-world culture) as indisputably the greatest native voice yet heard from America. Emphatically great, magnanimous, I always find him; in his faults as in his merits there is never any bitterness of heart or mind. And even the greatest faults of the great-hearted are more sanative than the petty virtues of the mean."

GEORGE SAINTSBURY.

In *The Academy* for October 10, 1874, appears a review of *Leaves of Grass*, six columns in length, by Mr. Saintsbury. He writes :—

"There are few poets who require to be studied as a whole so much as Walt Whitman . . . It is impossible not to notice his exquisite descriptive faculty, and his singular felicity in its use. Forced as he is, both by natural inclination, and in the carrying out of his main idea, to take note of 'the actual earth's equalities,' he has literally filled his pages with the songs of birds, the hushed murmur of waves, the quiet and multiform life of the forest and the meadow. And in these descriptions he succeeds in doing what is most difficult, in giving us the actual scene or circumstance as it impressed him, and not merely the impression itself. This is what none but the greatest poets have ever, save by accident, done, and what Whitman does constantly, and with a sure hand. . . . No Englishman, no one indeed, whether American or Englishman, need be deterred from reading this book, a book the most unquestionable in originality, if not the most unquestioned in excellence, that the United States have yet sent us."

RICHARD HENGIST HORNE.
Author of "Orion," etc.

A STAR OVER NIAGARA.
Brief Colloquy of Two Spirits.

BLAKE.

More form, and less of catalogues, brave Walter,
A cumulative rush of powers
O'erwhelms design. Give to Art's flowers
A spirit more ethereal.

WHITMAN.

No defaulter
Am I, pure star !—but my waves boil to hear
  Echoes of sham-psalms, o'er aesthetic tea,
While pantomine shines foul round many an altar,
  And saintly-sensual courtships leer,
Or half-born poets woo the fruitless tear,
  Lost to our nature's cosmic energy.
    Star of rare beams ! by thee
All sons of art should better learn to steer
Thou (living) man of men, uncapable of fear.

BLAKE.

Flow thine own way. Let the Great Baby jeer,
Or pass : the living truth it doth not see.

From "Cosmo de Medici, An Historical Tragedy and other Poems" (3rd edition, 1875), p. 157.

STANDISH O'GRADY.

Mr. Standish O'Grady (Author of "A History of Ireland," etc.), under the pseudonym of "Arthur Clive," contributed to *The Gentleman's Magazine* for December, 1875, an article entitled "Walt Whitman the Poet of Joy," from which the following is an extract :—

"Under a mask of extravagance and of insane intensity, Whitman preserves a balance of mind and a sanity such as no poet since Shakespeare has evinced. If his sympathies were fewer he would go mad. Energy and passion so great, streaming through few and narrow channels, would burst all barriers. His universal sympathies have been his salvation, and have rendered his work in the highest degree sane and true. He is always emphatic, nay, violent, but then he touches all things. Life is intense to him, and the fire of existence burns brighter and stronger than in other men. Thus he does his reader service : he seems out of the fulness of his veins to pour life into those who read him. He is electric and vitalising. All nature, books, men, countries, things, change in appearance as we read Whitman ; they present themselves under new aspects and with different faces . . . He has what Wordsworth lost, and in his old age comes trailing clouds of glory—shadows cast backward from a sphere which we have left, thrown forward from a sphere to which we are approaching . . . He is the noblest literary product of modern times, and his influence is invigorating and refining beyond expression."

PROFESSOR TYRRELL.

Mr. Tyrrell, now Regius Professor of Greek in the University of Dublin, delivered in 187 (?) a public lecture—one of the series of "Afternoon Lectures"—in Dublin on Walt Whitman. It was characterised by strong and discriminating admiration of Whitman. The lecture has not been published.

PETER BAYNE.

Mr. Bayne contributed an article entitled "Walt Whitman's Poems" to *The Contemporary Review* for December, 1875. It is wholly adverse to Whitman's claims as a poet. "If I ever saw anything in print," writes Mr. Bayne, "that deserved to be characterized as atrociously bad, it is the poetry of Walt Whitman. . . . The secret of Whitman's surprising newness—the principle of his conjuring trick—is on the surface. It can be indicated by the single word 'extravagance.' In all cases he virtually, or consciously, puts the question, 'What is the most extravagant thing which it is here in my power to say !' Incapable of true poetical originality, Whitman had the cleverness to invent a literary trick, and the shrewdness to stick to it. As a Yankee phenomenon, to be good-humouredly laughed at, and to receive that moderate pecuniary remuneration which nature allows to vivacious quacks, he would have been in his place ; but when influential critics introduce him to the English public as a great poet, the thing becomes too serious for a joke."

EDMUND W. GOSSE.

Mr. Gosse, reviewing Whitman's "Two Rivulets," in *The Academy*, June 24, 1876, writes ·—

" Between the class that calls Whitman an immoral charlatan bent on the corruption of youth, and the class that calls him an inspired prophet, sent, among other iconoclastic missions, to abolish the practice of verse, there lies a wide gulf. One would like to ask if it be not permitted that one should hold, provisionally an intermediate position, and consider him a pure man of excellent intentions, to whom certain primitive truths with regard to human life have presented themselves with great vividness, and who has chosen to present them to us in semi-rhythmic, rhetorical language, which rises occasionally in fervent moments, to a kind of inarticulate poetry, and falls at others into something very inchoate and formless. . . The ethical purpose of the book ['Memoranda during the War']—and it is needless to say that it has one—manifestly is to exemplify in a very tragical passage of real life the possibility of carrying out that principle of sane and self-sacrificing love of comrades for one another which Whitman has so often celebrated in his most elevated and mystical utterances. It is the old story of Achilles and Patroclus transferred from windy Troy to the banks of Potomac. It is conceivable that when all Whitman's theories about verse and democracy and religion have been rejected or have become effete, this one influence may be still at work, a permanent bequest of widened emotion to all future generations.

PROFESSOR CLIFFORD.

The late Professor Clifford, in his article "Cosmic Emotion" (*The Nineteenth Century* for October, 1877), uses passages from *Leaves of Grass* to illustrate his statements with respect to the emotion which is felt in regard to the universe or sum of things viewed as a cosmos or order, introducing the first quotation with the words—"So sings one whom great poets revere as a poet, but to whom writers of excellent prose, and even of leading articles, refuse the name." I copy the following from an American paper, *The New Republic* (Camden), March 27, 1875 :—"There may be mentioned a late lecture in St. George's Hall, London, by Professor Clifford . . . on "The relation between the Sciences and Modern Poetry," in which the Professor, reading mostly from the pieces of Whitman (the report in the English paper says "amid hearty and general applause"), ... pronounced him the only poet whose verse based on modern scientific spirit is vivified throughout with what Professor Clifford terms the 'cosmic emotion.' "

T. W. R. ROLLESTON.

Mr. Rolleston (translator of "The Encheiridion of Epictetus," Kegan Paul & Co., 1881) contributed a poem "On Walt Whitman's *Leaves of Grass*" to the second volume of *Kottabos* (1877). The following is a stanza :—

" Songs for the whole wide earth are thine,
　　Limitless as the clear sunlight :
What bridal hymns of love divine !
What converse with the mystic night !
What tempests of the woods and seas !
In passions mightier than these,
　　What wild and fierce delight
When through the throng'd exulting street
Thunder'd the tramp of soldiers' feet."

Recently Mr. Rolleston has lectured in German, and before a German audience in Dresden, on Walt Whitman. The lecture is published (Ueber Wordsworth und Walt Whitman : Zwei Vorträge gehalten vor dem Literarischen Verein zu Dresden von H. B. Cotterill und T. W. Rolleston. Dresden : Carl Tittman, 1883). He writes :—"Walt Whitman ist Verfasser des erstaunlichsten literarischen Werkes der Gegenwart, sein Erscheinen ist für die Literatur, für die Religion ein epochemachendes. . . . . Es finden sich in Whitman's Werke drei wunderlich zusammen verbundene Eigenschaften, welche denselben einen dauernden Werth unter den Menschen versichern. Man vernimmt bei ihm erstens die Wirkungen

eines Verstandes von einer Tiefe, einem Umfange, der, wenn wir uns zu
seiner Ergründung richtig anstrengen, uns als mehr und mehr erstaunlich
erscheint, je mehr wir hineinzudringen vermögen. Zweitens haben wir
einen Reichthum der Poesie, deren Schönheit nur um so tiefer und dauernder
wirkt, weil sie niemals zu einem Ziel und Zweck gemacht worden ist. Und
zuletzt findet der geeignete Leser etwas noch seltener noch werthvoller als
Verstand oder Poesie—er findet dass ein zauberhafter, unbeschreiblicher,
persönlicher einfluss aus diesen Blättern hervorströmt, er wird nicht mit
einem Buche in Verbindung gesetzt, soudern mit einem Menschen, mit
einem Freunde, dessen Geist auf den unsrigen—durch nichts, das wir eine
Lehre nennen können, durch blosses Zusammensein—verstärkend, erhabend,
reinegend und befreiend wirkt" (PP. 59-60).

HERBERT J. BATHGATE.

Mr. Bathgate contributed an article entitled "Walt Whitman" to the
"Papers for the Times, on Literature, Philosophy, and Religion" (London ·
E. W. Allen) for Sept. 1st, 1879, from which the following is an extract :—
"Throughout the whole of the remarkable *Leaves of Grass* and his other
numerous poems, Whitman sings with a joyous swing the dignity and greatness of Man and his Body. . . He has been charged with the rankest
materialism, but the truth is exactly the reverse. He is entirely and wholly
spiritual. . . One would say he was Titanic, but that the word has something dark and fearsome about it, and Whitman is pre-eminently joyous and
hopeful, and taking this into consideration, one readily sees that he belongs
to Emerson rather than to Carlyle. But all classification is useless, and
Whitman stands alone."

JOHN TODHUNTER.

"The present age has produced three great poets of Democracy—three
men whose utterances are full of prophetic fervour, and who seem to gaze
forward into the future with eyes that lighten with the vision of some boundless hope for mankind—Shelley, Victor Hugo, and Walt Whitman. . . .
Walt Whitman is neither, like Shelley, a dreamer aloof from every-day life,
in pursuit of ethereal abstractions, of a 'something removed from the sphere
of our sorrow,' nor is he like Hugo, led into extravagance by love of theatrical
effect. He is rather the idealist of real life, in every common event of which
his full-blooded imagination discerns an underworking spiritual force—'a hope
beyond the shadow of a dream.'" (1880) "A Study of Shelley" (C. Kegan
Paul & Co.), pp. 1, 2.

ROBERT LOUIS STEVENSON.

[From the Preface to "Familiar Studies of Men and Books," which contains an article on Walt Whitman.] "I cannot help feeling that in this
attempt to trim my sails between an author whom I love and honour and a
public too averse to recognise his merit, I have been led into a tone unbe-
coming from one of my stature to one of Whitman's. But the good and the
great man will go on his way not vexed by my little shafts of merriment. . .
It will be enough to say here that Whitman's faults are few and unimportant
when they are set beside his surprising merits. I had written another paper
full of gratitude for the help that had been given me in my life, full of enthusiasm for the intrinsic merit of the poems, and conceived in the noisiest
extreme of youthful eloquence. The present study was a rifacimento ; . .

the result is cold, constrained, and grudging. In short, I might almost every-where have spoken more strongly than I did."

The Essay on Whitman closes with the following words :—

"My reader who bears in mind Whitman's own advice and 'dismisses whatever insults his own soul,' will find plenty that is bracing, brightening, and chastening to reward him for a little patience at first. It seems hardly possible that anyone should get evil from so healthy a book as the *Leaves of Grass*, which is simply comical wherever it falls short of nobility ; but if there be any such, who cannot both take and leave, who cannot let a simple opportunity pass by without some uncouth and unmanly thought, I should have as great difficulty, and neither more nor less, in recommending the works of Whitman as in lending them Shakespeare, or letting them go abroad outside the grounds of a private asylum." (1882) "Familiar Studies of Men and Books." Pp. 127-128.

JOHN RUSKIN.

A sentence of Mr. Ruskin's—that Whitman's poems "are deadly true—in the sense of rifles—against our deadliest sins," has been often quoted ; I find some additional words of Mr. Ruskin's given by Mr. Molloy in his article on Whitman in *Modern Thought* for September, 1882, from which I extract what follows :—"Speaking of Whitman's poems, he declares the hostility they have excited is because 'they are deadly true—in the sense of rifles—against our deadliest sins.' This brief and characteristic sentence is sufficient in itself to indicate the value in which he holds the American poet. . . . 'I know that I should have said more about Walt Whitman's poems,' Mr. Ruskin said to me in writing of the subject, 'had not I felt that in him, as in Emerson, the personal feelings of the writer were thought of as too impor-tant,—it is the calamity of Republican patriotism to teach this error as if it were a duty."

H. B. COTTERILL.

From "An Introduction to the Study of Poetry," pp. 21-22 (Kegan Paul & Co., 1882).

"One of the finest examples, in any poet that I know, of this faculty of exciting an emotional feeling by mere association with material things, is the following. It is written by Walt Whitman, the American poet ; for though many deny him the name of poet, and in the highest sense of the word he may not be one of the completest poets, yet I have no hesitation in saying that, especially in this power of associating appearances, which *tends* to draw our minds from the less to the greater, from the lower form of the finite to a higher form, he is a great poet." [Quotations follow from the "Song of the Broad-Axe."]

FITZGERALD MOLLOY.

Mr. Molloy contributed an article of sixteen columns, entitled, "Leaders of Modern Thought, No. xxvii. Walt Whitman," to *Modern Thought* for September, 1882. "Walt Whitman," he writes, "was the outcome of a great era and a great country—they worthy of him in all things, he worthy of them ; and as a poet and a prophet he sings of all that he sees in the present, and of the future, peering beyond the surface of things, and crying aloud of the changes to come in the fulness of time. . . . Perhaps the most striking feature in his poems is the wonderful buoyant sense of delight he feels in all things—a healthy manly enjoyment of life and all that life holds and external nature presents. . . . But there is far more to be found in his poems than the glorification of Nature. A lesson which they teach over and over again is the worth and grandeur of manhood in its highest forms ; of man living openly, fearlessly, true withal to his instincts, honestly, lovingly, sacrificing self-interests for his neighbour's good or the common good, living in the spirit of liberty, equality and fraternity."

PROFESSOR NICHOL.

" Walt Whitman is undoubtedly a writer of great force, but he is ruined as an artist by his contempt for art. . . . He has a teeming brain on a big body, and he tosses everything that the one or the other engenders into his powerful or monstrous book. . . . . His moral excellences are his absolutely unaffected democratic philanthropy ; a confidence like Shelley's in the world's great age beginning anew—like that of Burns, in all the dwellers on its surface being brothers at last ; and his intense pathetic sympathy with his fellow-workers under every form of struggle, sickness, or sorrow. . . . Half the drum-taps are clarions ; the rest dirges or idylls, which only fall short of masterpieces because their passionate regrets are expressed in stammering speech. Few nobler laments have been written in America than 'Lincoln's Burial Hymn.' . . . But even in Whitman's best work there is constantly some provoking rudeness that jars, as if a piece of glass had got into our bread ; we must take him as he is, a benevolent but unteachable egotist, who has been told that he writes like the Hebrew prophets till he has come to believe it, and regards any other criticism as profanity."—" American Literature : an Historical Sketch," by John Nichol, LL.D., 1882, pp. 210-213.

G. C. MACAULAY.

" If we were asked for justification of the high estimate of this poet, which has been implied, if not expressed, in what has been hitherto said, the answer would be perhaps first, that he has a power of passionate expression, of strong and simple utterance of the deepest tones of grief, which is almost or altogether without its counterpart in the world. . . His morality is almost comprised in the one word 'health,' of body and health of soul, the healthy and the sane man to be the ultimate standard. These are Greek ethics, and the maxim on which they seem to be based—'Whatever tastes sweet to the most perfect person, that is finally right'—is thoroughly Aristotelian. . . The body is sacred as well as the soul, and to assert its sacredness is the purpose of his sometimes outrageous physiological details, which can hardly have the desired effect, but are clearly not meant, nor indeed adapted, to minister to vicious tastes ; they may disgust, but they can hardly corrupt. There is indeed something in this tearing away of veils, which, however justly it may offend true modesty, is to unhealthfulness and pruriency as sunlight and the open air ; they shrink from the exposure, and shiver at the healthy freshness . This man's nature is itself as healthy as the sea, which endangers not us with all the fevers deposited in it." " Walt Whitman," an article in *The Nineteenth Century* for December, 1882.

THE SCOTTISH REVIEW.

The *Scottish Review* for September, 1883, contains an article of twenty pages, entitled, " Walt Whitman." The following is an extract :—

"Whatever our estimate of Whitman's writings may be, Whitman himself is unquestionably a notable figure, certainly one of the most notable America has produced. . . . They [the sources of his power] are to be found not so much in his art, for as an artist he is in some respects confessedly weak, but in the lofty purpose by which he is inspired, and in the ardent and almost fierce enthusiasm with which he has from first to last devoted himself to it. This purpose, to put it in the fewest words, is nothing less than to inaugurate in America, by means of a genuinely native imaginative literature, a new era of intellectual and spiritual development. . . . Whitman is preeminently a poet of the modern world. No other has more thoroughly adopted the conclusions of science, or made a more splendid and impressive use of them in his writings. Not unseldom they give a vastness and grandeur to his thought, which is well-nigh overwhelming. At the same time he is very far from being in any sense or degree a materialist. The supremacy of the spiritual he always loyally, and sometimes ostentatiously, recognises.

His works are pre-eminently suggestive. Any finished picture he seldom presents. His poems are rather suggestions, arousing the reader and leading him on and on, till he feels the fresher air of a freer thought breathing around him, and sees spreading out before him the limitless and unknown."

EDWARD CARPENTER.

In 1883 appeared a volume of poetry entitled "Towards Democracy," by Mr. Edward Carpenter, the inspiration of which comes in a great degree, both as regards substance and form, from Whitman.

WILLIAM WATSON.

Author of "The Prince's Quest," and "Epigrams of Art, Life, and Nature" (1884).

> To WALT WHITMAN.
> Some find thee foul and rank and fetid, Walt,
>   Who cannot tell Arabia from a sty.
> Thou followest Truth, nor fearest, nor dost halt;
>   Truth : and the sole uncleanness is a lie.
>   Epigram lxxxii. of "Epigrams of Art, Life, and Nature."

DR. C. VILLIERS STANFORD.

At the Norwich Musical Festival, 1884, was given an Elegiac composition by Dr. Stanford, to words by Walt Whitman.

WILSON & M^cCORMICK'S

BOOK ⚘ LIST.

Saint Vincent Street   GLASGOW.

Post 8vo, Cloth. With Portrait. Price 10s. 6d.

Leaves of Grass.

By WALT WHITMAN.

Comprises all the author's Poetical Works down to date (last of 1882), over Three Hundred Poems : has been the growth of many successive accumulations and issues—this being the ninth : includes all and several of the original Brooklyn '55, the New York '57, the Boston' 61, the Washington' 73, Camden '76, and Boston '81 Editions.

The author himself considers this issue of *Leaves of Grass* the only full and finally authentic collection of his poetry. Contains characteristic portrait (fine steel engraving) of the Poet, from life, in 1856.

' Ruskin has recently eulogised it, declaring that "it carries straight and keen as rifle-balls against our deadliest social sins." Thoreau ranked it with the mighty Oriental Poems, and pronounced it the supreme expression of American democracy, and its author the greatest democrat the world has ever seen. Emerson literally exhausted panegyric upon it in his letter of 1855, incidentally calling it "the most extraordinary piece of wit and wisdom America has yet contributed." '—*New York Tribune.*

Post 8vo, Cloth. With Portrait. Price 10s. 6d.

Specimen Days and Collect.

By WALT WHITMAN.

Author of Leaves of Grass.

A full compendium of the author's prose writings, old and new. Gives Whitman's early days on Long Island, and young manhood in New York City—Copious War and Army-Hospital Memoranda (1862-65), Convalescent out-door Notes in the Country (1876 81)—Visits in Boston—Some Literary Criticisms—Carlyle from American points of view—Poetry To-Day in America—Prefaces to 'Leaves of Grass,' 1855, 1872, 1876—Death of Abraham Lincoln —Loafing in the Woods—The Women of the West—Jaunts over the great Plains, and along the St. Lawrence and Saguenay, etc. The 'Collect' includes *Democratic Vistas* and all his political and critical writings. The volume contains a fine heliotype portrait of the 'good gray poet.'

'Amid the notes on external Nature, on the songs and habits of birds, on the trees, the skies, the stars, of which a great part of the volume is composed, so rare and slight is the mention of his infirmities that we might forget that the idyll was composed by a half-paralyzed man.'—*Westminster Review.*

Crown 8vo, Cloth. Price Six Shillings.

Inchbracken: a Novel.

By ROBERT CLELAND.

' "Inchbracken" is a clever sketch of Scottish life and manners at the time of the "Disruption" or great secession from the Established Church of Scotland, which resulted in the formation of the Free Church. . . . The story is well and simply told, with many a quiet touch of humour, founded on no inconsiderable knowledge of human nature.'—*Westminster Review.*

'The villain of the story is a most detestable hypocrite, who acts as clerk—or whatever the official may be called—to the Free Church congregation. Happily there are better beings in the book. Some of the sketches of character are happily touched, and the dialogue is commonly well managed.'—*Spectator.*

Preparing for Publication. Crown 8vo, Cloth. With Portraits and Illustrations.

Walt Whitman.

By RICHARD MAURICE BUCKE. With ADDENDA

BY PROF. EDWARD DOWDEN, LL.D.

'Whitman is pre-eminently a poet of the modern world. No other has more thoroughly adopted the conclusions of science, or made a more splendid and impressive use of them in his writings. Not unseldom they give a vastness and grandeur to his thought, which is well-nigh overwhelming. At the same time he is very far from being in any sense or degree a materialist. The supremacy of the spiritual he always loyally, and sometimes ostentatiously, recognises. Though almost Greek in his sympathy with nature, and notwithstanding the manner in which he has sung of man's physical constitution, the position which he assigns to the soul is always incomparably higher.'—*Scottish Review.*

'We know Whitman better after having read Dr. Bucke's book ; we feel, through his words, the powerful fascination of the man. . . . If I were to put it in my own way, I should say that Whitman's feeling for the spiritual, as involved in and emerging out of what is natural and even material, gives their peculiar quality to his writings. And accordingly he is at once a mystic or transcendentalist and the keenest of observers.

Like Wordsworth, like Mr. Browning, Whitman has lived long enough to see indifference and opposition yield, and a kind of cult (not perhaps always of the wisest) take their place. The edition of "Leaves of Grass" published last year, without the omission of a line or word, was all sold in one day, and there has been quite a general and steady sale since. Dr. Bucke brings together some of the praise and dispraise of a quarter-of-a-century as found in Reviews and Magazines. This volume reprints Mr. O'Connor's fervid and fiery pamphlet, ''The Good Gray Poet,'' with an added letter dated February 1883. Beside portraits of Whitman, portraits of his father and mother are given, with drawings of the ancient burial-grounds of the Whitmans and Van Velsors. Those who care for Whitman will find much to interest them in Dr. Bucke's various gatherings, as well as in his personal record of facts and of impressions.'—*Academy.*

3

Post 8vo, Cloth. Printed on hand-made paper. Price 6s.

Wayside Songs : with other Verse.

'The best of the "Wayside Songs" show lyric impulse, associated with some amount of descriptive fancy.'—*Athenæum.*

'This volume shows some real lyrical power. Now and again there is a "lilt" in the verse which makes us feel that the author has at least approached to the secret of song-writing.'—*Spectator.*

'Undoubtedly the author of "Wayside Songs" is a poet, and a poet gifted with a lyrical capacity which is considerably above the average. His love of nature is almost equal to that of Herrick, Wordsworth, or Bryant, and his verse seems to flow forth at a touch, and to move along as easily and melodiously as a brook.'—*Glasgow News.*

'There is in almost every page the true touch of the poet ; deep sympathetic insight, light, airy, and graceful turns of thoughts, which at times reminds you of Locker, although in justice to the author we must confess that everything which passes through his hand, or rather brain, has its own peculiar tinge.'—*Dundee Advertiser.*

'Some of the lyrics in this volume are little gems.'—*Literary World.*

Second Edition. Fcap. 8vo, Cloth. Price 2s. 6d.

Song Drifts.

'Whoever the author of "Song Drifts" may be, he has mastered some of the most vital secrets of poetic art. He possesses a rare command of rhythm and of musical expression, which would go a long way to commend his verse, even if it possessed no higher qualities. But in most of the tiny lyrics which make up this volume, there is also discernible a rich imaginative power, while, just as the theme is grave or gay, the lines are alive with cheerfulness or full of true and tender pathos. Where all is so good, quotation would be an invidious task ; but we can cordially recommend "Song Drifts" to all lovers of really good poetry.'—*Scotsman.*

'There is much music, tender thought, and poetic fancy in "Song Drifts." Many of the songs would be welcome from the hands of a clever composer.'—*Morning Post.*

Fcap. 4to, Cloth. Frontispiece and Portraits of the Sultans. Price 15s. Forty-five (numbered) Copies on Dutch hand-made paper, bound in parchment, with elaborate Moorish Design in gold and colour, 31s. 6d. A few of the latter remain.

Ottoman Poems.

TRANSLATED INTO ENGLISH VERSE IN THE ORIGINAL FORMS.

WITH INTRODUCTION, BIOGRAPHICAL NOTICES, AND NOTES.

BY E. J. W. GIBB, M.R.A.S.

'It reveals a picture of literary endeavour unfamiliar to us because it is so remote from our own ideas. It shows, too, in what varied shapes the intellectual life of a people presents itself. It is true that the peculiar form of these compositions is greatly due to the pervading influence of Islam and to the imitation of Persian poetry already referred to, but there is something in the genius of the Turks themselves which allows them to assimilate these mystical conceptions, and to adopt a like treatment of language. If Mr. Gibb begins five centuries ago, and gives specimen after specimen, age after age, it must be borne in mind that at this very day the same literary system and workmanship are in full vigour. . . In this sense, Mr. Gibb's volume is a curious study of Turkish life. He supplies a chronological table of Sultans, scrupulously marking all those who are recorded as poets, and those so marked outnumber those unmarked. The biographical notices show that the poets are taken largely from the political class, or were engaged in public life. The casual details supplied regarding poetesses will be interesting to the reader, and make him wish that the author had given more in illustration of the position of women in Turkey so much misapprehended abroad. The biographical notices and the notes are so written that they form an attractive portion of the book.'—*Athenæum.*

'Here we may wish for a little more, and there for a little less ; but the chief sentiment of all who read this charmingly printed and edited volume—with its interesting if somewhat pugnacious intro-duction, its essays on Turkish poetic literature and metres, and its biographical and explanatory notes—must be gratitude to the pioneer. Mr. Gibb is the first to bring Ottoman poetry within that comfortable reach which the English reader demands. Others may use his work and improve upon it, but meanwhile he is the first ex-ponent of Ottoman poetry to a faithless generation who know not Turkish.'—STANLEY LANE-POOLE in *Macmillan's Magazine.*

Post 8vo, Cloth.   Printed on hand-made paper.   Price 7s. 6d.

The Praise and Blame of Love : with other Verse.

'Far be it from us to announce "a new poet" with blare of trumpet and waving of banners. *Ne fait pas ce tour qui veut* either in the way of being a new poet or discovering one. But the author of *The Praise and Blame of Love* is, at any rate, worth pointing out to those who take an interest in poetry as a person on whom an eye should be kept.'—GEORGE SAINTSBURY in *The Academy.*

'Who would not envy such an attire for the offspring of his muse? Seriously, the book is a beautiful specimen of modern printing, and the sunflower on the title-page, though not perhaps a very startling emblem just now, almost persuades us to be æsthetics. The best lines in the book are in a Scottish version of the famous ninth ode of the third book of the 'Odes of Horace.' *Westminster Review.*

'The writer has the art of producing firm and sonorous Iambics.' *Scotsman.*

Demy 8vo, Sewed.   Price 1s.

How Glasgow Ceased to Flourish:

A TALE OF 1890.

Third Edition.   8vo, Sewed.   With Steel Engravings.   Price 1s.

'To the Highlands! or, A Ten Days' Tour in Scotland.

'These memoranda of a tour are written in a style far removed from that which seems natural to compositions where "all things and several others" are dealt with, and as humorously-written notes, interspersed with appropriate quotations from the poets known and unknown, is to be recommended to holiday tourists bent on pleasure.'—*Glasgow News.*

6

New Edition. Fcap. 8vo, Cloth. Price 2s. 6d. A few Copies on hand-made paper. Price 5s.

Thoughts in the Cloister and the Crowd.

By SIR ARTHUR HELPS, K.C.B.

Author of *Friends in Council*.

'A charming little reprint of the author's earliest work.'—*The Modern Review*.

'He is a mediator always, and often an apologist for human nature and human perversity ; nevertheless his belief in the good remains. In one sentence here he characteristically condemns the *nil admirari* attitude.'—*British Quarterly Review*.

'A little volume, which is beautifully printed and got up, is a reprint of the late Sir Arthur Helps' earliest work, "Thoughts in the Cloister and the Crowd," which was first published in 1835. It is a series of brief but thoughtful utterances on a wide range of subjects, revealing the extensive culture, the knowledge of human nature, the innate charity, and the gentle humour of this pleasant writer in a very acceptable form.'—*Scotsman*.

'We claim a high place for "Thoughts in the Cloister and the Crowd" when we say that it and "Guesses at Truth" may be placed side by side upon one shelf.'—*Glasgow Herald*.

'For many years the book has been very scarce, and lovers of Sir Arthur Helps who wished to perfect their sets of his writings have in many instances been obliged to dispense with this one. They will be glad to learn that a new edition of it has this week been published by Messrs. Wilson & McCormick of Saint Vincent Street, who have brought it out in a very attractive form.'—*North British Daily Mail*.

'The dainty little volume which Messrs. Wilson & McCormick have just issued from the press will be welcomed for more reasons than one. In the first place, it has been prepared with such evident care and taste that it may be welcomed on that score alone as a sample of what its publishers can do, and an earnest of what we may expect from them in the future. . . . There are in "Thoughts in the Cloister and the Crowd" passages which are hardly equalled for keen terseness and sagacity in any of his other works.'—*Glasgow News*.

12mo, Cloth. Thirty Maps and Plans. Price 6s.

The Highlands of Scotland

AS FAR AS LAIRG, LOCHINVER, AND STORNOWAY.

By M. J. B. BADDELEY, B.A.

'There was still room for a guide to Scotland of moderate size, real utility, and complete intelligibility, and that has been satisfactorily supplied by Mr. Baddeley, in the second volume of his Thorough Guide Series.—We have tested the guide in many places with which we are familiar, and have found it quite trustworthy, decidedly practical, and wisely discriminating. Mr. Baddeley's directions as to getting to a place, so far as we have tested them, may be implicitly followed, and are evidently the result of his own experience.'—*Times.*

12mo Cloth. Numerous Maps, tinted to show elevation. Price 4s.

Northern Highlands and Islands

FROM INVERNESS AND GAIRLOCH TO THE NORTH OF SHETLAND.

By M. J. B. BADDELEY, B.A.

'Baddeley's "Northern Highlands and Islands" is one of the "thorough-guide" series published by Messrs. Dulau & Co., of London, and Messrs. Wilson & M°Cormick, of Glasgow. The present supplements the former volume, which conducted the tourist as far as Lairg, Lochinver, and Stornoway. This covers from Inverness and Gairloch to the extreme north of the Shetland Islands, containing full descriptions of Inverness, Loch Maree, Gairloch, and of the places and country northward thereof in the counties of Inverness-shire, Ross, Cromarty, Sutherland, and Caithness; also of the Orkney and Shetland Islands, and the districts of Forres, Elgin, Nairn, and Speyside, and the approaches to the Northern Highlands from Edinburgh, Glasgow, and Aberdeen. The letterpress is terse and yet lively, the distances are carefully stated, the notes about conveyances, fares, hotel charges, &c., are never omitted. The maps are the strong point of this, in all respects, admirable guide-book, and than these maps it is not possible to desire anything more clear and workmanlike.'—*Glasgow Herald*

Geology and the Deluge.

By THE DUKE OF ARGYLL.

Demy 8vo, Sewed.   Price One Shilling.

The Economics of Fair Trade.

By W. R. HERKLESS, M.A.

'Mr. Herkless is a Free Trader, but he tries to show that there is a real difference between the motives of the Fair Trader and the Protectionist.'—*Glasgow Herald.*

8vo, Cloth.   With Illustrations.   Price 6s.

Iberian Sketches:

TRAVELS IN PORTUGAL AND THE NORTH-WEST OF SPAIN.

By JANE LECK.

WITH ILLUSTRATIONS BY ROBERT GRAY, F.R.S.E.

Third Edition.   Demy 8vo, Sewed.   Price 1s.

John Ruskin: his Life and Work.

By WILLIAM SMART, M.A.

' "Modern Painters," the "Seven Lamps of Architecture," and the "Stones of Venice" will last as long as our language for their beauty of style, their elevating criticism, and the grasp and extent of their erudition.   But when Mr. Smart endeavours to support the theory that Mr. Ruskin as a philosopher and political economist is as sound and trustworthy a guide as he is as an art critic, we think statements are being advanced which are certainly new but which cannot be maintained.'—*Westminster Review.*

Demy 8vo, Sewed.   Price 1s.

A Disciple of Plato: a Critical Study of John Ruskin.

By WILLIAM SMART, M.A.

With a Note by Mr. Ruskin.

'Mr. Smart's aim in this handsome pamphlet is to show that in some of his leading doctrines Mr. Ruskin is a follower of Plato.'—*Scottish Review.*

Crown 8vo.   Illustrated.   Price One Shilling.

Tourists' Guide to Islay.

WITH DIRECTORY OF THE ISLAND,

And Descriptive Excursions to Places of Interest, Instructions for the Angler to the various Fishing Lochs, etc., etc.

Demy 8vo, Sewed.   Price Sixpence.

Wealth: Definitions by Ruskin and Mill Compared.

[Out of Print.

A NEW MAP OF THE ISLAND OF ARRAN.

Coloured, price Sixpence.   In neat cloth case and mounted on linen, 1s.

Map of Arran for Tourists and Pedestrians.

FROM ORDNANCE SURVEY.

A BOOK OF HIGHLAND SKETCHES.

Second Edition.   Square 16mo, Sewed.   Price One Shilling.

From the Clyde to the Hebrides:

SKETCHES BY THE WAY.

'To those who contemplate a trip to the West Highlands, we would recommend a little volume of sketches recently published by Messrs. Wilson & McCormick, of Glasgow.   The book consists of over seventy pen-and-ink drawings of places of interest visited by Mr. MacBrayne's well-known steamers.   Humorous and full of amusing glimpses of tourist-character, these "Sketches by the Way" should serve as an admirable souvenir to carry away with one on his return from the far North.   The book seems to have already met with considerable success, for it is now issued in a second edition.'—*Moffat Times.*

Crown 8vo, Sewed.   Illustrated with upwards of Twenty-one Original Sketches.   Price One Shilling.

A Day in the Columba: a Summer Idyll.

'In easy glowing verse the anonymous author of this brochure describes the tourist's experiences on board the beautiful steamer *Columba,* and the scenery that opens up to his delighted vision, during the journey from Glasgow to Ardrishaig.   A number of capital etchings of the officers and principal parts of the ship, together with some of the scenery, greatly enhance the value of the little book.   Many who read it will thereby be led to make the trip, while to those "who have been there and still would go" it will make an excellent souvenir.'—*Literary World.*

Demy 8vo, Sewed.   Price Sixpence.

Thomas Carlyle: his Life & Work.

By WILLIAM MARTIN.

In One Volume, 8vo, Cloth, Subscription Price, 7s. Impression limited to 300 Copies.

THE STORY OF JEWAD

A TURKISH ROMANCE

By 'ALĪ 'AZIZ EFENDI of CRETE

Translated into English by

E. J. W. GIBB, M.R.A.S.

Author of *Ottoman Poems*, etc.

MESSRS. WILSON & McCORMICK have the pleasure to announce their intention to publish by subscription, a new work by the Author of *Ottoman Poems*.

The volume is a romance dealing with the adventures of a young magician named Jewād, who wanders through various countries seeking to do good. The Author, 'Alī 'Aziz Efendi of Crete, who died near the close of last century, was learned in Eastern philosophy, and has put into his work several curious details concerning magic ceremonies and Oriental spiritualism. As is the case in so many Eastern works of fiction, there are incidental to this romance many secondary tales, which are not less interesting than the leading story itself. The manners and customs described, or alluded to, are those of the author's own time, and they serve to show the esteem in which the occult sciences and their professors used to be held in the Levant, as also to give a glimpse into a section of life in the Ottoman capital long before the introduction of the modern reforms, and while Constantinople was still a thoroughly Oriental city.

So far as the publishers are aware, the work has never till now been translated into any European language. The impression will be limited to 300 copies, and the right reserved to raise the price now fixed should it be found necessary. [*In the Press.*

GLASGOW: WILSON & McCORMICK, SAINT VINCENT STREET.

12

CPSIA information can be obtained at www.ICGtesting.com
Printed in the USA
BVOW06s1218070116

432102BV00026B/368/P